AF305169

# The Environment and International History

# NEW APPROACHES TO INTERNATIONAL HISTORY

**Series Editor:** Thomas Zeiler, Professor of American Diplomatic History, University of Colorado Boulder, USA

## Series Editorial Board:

Anthony Adamthwaite, University of California at Berkeley (USA)
Kathleen Burk, University College London (UK)
Louis Clerc, University of Turku (Finland)
Petra Goedde, Temple University (USA)
Francine McKenzie, University of Western Ontario (Canada)
Lien-Hang Nguyen, University of Kentucky (USA)
Jason Parker, Texas A&M University (USA)
Glenda Sluga, University of Sydney (Australia)

*New Approaches to International History* covers international history during the modern period and across the globe. The series incorporates new developments in the field, such as the cultural turn and transnationalism, as well as the classical high politics of state-centric policymaking and diplomatic relations. Written with upper-level undergraduate and postgraduate students in mind, texts in the series provide an accessible overview of international diplomatic and transnational issues, events, and actors.

## Published:

*Decolonization and the Cold War*, edited by Leslie James and Elisabeth Leake (2015)
*Cold War Summits*, Chris Tudda (2015)
*The United Nations in International History*, Amy Sayward (2017)
*Latin American Nationalism*, James F. Siekmeier (2017)
*The History of United States Cultural Diplomacy*, Michael L. Krenn (2017)
*International Cooperation in the Early Twentieth Century*, Daniel Gorman (2017)
*Women and Gender in International History*, Karen Garner (2018)
*International Development*, Corinna Unger (2018)
*The Environment and International History*, Scott Kaufman (2018)

## Forthcoming:

*The International LGBT Rights Movement*, Laura Belmonte
*Scandinavia and the Great Powers in the First World War*, Michael Jonas
*Canada and the World since 1867*, Asa McKercher
*Reconstructing the Postwar World*, Francine McKenzie
*The History of Oil Diplomacy*, Christopher R. W. Dietrich
*The Nineteenth Century World*, Maartje Abbenhuis and Gordon Morrell
*Global War, Global Catastrophe*, Maartje Abbenhuis and Ismee Tames

## Series Editor Preface

*New Approaches to International History* takes the entire world as its stage for exploring the history of diplomacy, broadly conceived theoretically and thematically, and writ large across the span of the globe, during the modern period. This series goes beyond the single goal of explaining encounters in the world. Our aspiration is that these books provide both an introduction for researchers new to a topic and supplemental and essential reading in classrooms. Thus, *New Approaches* serves a dual purpose that is unique from other large-scale treatments of international history; it applies to scholarly agendas and pedagogy. In addition, it does so against the backdrop of a century of enormous change, conflict, and progress that informed global history but also continues to reflect on our own times.

The series offers the old and new diplomatic history to address a range of topics that shaped the twentieth century. Engaging in international history (including but not especially focusing on global or world history), these books will appeal to a range of scholars and teachers situated in the humanities and social sciences, including those in history, international relations, cultural studies, politics, and economics. We have in mind scholars, both novice and veteran, who require an entrée into a topic, trend, or technique that can benefit their own research or education into a new field of study by crossing boundaries in a variety of ways.

By its broad and inclusive coverage, *New Approaches to International History* is also unique because it makes accessible to students' current research, methodology, and themes. Incorporating cutting-edge scholarship that reflects trends in international history, as well as addressing the classical high politics of state-centric policymaking and diplomatic relations, these books are designed to bring alive the myriad of approaches for digestion by advanced undergraduates and graduate students. In preparation for the *New Approaches* series, Bloomsbury surveyed courses and faculty around the world to gage interest and reveal core themes of relevance for their classroom use. The polling yielded a host of topics, from war and peace to the environment; from empire to economic integration; and from migration to nuclear arms. The effort proved that there is a much-needed place for studies that connect scholars and students alike to international history, and books that are especially relevant to the teaching missions of faculty around the world.

We hope readers find this series to be appealing, challenging, and thought-provoking. Whether the history is viewed through older or newer lenses, *New Approaches to International History* allows students to peer into the modern period's complex relations among nations, people, and events to draw their own conclusions about the tumultuous, interconnected past.

*Thomas Zeiler, University of Colorado Boulder, USA*

# The Environment and International History

SCOTT KAUFMAN

BLOOMSBURY ACADEMIC
LONDON • NEW YORK • OXFORD • NEW DELHI • SYDNEY

BLOOMSBURY ACADEMIC
Bloomsbury Publishing Plc
50 Bedford Square, London, WC1B 3DP, UK
1385 Broadway, New York, NY 10018, USA

BLOOMSBURY, BLOOMSBURY ACADEMIC and the Diana logo are trademarks of
Bloomsbury Publishing Plc

First published in Great Britain 2018

Copyright © Scott Kaufman, 2018

Scott Kaufman has asserted his right under the Copyright, Designs and Patents Act, 1988,
to be identified as Author of this work.

For legal purposes the Acknowledgments on p. xi constitute an extension
of this copyright page.

Cover image © Fallen trees in the state of Amazonas Brazil, 2004. (© Paulo Fridman /
Alamy Stock Photo)

All rights reserved. No part of this publication may be reproduced or transmitted
in any form or by any means, electronic or mechanical, including photocopying,
recording, or any information storage or retrieval system, without prior
permission in writing from the publishers.

Bloomsbury Publishing Plc does not have any control over, or responsibility for, any
third-party websites referred to or in this book. All internet addresses given in this
book were correct at the time of going to press. The author and publisher regret any
inconvenience caused if addresses have changed or sites have ceased to exist,
but can accept no responsibility for any such changes.

A catalogue record for this book is available from the British Library.

A catalog record for this book is available from the Library of Congress.

ISBN: HB: 978-1-4725-2722-6
PB: 978-1-4725-2505-5
ePDF: 978-1-4725-2902-2
eBook: 978-1-4725-2703-5

Series: New Approaches to International History

Typeset by Deanta Global Publishing Services, Chennai, India
Printed and bound in Great Britain

To find out more about our authors and books visit www.bloomsbury.com and
sign up for our newsletters.

*To My Sister and Brother-in-Law*
*Heather Kaufman and Steve Moore*

# CONTENTS

# LIST OF ILLUSTRATIONS

# ACKNOWLEDGMENTS

This book originated from an offer by Tom Zeiler, a professor of history at the University of Colorado, to participate in a series of books he was editing for Bloomsbury Press. Having done some work related to US environmental history, I regarded a manuscript on international environmental diplomacy as a natural extension of my earlier research. I therefore requested and received the opportunity to write this work.

Because *The Environment and International History* is a synthesis of secondary materials, I relied heavily on the holdings of the Rogers Library at Francis Marion University as well as interlibrary loan. The state of South Carolina's PASCAL system—an intrastate catalog of college and university libraries—was immensely helpful, as was Steve Sims, the head of Access Services at Rogers Library, whom I probably overworked ordering items for me from interlibrary loan.

Francis Marion University (FMU) has been ranked by the *Chronicle of Higher Education* as one of the best academic institutions at which to work in the United States, and it has been a pleasure to call FMU home. The administration, from President L. Fred Carter down, has been very supportive of my research, as have my colleagues in the Department of History. I cannot express enough my appreciation to them.

Emma Goode, the commissioning editor at Bloomsbury Publishing, has been a wonder with whom to work. My thanks go out as well to the peer reviewer of the manuscript, who offered terrific suggestions for revisions. Jeff Novak, a friend who is an expert on plant, water, and soil conservation with the U.S. Department of Agriculture, read over a portion of the manuscript, and my brother-in-law, Steve Moore, who works with the U.S. Army Corps of Engineers, provided some helpful insights.

In addition to Steve, I want to thank my father, Burton Kaufman, my stepmother, Jane Bloom, and my sister, Heather Moore, for their love and support. But most of all, I want to thank my wife, Julie, for putting up with me as I turned my office into what I call "organized chaos" as I researched and wrote this manuscript.

# PREFACE

In June 2017, US president Donald Trump announced his decision to withdraw from the 2015 Paris climate agreement. Signed by 195 countries, it was one of the most far-reaching accords aimed at addressing climate change, a subject that had drawn intense international attention for at least a generation because of its impact on the global environment. Trump's pronouncement was expected. He had been elected in 2016 on a platform that called for a more unilateral, America-First foreign policy, and he had denounced Paris as harmful to the US economy. Even so, his statement greatly disappointed the world community, particularly because the United States was one of the planet's leading emitters of climate-changing greenhouse gases. Trump declared three months later that he would not leave the accord, but he added that he was open to renegotiating it, thus leaving uncertainty as to where America stood.[1]

Trump's statement reflected what has been an overarching challenge facing multilateral efforts to protect the global environment, that of giving environmental protection a priority on par with what are oftentimes regarded as more important social, economic, political, or military concerns. Within this broader anthropocentric theme are several subthemes. The first is that finding a means of balancing internationally accepted regimes to tackle specific environmental challenges with the desire of each country to defend its own interests. This is a quandary predating the modern environmental movement that emerged in the 1960s.

The second is that of North-North and North-South divides. Developed countries (DCs) of the "North" did not necessarily agree among themselves as to what steps to take insofar as environmental protection efforts. Even more vigorous was the dispute that pitted the North against the lesser developed countries (LDCs) of the "South." Following the Second World War, one-time colonies became independent and adopted initiatives that emphasized economic growth. In the meantime, a wave of environmentalism spread through the North, driven by the realization that radioactive fallout and pesticides posed a threat to flora, fauna, and humans; that agricultural output was unlikely to keep up with a rapidly growing human population; and that leading a good life required a healthy environment. DCs established new government agencies and signed multilateral agreements designed to protect humans' well-being, and to conserve flora and fauna for humans' enjoyment. That environmental movement in the North soon encompassed other concerns, among them hazardous waste, depletion of the ozone layer, and climate change. DCs encouraged LDCs to follow their lead on environmental regulation. While not opposed to protecting the environment, lesser developed nations regarded their more developed counterparts' ostensible altruism an affront to national sovereignty, an attempt to perpetuate the South's dependency on the North, and, given the amount of waste and atmospheric pollution produced by DCs, hypocritical.

The final subtheme is that of military conflict. The inability of humans to find peaceful solutions to their differences has led to innumerable armed clashes, some of them global in nature and others that risked becoming so. The natural environment affects and is affected by the bombs and artillery used in these conflicts, by the movement of troops and vehicles, and by the construction of fortifications, roads, and bases. Likewise, the terrain and weather conditions can influence military operations. But wars can also have an impact hundreds or even thousands of miles from the front. Additionally, armed conflicts are diversionary. On the one hand, they take attention away from efforts to protect the environment. On the other hand, they can send resources elsewhere that might otherwise be put toward exploitation of the planet's flora or fauna.

In examining efforts to defend the environment—or the harm done to it— in an international historical context, this book will define "environment" broadly, placing within it not only living organisms but Earth's atmosphere and topography. In this respect, "environment" is broader in scope than "ecology," which describes the distribution and abundance of animals. Instead, the definition used is similar to that of "ecosystem," which is a community of organisms interacting with one another and with their physical (living and nonliving) environment.

Moreover, it would do a disservice to both readers and those involved in international environmental affairs to restrict this study solely to the actions of nation-states and their leaders. Individuals working outside of government circles, including hunters, scientists, and authors, could and did influence policymaking at the national and multinational levels. The same is true with international financial institutions, which have tended to emphasize development over environmental protection, and nongovernmental organizations, whose topic-oriented expertise has been able to sway opinion and the language appearing in multilateral environmental agreements.

In examining the themes that have influenced international environmental policies, as well as those who have been involved in them, this book will begin with the lead-up to what became the first international environmental agreement, the 1900 Convention for the Preservation of Wild Animals, Birds and Fish in Africa, and end with the Paris climate accords. Neither of these pacts, nor the dozens of others signed between them, have succeeded in resolving fully the myriad of environmental issues that continue to confront those within and outside the highest levels of diplomatic circles. Accordingly, the conclusion will provide not only a summary of accomplishments but an overview of the numerous challenges that remain.

# Anthropocentric environmentalism

In 1900, delegates from Great Britain, France, Germany, Portugal, Italy, and the Belgian Congo arrived in London for a first-of-its-kind meeting. The topic was not principally military or commercial, but nature itself. The expansion of European colonial possessions in Africa, in combination with the arrival of numerous Europeans, had increased the number of animals on that continent that were hunted for trophies, feathers, meat, pelts, or ivory. In other cases, the Europeans brought their own animals with them, such as sheep, and killed any indigenous fauna that posed a threat to their herds. Consequently, the population of indigenous animals such as the ostrich, lion, and rhinoceros had declined, or, in the cases of the blue antelope and a zebra called the quagga, were entirely wiped out.[1] In the hope of preventing the extinction of prized fauna, the representatives in London signed that May the Convention for the Preservation of Wild Animals, Birds and Fish in Africa.

The convention divided African animals into five "schedules." Those on schedules 1 through 4 were worthy of preservation because they were useful to humans, were rare or had not yet reached adulthood, or were females with young. Among the fauna on these lists were owls, giraffe, ostriches, apes, zebra, elephants, and hippopotamuses. Those animals on schedule 5, such as baboons, crocodiles, otters, and poisonous snakes, were labeled as pests that could be killed at will, no matter what their age. Hunting would be limited to particular times of the year and only to those with licenses. Banned were certain methods of hunting, including poison, dynamite, and nets. Finally, the convention called for establishing reserves on "sufficiently large tracts of land" to permit more sizable animals to engage in their natural migrations.[2]

The convention, as was the case with other environmental agreements reached in the first two decades of the 1900s, was largely anthropocentric in nature—that is, its prime purpose was to protect the interests of humans rather than safeguard the well-being of the animals. Moreover, despite the apparent support the agreement had among Europe's major powers, most of those who attended the meeting in London failed to ratify it. Yet the convention was significant. For one, it reflected the influence of a burgeoning interest in environmental protection in parts of Europe as well as the United States. Additionally, it gave hope to individuals in and out of government on both sides of the Atlantic that it might be possible to enact similar multilateral agreements. Indeed, for over a decade, those seeking to protect the environment could point to the signing and ratification of a number of bilateral or multilateral environmental treaties. The First World War put a halt to what momentum the international environmental movement had, but the end of that conflict generated an expectation of its revival.

## Placing (European) humans first

Although the Convention for the Preservation of Wild Animals, Birds and Fish in Africa was the planet's first international environmental agreement, it was not the earliest attempt to protect the environment, even if those previous efforts were not necessarily aimed at preventing harm to flora or fauna. Ancient Rome made some effort to control smoke that damaged buildings in the city and harmed people living in its wealthier neighborhoods. But it was Great Britain that may have passed the earliest environmental law, specifically an ordinance barring the use of sea coal. A "dirty" type of coal, sea coal, produced along with heat a significant amount of soot. It was the resulting pollution that prompted King Edward I to enact the law in 1273. When that initial effort failed to reduce the amount of smoke that placed a pall over London, Edward in 1307 issued a royal proclamation prohibiting the use of coal in furnaces. The effectiveness of such legislation, though, is in doubt, for the use of coal in England continued to increase during the 1400s and 1500s.[3]

Other early environmental laws concerned protection or regrowth of forests. German king Albert I (1298–1308) and his successor, Henry VII (1308–13), enacted ordinances safeguarding some forests and requiring the reforestation of other agricultural lands that once were tree covered. But like Edward I's proclamation, the purpose of these in Germany was not to protect the environment. Rather, it was to guarantee lumber for housing, tools, weapons, and fuel. Similarly, the purpose of a forest code passed by the French government in the 1300s was to ensure a supply of wood for the navy.[4] A common theme to these environmental laws was their anthropocentric nature. What mattered most was not protecting the environment as an end in itself, but making sure that any harm to the environment did not affect the well-being of the human population.

At the time of the passage of these laws, Europe was on the verge of the Renaissance, a period of cultural, technological, and scientific innovation. One of the consequences of this era of world history was to give Europeans the desire and ability to head into uncharted parts of the world. An age of exploration got underway, as British, French, Dutch, Portuguese, and Spanish sailors headed into the unknown, hoping to achieve one or more of the "three Gs": God, gold, and glory—spreading Christianity, making money, and winning prestige for themselves and their home countries.

European exploration and colonization had significant, and oftentimes devastating, environmental effects. In the Azores, the Portuguese, who arrived in the 1420s, burned down trees to make room for grazing animals and sugarcane. On one of the islands, a new arrival let loose rabbits, which reproduced and ate both the indigenous flora and the even the settlers' crops. On the Canary Islands, the Spanish brought with them animals and plants, and also engaged in producing sugar. Here too, the native flora and fauna were all but destroyed. Furthermore, on both the Azores and Canaries, the lack of trees encouraged erosion, which interfered with the flow of streams vital to the Europeans' agricultural pursuits.[5]

These stories repeated themselves elsewhere. The British discovered that sugar depleted the soil's nutrients at a slower rate than the tobacco they were growing in North America, and therefore removed trees on the Caribbean islands of Barbados and Jamaica to make way for sugarcane. The Dutch, who established a colony on the Indian Ocean island of Mauritius in 1638, had eliminated by the end of the century most of the palms, and brought with them rats, goats, dogs, and pigs that began to roam the island, propagate, and kill many of the native plants and animals. The French, who claimed Mauritius in 1715, determined that a significant number of the trees were excellent for shipbuilding, leading the colonial government to bring in slaves and oxen to facilitate lumber operations. The Portuguese, claimants of Brazil starting in 1500, began to use that colony's numerous rivers to penetrate its interior and clear land for sugar plantations, forcing the local Indian populations into slavery. Portuguese and Spanish traders in Brazil discovered turtle eggs, and turtle and manatee meat, which were in high demand in Europe. In turn, they killed large numbers of those animals, depriving the indigenes of important sources of protein.[6]

Enslavement and destruction of wildlife were two causes of the toll European colonization took on the indigenous human populations. War was another, particularly as Europeans claimed the possessions of the locals. Nothing, however, had as great an impact as disease. Of those deadly pathogens, one of the most easily spread was smallpox, but there were other Old World illnesses that ravaged the New World, among them typhus, measles, and whooping cough. So many unknown diseases outside Europe precipitated a demographic disaster. In less than a half-century after Christopher Columbus arrived on the Caribbean island of Hispañola, virtually the entire Taino population had died. In central Mexico, the home of the Aztec Empire, the population fell from an estimated 18–30 million in 1519—the year the conquistador Hernán Cortés landed—to only about 1.5 million by 1600. Likewise, the Aborigines of Australia and Maori of New Zealand suffered terribly after the arrival of Europeans. One historian estimates that on average, each indigenous society in the New World alone lost nine-tenths of its population to disease following first contact with Europeans.[7]

These exploratory voyages by the start of the eighteenth century had brought Europeans to every continent, and they had charted parts or all of the coastlines of each continent. In some cases, such as in the Americas, they had surveyed large portions of the interior and staked claims to those lands. Africa was a notable exception: about 90 percent of it remained unclaimed by Europeans as late as the 1870s.[8]

## Scrambles in Africa, the Americas, and the Pacific

One reason why Europeans in the last quarter of the nineteenth century took a greater interest in Africa was industrialization. By the early 1800s, economic prosperity, a growing population, and higher demand for commodities in Great Britain had generated what became known as the First Industrial Revolution. The iron industry saw some growth at this time thanks to the recent development of the steam engine, but it was the textile industry that witnessed the greatest expansion. A cooperative banking sector provided the liquidity to support these firms, and a growing railroad system assisted manufacturers in shipping their commodities to markets or ports.

As significant as the First Industrial Revolution was, the Second that was underway by the last quarter of the 1800s proved even more so. By then, the technological innovations taking place on the British Isles had spread to continental Europe and the United States, be it because of industrial espionage, the use of patents, or the widespread sale of technical and trade books that offered descriptions of the new machines. Factories sprung up near places with large coal deposits that could be tapped for power. Railroads continued to expand on both sides of the Atlantic and were constructed on other continents, including in India, South Africa, Argentina, Japan, and China. The use of refrigeration in rail cars and ships appeared in the 1870s, permitting the conveyance of formerly perishable items. Ocean-going vessels became bigger and moved goods more quickly thanks to the use of iron and then steel hulls; the shift from sail to steam to oil provided energy to increasingly powerful engines; screw propellers instead of paddlewheels; and new waterways such as the Suez and Kiel canals, which reduced the time and cost of transportation. Whereas a US clipper ship that relied on sails could in the 1860s carry 5,000 tons of cargo across the

Atlantic Ocean in under two weeks, by the late 1880s, a steam-driven vessel could handle more than twice that amount, yet make the same run in about six days.[9] These innovations in transport, alongside wider employment of the telegraph—including the laying of the first trans-Atlantic telegraph line in 1866—allowed people to share their discoveries over longer distances in ever shorter periods of time, further hastening industrialization. So did a pool of immigrants who, inspired by the possibility of work or access to cheap land, left their home countries to seek a new life elsewhere.

Industrialization, and the desire for new markets or improving one's economic status, had profound implications for Africa, as did the discovery in the 1700s of quinine as a treatment for malaria, an oftentimes tropical disease spread by mosquitoes. Although Europeans for centuries had had contact with numerous African kingdoms, from which they acquired slaves in return for manufactured goods, that commercial relationship by the mid-1800s had begun to change. European countries had banned slavery, but explorers and missionaries who traveled to Africa disseminated information regarding raw materials that could feed Europe's expanding industry and trade. Driven by these economic motives and a desire to enhance their great power status by grabbing new territory, and having behind them superior firepower, Europeans began to carve up Africa. By the time the twentieth century got underway, they had asserted control over 90 percent of that continent, with Great Britain claiming the largest share.[10]

Industrialization had similar impacts in the United States. In 1860, a year before its civil war broke out, the United States was already the fourth largest industrial country. It had vast areas of unoccupied lands—"unoccupied" as defined by the many white Americans who did not consider the interests or well-being of Native Americans. Its population by 1900 was seventy-six million, more than double what it had been forty years earlier, and included millions of recently arrived immigrants. An ever-growing number of its citizens migrated to the cities to find work in its new and expanding industries, so that by 1920, just over half of Americans lived in an urban area. To support their population and feed their factories, American officials encouraged their citizens to move onto the Great Plains, where farmers raised wheat on land that had only a narrow layer of topsoil; started to drain the Florida Everglades in the 1880s; endorsed the cutting down of billions of feet of lumber for fuel and construction; and, as wood declined in availability, turned to coal and oil. In so doing, Americans transformed the landscape, removing trees that prevented erosion and provided homes to animals, killing most of the wading birds in the Everglades, moving tons of earth to expose the coal underneath, and pumping into the air large amounts of soot.[11] Similarly, the United States joined the imperialist urge. In the name of economic well-being, power status, national security, or racial superiority, US officials, through negotiation or war, acquired islands in the Pacific and Caribbean, including Samoa, Hawaii, the Philippines, and Cuba.

# Enter the environmentalists?

Prior to the Scramble for Africa, some European scientists and colonial officials had begun to take issue with the environmental destruction they witnessed, though it was not uncommon for the arguments they used to have anthropocentric qualities. Authorities of the Cape Colony, established by the Dutch East India Company in the 1650s in what later became South Africa, regarded it as important to protect the indigenous flora in part because it could have medicinal properties. Englishman Stephen Hales rejected a long-standing claim that deforestation benefited human health, contending instead that vegetation improved air quality. His critique offered a foundation for what became the theory of "desiccation"—an early version of the theory of climate change—that deforestation generated less rain, greater flooding when storms took place, and a decline in the flow of streams. His conclusions influenced others, such as French botanist Henri-Louis Duhamel du Monceau. Horticulturalist Pierre Poivre, the administrator of French-controlled Mauritius, constructed a botanical garden on that island to combat the deforestation occurring there. Alexander Beatson, the governor of the British colony of St. Helena from 1808 to 1813, became aware of the work taking place in Mauritius and the argument regarding desiccation, and instituted a reforestation effort.[12]

In the United States, too, a backlash against environmental harm began to emerge. In 1864, George Perkins Marsh used scientific data to demonstrate the impact humans had on life on the planet in his book, *Man and Nature*. Marsh rejected the idea that mankind had the right to exploit the environment. "Wherever he plants his foot," he wrote, "the harmonies of nature are turned to discord. . . . Indigenous vegetable and animal species are axteripated, and supplanted by others of foreign origin." Such changes, he warned, precipitated tremendous harm to the natural order. His solution became known as conservation: it was the duty of humans to manage the earth's resources so that they would be available to future generations. These conclusions in certain respects were not new or profound, as they reflected to some extent the desiccationist theory that had been around for a century. But Marsh was the first person to demonstrate clearly the interdependence of human society and the environment, and to warn that without proper management, nature would conquer humans.[13]

*Man and Nature* reinforced an ongoing assumption that humans' know-how could defend the environment in ways beneficial to them. Of particular concern to both scientists and colonial officials were forests, given the importance of trees for both construction and fuel. By the 1700s, states in what was to become Germany had emerged as leaders in the field of scientific forestry. Adopting a quantitative methodology, German foresters assumed it was possible to look at a forest and estimate both the age and weight of trees. By restricting which of those trees could be cut, the forest could indefinitely sustain  humans' needs. The Germans applied this system of forest management not only to their colonies, but to those of other European powers that believed German expertise could protect their forest resources. With German assistance, the Dutch imposed restrictions on the felling of trees in their East Indies colony. For the first half of the 1800s, Germans oversaw the Forest Department of British-controlled India, from which that knowledge was transferred to England itself and throughout the British Empire.[14]

Among those influenced by the German model of forestry as well as by Marsh was the American Gifford Pinchot. A graduate of Yale University, Pinchot had been inspired by Dietrich Brandis, a German botanist and advocate of scientific forestry who had overseen India's Forest Department. Pinchot became friends with Theodore Roosevelt who, four years after becoming president of the United States, appointed him as the first chief of the U.S. Forest Service, a post he held until 1910. To Pinchot, it was important to protect the forests "not . . . because they are beautiful . . . or because they are refuges for the wild creatures of the wilderness. The forests are to be used by man. Every other consideration comes secondary."[15] In 1900, he helped establish a forestry school at Yale, where students could learn about Europe's scientific methods.

By the turn of the twentieth century the term "conservation" had come to describe virtually any form of environment protection. However, in the 1800s, the word "preservation" found common usage, and, indeed, there was a difference between conservationism and preservationism. To the former, defending nature was a means to protect the welfare of humankind. To preservationists, such as American writers Ralph Waldo Emerson and Henry David Thoreau, and British poets Edward Carpenter and William Wordsworth, protecting the environment was an end in itself. This did not mean avoiding all contact with protected wilderness. Rather, preservationists wanted to keep those landscapes free of human manipulation so that people could enjoy them during hiking or camping excursions. Among those inspired by the words of Emerson and Thoreau was John Muir, a Scottish immigrant raised in the US state of Wisconsin and who founded the environmental nongovernmental organization (NGO) Sierra Club in 1892. Rejecting Marsh's assertion that the environment existed for human use, he wrote in 1916, "Nature's object in making animals and plants might possibly be first of all the happiness of each one of them, not the creation of all for the happiness of one. Why should man value himself as more than a small part of the one great unit of creation?" In the United Kingdom, the words of individuals like Carpenter and Wordsworth influenced to some degree environmental groups such as the Selborne Society, the Coal Smoke Abatement Society, and the National Trust.[16]

Preservationists had some success. The United States became the site of the world's first national park, Yellowstone, established in 1872, and Muir himself assisted in the creation of Yosemite National Park in 1890. The American model inspired others to follow suit: the British colonial government in Australia set aside land in 1879 for Royal National Park— the planet's second oldest national park. In 1885, Canada established Banff National Park and, a year later, Yoho National Park.

Yet conservationism, driven by the principle of scientific management, held the upper hand over preservationism in the United States and much of the world. For instance, following a major earthquake that struck San Francisco in 1906 and cut much of its water supply, Pinchot, Muir, and their allies fought over a proposal to dam the Tuolumne River in Yosemite Park and create a reservoir in the Hetch Hetchy Valley that would serve San Francisco's population. Preservationists argued that the dam would destroy the natural beauty of the valley, but conservationists, who insisted that the most important consideration was the welfare of San Francisco's residents, won out in 1913.[17] In Europe and its colonies, the demand for raw materials and markets, and a desire to protect one's status as a great power, gave conservationists the edge over preservationists. Scientific conservation inspired the French in 1862 to establish forest reserves in what later became Vietnam. British authorities endorsed passage of the Indian Forest Act in 1865 and, thirteen years later, the Forest Tree Act in South Australia.[18]

## To the 1900 convention

The language of protecting the environment for human benefit included not just flora, but fauna. As they pushed ever more into Africa, Europeans found an animal population that was highly diverse and appeared limitless, not realizing that it had been shaped in many ways by the indigenous peoples who maintained herds of cattle; used fires to clear growth for pastures and control the tsetse fly that spread a dangerous disease called trypanosomiasis; and grew crops to maintain their populations. Instead, as British biologist Sir Julian Huxley commented as late as 1929, Africa was "a continent which had hardly changed in the last five hundred years."[19]

This disconnect between Europeans' amazement with the richness of Africa's bounty and the ways in which the indigenous peoples had helped mold it reflected racial and cultural stereotypes witnessed nearly everywhere European settlers and their ancestors set foot. German Southwest Africa's colonial government favored the removal of the local Herero and Nama populations onto poorer quality land because, having bought into desiccation theory, its leaders believed that the indigenous peoples were responsible for droughts by cutting down far too many trees and bushes for fences, fires, and housing. In the United States, many white Americans argued that Native Americans did not know how to use the land properly.[20] In turn, the Bannock, Crow, and Shoshone Indians found themselves displaced with the creation of Yellowstone National Park. Following the establishment of Glacier National Park in 1910, the US government saw to it to exclude the Blackfeet Indians.[21] Similarly white Americans from the early 1800s and into the 1900s believed the lack of land claims by the indigenes of Latin America was the result of "a debased people . . . willing to live in an indolent standoff with nature because they lacked the moral stamina to conquer it." Using language akin to that of whites in North America, Europeans in Australia and New Zealand asserted that the "uncivilized" Aborigine and Maori peoples were "doomed" to find themselves displaced "in the 'struggle for life.'"[22]

That disconnect between whites and indigenes included the hunt. Many Europeans at the turn of the twentieth century were influenced by Victorian social mores. They originated in Great Britain, where the First Industrial Revolution created a new class of wealthy individuals whose economic well-being was not based on land ownership. However, they purchased large swaths of acreage to use for hunting game and got enacted legal statutes limiting access to that acreage only to members of the elite. The hunt on these "game farms" were well organized and extravagant, with beaters used to get birds out of their hiding places, or men on horseback, aided by dogs, tracking down foxes. Additionally, the participants imposed rules on themselves to ensure the quarry had a "sporting chance" of getting away. As firearm technology improved, they added more decrees. For instance, it was "unsporting" to shoot "a sitting bird"; bringing down one in flight became the goal.[23]

The Victorian hunt spread elsewhere in Europe and beyond. Killing animals for sport in places like Africa and India became a status symbol, particularly among the British and Germans. Moreover, it came to be seen as a form of military training, one that would make men physically stronger, more able to handle "unhealthy climates," and, in the name of protecting the British Empire, more prepared to kill those who posed a threat to the motherland and its interests. Through photographs, novels, speeches, and trophy exhibitions, the adventures of European hunters like W. D. M. Bell and Arthur Neumann nurtured nationalism at home and further imperialist expansion.[24]

It would be wrong to state that hunting was solely a phenomenon of the elite or of Europeans. Those who were less well-off and traveled to Africa wanted to make a better life for themselves too. They looked for gemstones, sought employment in any number of corporate entities, or started plantations, where they grew coffee, bananas, or other products for export. The rapid growth of the European population necessitated the construction of not just additional towns but railroads to link the settlements together and with commercial operations, which opened the door to developing further population centers. Those same railroads made it easier for a settler not of the upper classes to engage in hunting of his own. In North America, Americans adopted some elements of the Victorian hunt. But the rifle also was used to kill vermin that posed a threat to one's livestock or crops, or to retain aspects of the pioneer spirit that seemed to be disappearing as ever more Americans moved to cities to get work in the country's booming industrial sector.[25]

Whether a member of upper crust or not, Europeans had a difficult time understanding, indeed accepting, indigenous peoples' concept of the hunt. To them, a "true sportsman" shunned wanton killing. Even a person who shot dozens of animals considered "vermin" without just cause was one to receive criticism. White Europeans frowned on Africans' use of nets, traps, and, increasingly, muzzle-loading rifles to engage in what the newer arrivals perceived as senseless destruction. To the British the Kamba people of Kenya did not need game on which to survive and considered it "illegitimate" for them to hunt outside their home territory. They failed to grasp that the Kamba turned to hunting for survival when droughts destroyed their crops. Even those European officials who understood their fellow travelers were most responsible for the decline of Africa's animal populations saw every reason to exclude the indigenes in the name of preserving the fauna. Lord Delamere, one of the first Europeans to settle in Kenya and a leader among the colonists there, admitted, "It is easy enough to say natives have been centuries in Africa and have not exterminated the game, but that was under different conditions."[26]

The game the newcomers in Africa sought fell into several categories. The most prized were "trophy animals," including lions, rhinos, elephants, leopards, buffalo, eland, and giraffe. Of that list, the first five were especially coveted because they posed the greatest danger to humans or were the hardest to find. Ostriches also drew attention, not because they were menacing or elusive, but because their eggs and feathers were in high demand. "'Pot' animals," among them "smaller antelope," came next, for their meat offered both a source of protein and, when shipped, income for the settlers. Finally, there were "vermin." On that list one would find the carnivores, as they were the animals that killed the settlers' livestock, or the same quarry desired by hunters. Given that both lions and leopards were among Africa's meat eaters, they ended up being simultaneously "trophies" and "vermin."[27]

To prevent the decimation of fauna they wanted to highlight their own status or provide for their economic welfare, Europeans made a few early efforts to control hunting. The first imperial ordinance was in 1822 in the Cape Colony, which the British had seized from the Netherlands in 1806. While offering rewards for killing vermin, this 1822 law sought to protect the elephant, bontebok, and hippopotamus by imposing for them a closed hunting season, a license to hunt during open season, and protections for those that had not yet reached adulthood. The Transvaal in modern South Africa followed suit in 1846. Starting in 1856, the Cape Colony saw the founding of several forest reserves, though their purpose was less to protect the trees themselves and more to prevent the extirpation of the animal populations that lived in them. By the end of the century, protecting local wildlife had led to the concept of the nature reserve. Like a national park, a wildlife reserve would keep the environment in its natural state. The difference was that humans could visit national parks as tourists and photographers, while reserves separated people from the wildlife—though restricted hunting sometimes took place. The first of those sanctuaries, the Pongola, appeared in 1894 in the Boer-controlled region of southern Africa.[28]

By the time of the Pongola establishment, it appeared to many Europeans that a large number of the animals they hunted might soon go extinct. In 1872, Georg Schweinfurth, a German explorer and botanist, alerted those willing to listen about a rapidly declining elephant population in Africa. Within a decade, scientists, explorers, and hunters in the United Kingdom and Germany had joined him, warning of a "war of extermination" on the world's largest land mammal. That a growing number of tusks shipped out of Africa were smaller, and therefore likely came from younger or female pachyderms, suggested many of the mature and male elephants had been wiped out. Big-game hunters such as Frederick Selous started to champion conservation in the name of making sure that future generations had an opportunity to ply their trade. Even animals considered physically hideous became objects of glorification. "This useful scavenger," British politician and author Samuel Cronwright-Schreiner commented of the vulture, "seems repulsive seated near a dying carcass, so engorged at times that he can hardly rise from the ground. But see him in the air, and you look upon what is surely one of the most beautiful things in the world." The growing use of birds' plumage in dress, while popular among many Victorian women, sickened others, who considered it immoral. In the United Kingdom, they formed a number of NGOs, among them the Selborne Society and the Plumage League. Disease added to the worries of those desirous to protect Africa's indigenous fauna. Among the most dangerous was rinderpest, a virus that spread from the settlers' cattle to zebra, buffalo, and antelope.[29]

The possibility of Africa's animals disappearing spawned more intense efforts to protect them. Belgium's Congo Free State issued in 1889 restrictions on hunting elephants, and three years later, German Southwest Africa did the same for ostriches. Most significant, however, was a game ordinance enacted in 1896 by German East Africa's governor, Hermann von Wissmann. His inspiration came from two sources. One was an article he had read in a British magazine regarding the extirpation of animal species in Africa. The other was Yellowstone National Park. Just as German scientific management had influenced Americans like Gifford Pinchot, so the use of scientific management in the United States had inspired von Wissmann. Buffalo, once numbering in the tens of millions in the United States, had fallen victim to unchecked hunting, to the point that by the time of its creation, Yellowstone was the only place in that country with a free-ranging herd. To von Wissmann, the protection afforded to buffalo by Yellowstone was nothing short of the application of scientific management to animals, in this case, in the form of a game reserve.[30]

Von Wissman's law established two animal sanctuaries that did not ban hunting on them but restricted it to only a small number of people. On or off the reserves, those who wished to hunt had to pay for a license. The ordinance limited elephant hunting to professionals, required those

**PHOTO 1** Hermann Von Wissmann. *Credit: Dreamstime.*

professionals to pay a large fee, and imposed an additional charge for each elephant killed. No harm could come to elephants with tusks weighing less than three kilograms, or to females or their young. Conversely, the ordinance encouraged the extermination of animals regarded as "vermin," such as large cats, crocodiles, and wild pigs, by paying the hunter a bounty for each one. Reflecting the racial stereotypes of the day and the concept of what constituted true sportsmanship, von Wissmann prohibited indigenous peoples from using "nets, fire and other forms of driving game." His ordinance influenced the establishment of reserves in Britain's colonies in southern Africa. Among the most famous was the Sabi Game Reserve, created in 1898 in South Africa.[31]

It soon became clear that approaching the question of conservation one colony at a time would not work. As an example, British authorities had instructions to impound any elephant tusks smaller than five kilograms. Traders, though, found a way to get around the law by taking their booty into German- or Italian-controlled colonies, where they did not have to fear their haul would be seized. When the British urged the Germans to enact the former's regulations on tusks, Germany's colonial minister, Paul Kayser, replied that such a measure would only encourage smugglers to head to other European possessions, such as those in Portuguese hands.[32]

Realizing a multinational approach was necessary, von Wissmann in 1897 proposed to the British government an international agreement to protect Africa's game. The appeal to London made sense. Not only had the German experience with game reserves received notice in the United Kingdom, but two-thirds of the animals hunted in Africa were in Whitehall's colonies.

British prime minister Lord Salisbury liked the idea and, following further correspondence, proposed in 1899 holding the convention in London among all the powers with colonies in Europe. It was that gathering that witnessed the promulgation of the Convention for the Preservation of Wild Animals, Birds and Fish in Africa.[33]

In three respects, the convention's title was inaccurate. First, despite the mention of birds and fish, its focus was on land mammals. Indeed, much of the negotiations that led to the convention centered around one animal, the elephant. Second, the language of the convention, such as "to a certain extent" and "as far as it is possible" placed restraints on the degree to which preservation took place. Finally, it covered not all of Africa but only that part of the continent between 20° north and 20° south latitude. The northern demarcation line followed roughly along that separating the Saharan and sub-Saharan portions of the continent. That in the south was chosen because of the Second Boer War that had begun in 1899 between Great Britain, and the Boer republics of Transvaal and the Orange Free State, and which was still underway in 1900. By choosing these northern and southern boundaries, all or portions of numerous European colonies in Africa, among them German South West Africa, Portuguese East Africa, and Southern Rhodesia, were not covered. Furthermore, because the invitees represented only Europe and its colonies, two independent countries located within the scope of the convention, Liberia and Abyssinia, were not present.[34]

There were other shortcomings to the convention. Like von Wissmann's 1896 law, the 1900 convention sought to defend European hunters' interests by prohibiting the "use of nets and pitfalls for taking animals," both of them methods employed by African hunters. The overwhelming majority of indigenous people could not afford the licenses demand by the treaty, meaning that any animals they hunted for survival made them poachers. Due to resistance from the Portuguese and French over an effort by the British to restrict the commerce in feathers and tusks, the delegates removed certain birds from the list of those protected as well as a tariff on the export of all elephant tusks. Even those concessions were not enough. France insisted it would withhold ratification of the agreement unless Liberia and Abyssinia adopted it, but the Liberian government refused to accept any restraints on the hunting of elephants or leopards in the name of protecting locals' crops and domesticated animal herds. France's hardline position convinced the Belgian Congo also to forego ratification. With that, the agreement never officially went into effect.[35]

It would be wrong, however, to place the 1900 convention into the trash heap of history. It encouraged the establishment in Great Britain of an NGO, the Society for the Preservation of the Fauna of the Empire (SPFE). Its members included powerful individuals, among them Selous; Sir Henry Seaton Kerr, a hunter and member of the Conservative Party; and Sir Harry Johnston, a colonial official who had seen service in Cameroon, Mozambique, and Uganda. The SPFE's influence was enough that successive colonial secretaries met with its representatives in the years immediately after its founding. Less powerful NGOs appeared in continental Europe as well, such as the Game Protection Commission of the German Colonial Society and, in France, the Society for the Acclimation and Protection of Nature. Furthermore, mostly every colony revised its game laws to abide by the suggestions put forward in London, such as closed hunting seasons and protecting young animals. Finally, the treaty inspired the creation of other reserves, including the Luangwa in Southern Rhodesia, founded in 1904, and Giant's Castle, created three years later in Natal—later part of South Africa.[36]

The establishment of these wildlife sanctuaries was not always popular in the colonies. In some cases, European settlers reluctantly accepted them, assuming that once the fauna on them returned to sizable numbers, then they would be reopened for exploitation. In others, such as the Sabi, local farmers who wanted to use the reserve for cattle fought with game wardens, who resisted giving them that right. Another complaint was that the reserves provided safe havens for predators that destroyed livestock or animals that spread disease.[37]

It was the matter of disease that led not just farmers but colonial officials to cite the SPFE for hindering efforts to control the tsetse fly. A small insect of about 6–16 millimeters in length, the tsetse fly was a purveyor of trypanosomiasis, or "sleeping sickness," which attacks the nervous system and can lead to death. Native Africans had learned the fly preferred thick brush and had succeeded in controling it by removing the brush and turning it into grazing lands, or avoiding areas where the tsetse was known to exist. But the arrival of Europeans had removed many indigenes from their lands, thereby permitting once-grassy areas to become covered with the thickets the insect enjoyed. To open up fly-infested lands to settlers, British officials in eastern and southern Africa concluded the best solution was to kill off wild game, assuming the animals were responsible for the tsetse's spread. For instance, in 1901, from 1905 to 1908, and from 1910 to 1915, authorities in Southern Rhodesia suspended laws controlling the shooting of fauna. Because they deemed wild game as the culprit for trypanosomiasis's proliferation, colonial officers increasingly resisted the idea of establishing wildlife reserves in areas they controlled.[38]

## The 1902 bird convention

Although the Convention for the Preservation of Wild Animals, Birds and Fish in Africa gave priority to land mammals, its title demonstrated that the international community had by the early 1900s started to look at avian life. As was true with many land animals, birds were in high demand, and for similar reasons. Geese, ducks, and other waterfowl offered meat for consumption, while humans wanted cardinals, blue jays, and herons for their plumage.[39]

The consequences for the birds could be, and were, disastrous. Possibly the most famous example was the passenger pigeon. Once having numbers so large that they darkened the skies over the United States, they were a cheap source of protein. In Michigan, some counties shipped to the East Coast an average of one million pigeons annually.[40] By 1900, they were all but gone; in 1914, the last one died in captivity. Other species to disappear included the Labrador duck of the eastern United States and eastern Canada, and the great auk, which ranged from Greenland to Norway.

The movement to conserve birds and their habitat in the United States led to the creation in the 1880s of the first Audubon Society and an entomological bureau in the Department of Agriculture. From these initiatives emerged in 1905 both the founding of the National Audubon Society and the renaming of the entomological division the Biological Survey.[41] As a step toward protecting America's fowl, President Roosevelt in 1903 founded America's first wildlife sanctuary, Pelican Island National Wildlife Refuge in Florida.

European states lacked the information gathered by the Audubon Society and the Biological Survey, but the evidence there too pointed to the killing of large numbers of birds, whether it be on the continent or those shipped in from the colonies. Between 1887 and 1889, merchants sent about 2.7 million quail from Egypt, where most ended up on the tables of consumers in Great Britain and France. A demand for lark wings as a fashion statement led a single fashion shop in Paris to import 400,000 pair of them from Finland during a twenty-year period ending around 1907.[42]

It was German farmers and foresters who, in the late 1860s, first raised their voices about these numbers. A decade earlier, European botanists brought with them from the United States wine grapes and, unknowingly, an insect called the grape phylloxera that began to kill grapevines in Great Britain and continental Europe. German farmers and foresters argued that birds ate insects like the phylloxera, and the killing off of so many fowl endangered both forests and harvests. They appealed to both their government and that of Austria-Hungary. It happened that Germany and Austria-Hungary had long national traditions of protecting wild fowl, and the two commenced an effort in the 1860s to create a continental convention. Swiss and French officials joined the cause. In the 1881 International Phylloxera Convention, Austria-Hungary, Germany, France, Portugal, and Switzerland concurred that they would use American vines to stop the spread of the phylloxera. That agreement, though, did not offer protections for avian life. The 1902 Convention for the Protection of Birds Useful to Agriculture, signed by eleven European nations, did. Under its provisions, birds considered beneficial to farmers were off limits at all times, as were their nests, eggs, and offspring. About 150 species were placed on that list, among them the starling and some finches and thrushes. Other types of fowl could be killed or sold, but only during certain months of the year. Still others, including crows, magpies, and ducks, received no protections at all. Some European countries, including the United Kingdom, Norway, and Russia, refused to partake in it, but eleven ratified it, and it went into effect in 1905.[43]

# Marine life

The international cooperation that took place at the highest levels to defend fauna on land and in the air extended in the late 1800s and early 1900s to marine species. Whales provide one example. Numerous imperial nations, including the Norway, Spain, and France, had participated in whaling, but it was Great Britain which, taking advantage of its position as the world's preeminent maritime power, became the top whaling nation by the 1700s. The successful effort of London's American colonies to achieve independence saw Americans undertake pelagic (high seas) whaling themselves, and by the 1840s they had become responsible for about 70 percent of the global trade. In combination with a series of wars with Spain, the British found themselves largely cut out of South America's coastal waters. They therefore turned their attention to Australian and New Zealand waters, which Parliament had opened up for them at the end of the eighteenth century. The growing number of British whalers in the South Pacific also contributed to London's colonization of that part of the world.[44]

As the 1800s progressed, though, it appeared the whaling industry was headed toward its demise. Some whales, like blues, can weigh well over hundred tons, making them two or even three times the size of, and far more dangerous than, sperm whales. Because they had more blubber than fin whales, bowheads drew more attention from whalers. Fin whales were fast, making them hard to nab. Finally, some whale species, when dead, sank rather than floated. Hence, it was only a matter of time for the most desired whales, such as sperm and humpbacks, to fall perilously low in number, jeopardizing the whaling industry's future.[45]

But as the century progressed, the outlook became sunnier for whalers. New technology, including the exploding harpoon, improved steam-powered vessels, and the use of compressed air made it possible to kill more whales and to make sure those killed remained afloat so they could be collected later. Further developments, among them large factory ships, and, shortly after the First World War, the introduction of the "stern slipway" permitted the hunting and, while at sea, processing of ever-larger whales, and in greater numbers than before. By the early 1900s, the British and Norwegians had come to predominate the industry, with each responsible for nearly half of the whales caught around Antarctica—where many whales lived or went to feed during the summer months—alone.[46]

Of course, hunting whales mattered little if there was not a market for what could be made from them. Here, whaling had two trump cards. It

**PHOTO 2** Cutting into a sperm whale, 1903. *Credit: Library of Congress.*

was a global industry. Furthermore, there was worldwide demand for its products, meaning one could expect a lucrative return. Those products were numerous, and included piano keys, body creams, and lubricating oil. Even more popular, however, were margarine and soap. First developed in France in 1870 as a substitute for butter, margarine required the use of fat from cattle. But thanks to the development of hydrogenation at the turn of the twentieth century, by which hydrogen was combined with whale oil, it became possible to convert that oil into a solid fat which could replace that from cows. A similar process permitted the use of whale oil in soap. Statistics demonstrated consumers' appetite for these products. Some one million tons of margarine was manufactured in 1927, double the amount in 1913. The Unilever Group, formally established in 1930 by the merging of British soapmaker Lever Brothers and the Dutch margarine producer Margarine Unie, sold 450,000 tons of soap in Europe in 1929 alone.[47]

Walruses also found commercial use, but overhunting depleted the population to the point that Europeans and Americans joined Russians in targeting seals, whose pelts were desired as a result of the opening of the China market by the turn of the nineteenth century. Seals offered oil of their own, and their skin could be converted into leather goods like wallets, belts, and gloves. Seal hunts literally took place all over the globe, from the Aleutian Islands in modern-day Alaska to the southern tip of South America and the southern Indian Ocean. Despite the realization among some observers of the havoc sealers wrought on the globe's seal populations, there was little willingness to regulate the trade,[48] that is, until the late 1800s. By that time, there remained two large populations of seals, both in North America. One, made up of harp seals, resided in Newfoundland, Canada. Still hunted today, harp seals spend much of their time at sea. Females, however, will come up onto the nearby ice to have their young during a three-week period. With sought-after white coats, the pups became—and remain—prized by sealers, who clubbed and skinned them, sometimes removing the pelt while the animal was still alive.[49] The other large seal community was in the Pribilof Islands, located in the Bering Sea. It was here that the international community took its first steps toward controlling seal hunts.

Named after the Russian explorer Gavriil Pribilof, who discovered them in 1740, the Pribilof Islands are part of modern-day Alaska and are about two hundred miles north of Unalaska, the largest town in the Aleutian Islands. At the time Pribilof came upon the islands, they were home to an estimated three million Northern fur seals. Hunting of the animals began to diminish their numbers to the point that the Russians, who controlled Alaska, imposed regulations so that the commercially valuable animals did not disappear. However, after Russia sold Alaska to the United States in 1867, the number of animals killed increased, jeopardizing the herd. Pelagic sealing made matters even worse. Although US officials could restrict sealing along American shores, they could do little to stop the killing of fur seals when they left Alaska after pupping and headed toward Japan or down the US West Coast to California. The Japanese, Americans, Russians, and Canadians—the last, because of its quasi-colonial status, represented by Great Britain—began to argue among themselves over what to do as the seal population declined.[50]

In 1886, US president Grover Cleveland had authorized the arrest of British seal hunters in the Bering Sea, and his successor, Benjamin Harrison, warned he would do the same after his inauguration in 1889. The British, alongside the Russians—who also had a Bering Sea rookery, on Robben Island—sought a negotiated settlement with Washington, only to have the United States cut off talks and send revenue cutters to the area in 1890. The British formally protested and prepared to dispatch warships to protect their nationals engaged in seal hunts. Both nations avoided conflict, yet rumors of American preparedness to use force persisted into 1891. Word that the seal population was falling because of both land and pelagic hunting added to the sense of urgency. The result was an Anglo-American modus vivendi in June 1891 to impose a moratorium on sealing on the high seas until May 1892. On land, the United States permitted sealing as long as the number of animals killed did not exceed 7,500.[51]

Less than two weeks before their *modus* was to expire, the US and British governments signed a second one, continuing the restrictions on pelagic and land sealing. More important, they accepted the idea of having France act as arbiter to settle their differences. The Canadians, who worried about any financial losses they might suffer as a result of a more permanent settlement, got included in the new *modus* a provision stating that if the arbiter decided in favor of London, then Washington would offer compensation to Ottawa. If, however, the third party accepted the US position, then the British would recompense the Americans.[52]

In 1893, a seven-person tribunal called for a three-month hunting season, banned the use of firearms, and prohibited pelagic hunts within sixty miles of the breeding area, but this did little good given that the seals traveled well beyond the sixty-mile zone. When the United States barred its nationals from conducting high seas sealing around 1897, Canadian and Japanese sealers, who were not bound by the arbitration agreement, stepped in, further reducing the seals' numbers. Tensions among the parties increased, particularly after US officials in 1906 killed five Japanese poachers and imprisoned a dozen others.[53]

By this time, all four of the interested nations had reason to seek an agreement. In 1905, a nineteen-month-long war between Japan and Russia over rival claims to Korea and northeastern China ended with Japanese acquisition of formerly Russian territory, including Robben Island. Russia wanted to protect another seal rookery on the Commander Islands from Japanese hunters, and the United States sought to prevent extermination of the Pribilof colony. Great Britain was in the most difficult position. London was the world's most important center for preparing sealskins, and continued decline of seal numbers offered financial peril. At the same time, it had to consider the position of the Canadian pelagic sealing industry which, unable to compete against Japan's, had suffered monetarily and wanted an indemnity.[54]

When negotiations began in Washington in May 1911, the population of the Pribilof colony had fallen to 130,000 animals. Two months later, the Japanese, American, British, and Russian delegates hammered out the North Pacific Fur Seal Convention. It barred nationals of the four countries from engaging in pelagic sealing and left it up to each signatory to oversee hunting in rookeries on its territory. As both Canada and Japan were to lose the most financially from giving up sealing on the high seas, the United States and Russia provided remuneration based on a percentage of the seals killed. Japan, for its part, promised to pay the other parties a portion of the money it made from seal hunts. While the convention had a fifteen-year life span, the signatories agreed it would remain in effect after that point as long as none of them nullified it. Within a year, the Pribilof herd had grown, and by 1932, it numbered 1.2 million animals.[55] The convention offered what became a first step toward additional protections not only for seals but marine mammals in general.

# World war

Three years after the promulgation of the sealing convention, ongoing tensions among Europe's major powers erupted into all-out war. The competition for colonies; the division of the continent's key players into two major alliances; an ongoing arms race, particularly between Germany on the one hand and Great Britain on the other; growing militarist sentiment in Russia and Germany; and rising nationalism in portions of the Austro-Hungarian empire had increased the likelihood of some kind of conflagration. In June 1914, the assassination of Franz Ferdinand, the heir to the Austro-Hungarian throne, by a Serbian nationalist set in motion a series of declarations of war that quickly brought Europe's major powers into the first global conflict of the twentieth century.

It is a truism that war breeds environmental destruction. The Greek historian Thucydides wrote that during the Peloponnesian War, fought between the Greek city-states of Athens and Sparta from 431 to 421 BC, the combatants cut down trees to build palisades. The result was to leave much of the countryside barren, and vulnerable to soil erosion and flooding. Imperialist-minded European nations relied heavily on forests to build large sea-going merchant and military fleets. The fittings for those ships required wrought iron, which was melted using wood-burning fires. To make a single ton of that iron in the early 1700s required the equivalent of about ten hectares of forest. In the American Civil War, both Confederate and Union soldiers cut down trees, whether for railroad ties, bridges, or fuel for cooking. "It is wonderful how the whole country round here is literally stripped of its timber," wrote one Union officer. "Woods which, when we came here, were so thick that we could not get through them any way are now entirely cleared." The Sabi Game Reserve became overwhelmed by the Second Boer War, during which both sides shot and killed animals on the reserve to provide sustenance for their troops.[56]

Yet it would be wrong to assume that the relationship between humans and the environment during periods of military conflict is a one-way street. The environment has an influence on warfare. Rivers, mountains, and forests can make it difficult, if not impossible, for attacking armies to reach their intended targets, and they can provide cover for defending forces. Rain, sleet, and snow can turn dirt roads to mud, keep aircraft from flying, and make life miserable for soldiers. Germs, viruses, and parasites spread by insects or the elements can wreak havoc on both attacker and defender. One Union surgeon during the American Civil War commented, "Sickness among the troops rapidly increasing. Remittent fever, diarrhoea, and dysentery prevail. We are encamped in low, wet ground, and the heavy rains keep much of it overflowed. I fear that if we remain here long we shall lose many men by sickness."[57]

Soldiers fighting on both sides of the front lines in Europe during the First World War encountered similar conditions, including snow, rain, wind, heat, and the smell of rotting corpses. "We don't think of death, but it's the cold, the terrible cold!," wrote one French soldier in 1915. "It seems to me at the moment that my blood is full of blocks of ice." Wind was used to blow deadly gas toward enemy positions but could reverse itself and pose a threat to its source. Rats and lice infested the trenches, the former eating the food on which the troops relied or feeding off of human or animal corpses, and multiplying in number. Both, as well as mosquitoes, carried diseases, such as malaria, typhus, and "trench fever." Germs and viruses also posed a danger: between August 1917 and July 1918, for example, over 700,000 German troops suffered the effects of influenza.[58]

But the First World War was the first modern war in which more combatants lost their lives to bullets than illness, and it was here that the conflict devastated the environment. Trenches might be miles long, dug about twelve feet into the earth along a zigzag pattern to offer some protection for the defenders from incoming shells or ground attack. Not only did the process of constructing the trenches destroy the earth, but so did the incessant use of bombs, machine guns, and high-explosive artillery shells that left behind a moon-like setting devoid of life. Nothing better epitomized the war's devastation than "no-man's land," the area between the trenches that could be over two miles wide. Mary Borden, an American novelist who oversaw a French military hospital, captured such a scene in her poem "The Hill": "There were no trees anywhere, nor any grasses or green thickets, nor any birds singing, nor any whisper or flutter of any little busy creatures/There was no shelter for field mice or rabbits, squirrels, or men." To the present day, the remains of trenches can still be seen in parts of the European countryside. Moreover, some 460 square miles of French land remains off limits due to the release of arsenic and dangerous chemicals from shrapnel and unexploded ordinance.[59]

Countries and colonies far from the front were not immune to the war. Between 1916 and 1918, Great Britain cut down 50 percent of its forests to provide for its armed forces. Although the conflict did not affect the inland forests of Britain's India colony, Whitehall did procure timber from that territory's coast. In the United States, farmers transformed once rural, arid land into arable acreage so as to feed American and allied soldiers. Spruce wood, which was essential for the construction of airplanes, precipitated logging on parts of Washington State's Olympic Peninsula, and mining companies saw demand for their products increase substantially. Americans and Canadians put approximately six million hectares of grassland under the plow to meet Europeans' need for wheat. The removal of the grass loosened the soil, helping set the stage for the Dust Bowl that affected much of North America in the 1930s.[60]

Not surprisingly, the war hindered cooperative efforts aimed at environmental protection. In 1909, individuals desirous of protecting the planet's natural beauty met in Paris and proposed creating an international organization to safeguard the environment. With the endorsement of his country's government, Swiss explorer and naturalist Paul Sarasin, who in 1909 had helped found the Swiss League for the Protection of Nature, requested over a dozen European nations, as well as Argentina and the United States, to form such a body. Sarasin had reason for optimism. The conservation movement had become well established in the United States, Great Britain and its colonies, and in other European states. In May 1914, representatives from those European nations with colonies in Africa met in London for what one could consider a follow-up to the 1900 meeting. Again, the purpose was to place restrictions on the ivory trade in the name of protecting fauna. Slowing down the rate of progress was Germany's demand that restrictions on the sale of ivory had to go hand in hand with checks on the arms trade. The attendees failed to reach an acceptable compromise at the time the First World War began.[61] With that conflict's onset, Sarasin's dream of an international environmental organization fell by the wayside.

Similarly, talk of protecting whales went on hiatus. The rapid growth of that industry raised alarm bells in the British government that humans were pushing the animals toward extinction. London in March 1914 established a government committee to look into the matter, but the outbreak of the First World War put a halt to further movement. If anything, the war intensified the interest in whaling. In addition to its usefulness in the manufacture of soap and margarine, whale oil was sometimes an ingredient in making explosives. Hence, access to whale oil became tied to the Allies' national security. Norway had over the years expanded its presence as a global whaler to the point that by 1914, it produced just over 75 percent of all whale oil. The British government therefore pressed Oslo to give it sole access to that raw material. To the Germans, it became just as essential to prevent whale oil from reaching its enemies. On the British home front, the war witnessed the rationing of food and a search for substitutes for products such as cattle-based oils normally used in soap and margarine. For that reason, any trepidation that might have existed about using whale oil for those goods was swept aside.[62]

The war also affected animal life in Europe's colonies. Animal life on the Sabi reserve had begun to recover in the years following the Second Boer War. With the onset of the First World War, about 50 percent of the Europeans on the reserve's staff left to fight for their mother countries. Moreover, to cut costs, one-half of the Africans who worked for the reserve lost their jobs. In turn, Europeans and Africans began to hunt the animals on those lands.[63]

None of this is to suggest that the war brought an end to all international conservation efforts. Just as it was agitation within individual colonies that created the momentum that led to the Convention for the Preservation of Wild Animals, Birds and Fish in Africa, so concern about migratory fowl convinced Canadian and American officials to act. Two groups sought to protect avifauna. One was conservationists, including members of the Audubon Society. They railed particularly against "market hunters" who killed large numbers of birds to sell for food or to provide feathers to milliners. The second was recreational hunters. In the United States, they had their own lobbying organization, the American Game Protective and Propagation Association, which had the financial backing of gun manufacturers. Joining these groups in America was the Agriculture Department's Biological Survey. Gun manufacturers contended that they faced financial ruin if unregulated hunting killed off the prey gun buyers sought. A more common argument was that used in Europe: insect control. Although pesticides like sulfur had been in use since ancient times, they were also dangerous to humans, and chemical insecticides were in their infancy. Accordingly, American farmers and foresters relied on birds to kill pests that might destroy trees and crops. Yet it was those same birds, such as the downy woodpecker and Baltimore oriole, that hunters were killing in large numbers. Some states and provinces passed laws aimed at protecting those and other birds, but the ordinances lacked uniform enforcement. Consequently, pressure grew from conservationists for federal action. In 1913, the U.S. Congress passed the Migratory Bird Act, which banned the shooting of various types of insectivorous and migratory game birds during the spring months. States' rights advocates, though, challenged the law in dozens of court cases, claiming it was unconstitutional. By 1915, one of those cases had come before the U.S. Supreme Court.[64]

To overcome questions of constitutionality, conservationists sought to make the Migratory Bird Act part of a multinational treaty. The administration of President Woodrow Wilson reached the conclusion that such a goal would necessitate time-consuming diplomacy, during which the Supreme Court might void the 1913 law. Therefore, the White House approached Canada. Canada lacked the powerful lobbying organizations that sought to defend avian life, but the cabinets of each of the provinces liked the idea of a homogenous game law and gave their approval. In 1916, the Convention for the Protection of Migratory Birds went into effect.[65]

The convention was limited in scope, reflecting both the limited scientific background of the negotiators and the assumption that it was most important to cover only migratory fowl that were useful to humans or posed no harm. The agreement restricted open hunting to a maximum of three and a half months per year. It was up to each US state and Canadian province to choose the starting and ending dates, as long as they did not include the period March 10 to September 1 for the majority of game birds and February 1 to August 15 for shorebirds. It further established a ten-year "closed season" on some game birds considered in danger of extinction. The treaty permitted year-round hunting of certain bird species, such as murres, puffins, and auks, but imposed checks on the killing of other avifauna. In toto, the convention offered protections to about 540 different species. Yet over two hundred types of birds remained outside its scope, be it because they were not considered a protein source, did not eat pests, were birds of prey—and, hence, "vermin"—or did not migrate. Consequently, hawks, owls, quails, pheasants, and wild turkeys were ignored. Moreover, given that many species of avifauna migrated outside the protected area, there was no guarantee that those fowl leaving the United States or Canada would ever return. Additionally, even with efforts on both sides of the border to create reserves, such as Pelican Island National Wildlife Refuge, the 1916 convention was silent on the subject.[66]

## New hope?

There was reason for optimism that with the end of the First World War, the globe's leaders could turn their attention to other matters, including the environment. A conference sponsored by Great Britain estimated that 50 percent of the world's forest was managed by the practices long adopted in India, thereby providing a foundation for continued conservation efforts. Indeed, Australia in 1920 had established national goals for forest protection, and within two years after that, New Zealand had adopted a Forests Act. These actions, though, were taken at the national, not international, level. If anything, the evidence pointed to countervailing forces. As one example, the United States and Canada had proposed prior to the First World War's conclusion a multilateral conference on whaling, but the British balked, insisting other countries would use such a gathering to demand a piece of the pie. Moreover, since any effective international regulatory effort would have to include every whaling country, Argentina would have to be among the invitees. It would almost certainly use the conference as an opportunity to challenge British control of the Falkland Islands, an archipelago in the South Atlantic to which Buenos Aires also laid claim.[67]

The creation of the League of Nations, though, gave environmentalists hope. In 1919, the First World War's victors met in Paris to discuss the terms demanded of their wartime enemies and bring an official end to the globe's most devastating conflict up to that point. Having recalled the prewar progress made at the colonial, national, and international levels to protect flora and fauna, both individuals and international nongovernmental organizations (INGOs) believed the restoration of peace permitted a resumption of such efforts. Not affiliated with any state or international body and generally manned by volunteers who, because of their focus on a particular issue, could become experts on it, the concept of NGO had existed for some time. Two of the oldest that are still in existence today are the Royal Society for the Prevention of Cruelty to Animals (RSPCA), which was founded in 1824, and Anti-Slavery International, which traces its history back to the creation of the Anti-Slavery Society in Great Britain in 1823. The first environmental INGO was the International Union of Forestry Research Organizations, founded a year before the Sierra Club. The Treaty of Versailles signed at Paris, which established the League of Nations, heartened both NGOs and

INGOs.[68] Based in Geneva, Switzerland, and envisioned as an international organization that would maintain world peace, the League had three main organs: an assembly, in which all members had representation; a council, made up of the world's major powers; and a secretariat consisting of experts who would address particular issues. The one significant holdout was the United States, which refused membership during the League's lifetime.

It appeared to environmentalists that the League could address, if not solve, just about any global problem, including the wanton destruction of nature. Among those who felt that way were Sarasin and the members of RSPCA. To Sarasin, the return of world peace encouraged him to renew his call for a commission to defend nature and was pleased when the League's secretariat in 1919 endorsed the idea. The RSPCA for its part called for a multilateral agreement that would provide protections for internationally shipped domestic and wild animals.[69]

There were other reasons for Sarasin's and the RSPCA's sanguinity. The powers of Europe, once regarded as the guardians of "civilization," had demonstrated via the war their capacity to engage in acts of barbarity, including the deaths of thousands of soldiers on single days. Protecting nature, contended Sarasin, provided those countries and others willing to join them an opportunity to prove their "diplomatic capacity" and "cultural development." Moreover, there was no clarity as to what the League's power was, leaving open the possibility that the new organization would have the ability to oversee the enactment of national laws. The League Secretariat seemed to share such a vision, believing that protecting fauna was part of its broader mandate of promoting a more civilized society globally. Hence, working together, NGOs like the RSPCA and the League could create a better world, one where flora and fauna would enjoy national and international protections.[70] That optimism, however, was soon to fade.

# CHAPTER TWO

# From war through war

In 1921, Swedish prime minister Hjalmar Branting and Norwegian secretary-general of the Inter-Parliamentary Union Christian Lange received the Nobel Peace Prize for their efforts to promote world peace. Because of his desire to see a planet without conflict, Branting was a strong proponent of the League of Nations. "There is no reason why agreement on particular points should not be both possible and advantageous to the so-called neutrals and to one or more of the blocs, either existing or in the process of formation, within the League of Nations," he commented upon accepting the Nobel award.[1]

For environmentalists, "particular points" included subjects of concern to them, whether it be animals at risk of extinction from hunting or trees facing destruction because of the demand for lumber. Reality, however, quickly set in. The international issues the League had to tackle were numerous, ranging from human migration, disarmament, and slavery to potential political and military disputes, among them the events leading up to the Second World War. There was no way the secretariat could handle all of these matters as well as the conservation of nature, which was of far less interest to most of the organization's members. Moreover, the secretariat lacked the power to determine which subjects the assembly discussed. Rather, that responsibility fell to the League's members. In 1922, Swiss naturalist Paul Sarasin, who had hoped to create an international organization that would focus on environmental matters, realized the impossibility of the League overseeing such a body. Indeed, those topics with environmental overtones ended up in the hands of particular and less powerful sections of the League, such as those dealing with intellectual cooperation, economics, or communications.[2]

None of this is to suggest that the period between the wars proved static for conservation efforts. The idea of protecting the environment in the name of human welfare remained strong and was key to the League overseeing a convention to restrict whaling. Meanwhile, countries outside the auspices of the League signed both binational and multinational arrangements to protect life in the sea and air, and on land. In many cases, the signatories anticipated these agreements setting the stage for others. Just as the hope of the League serving as an instrument of environmental protection faded, however, so did the anticipation of new pro-conservation conventions. The rise of highly militaristic and nationalist dictatorships in Asia and Europe, in combination with growing tensions on both continents, served to slow further progress on conservation measures, and the onset of the Second World War in 1939 brought it to a complete halt.

The planet's second global conflict not only destroyed the vision of those who believed the League could maintain the peace but caused environmental destruction on a scale not seen before by humankind. Terrestrial life took the greatest beating, yet marine animals did not escape unharmed. More ominously, the war left behind chemicals and ordinance that to the present pose a threat to plant, animal, and human life. It also increased faith in the use of a pesticide known as dichlorodiphenyltrichloroethane (DDT), which would play a central role in fostering the modern environmental movement.

# Whaling

That the League believed it might do some good for the environment became apparent in 1924, when its leadership asked the organization's members to point to problems it might solve. One subject raised by a number of countries was whaling. Within a year, the League's economic committee had begun to look into the issue. There was good reason for concern. Next to right whales, the blue was the most popular for whalers, as it was the biggest species and the one that produced the most oil. Thanks primarily to the stern slipway, the number of blues killed had grown from 1,801 in the 1918–19 whaling season to 8,334 in 1927–28, and increased by another 4,400 a year later. Meanwhile, humpback whales had seen a dramatic decline compared to earlier years. In 1930–31, kills achieved a record of 34,662 blue whale units (BWUs)—a ratio that made the oil obtained from one blue whale equivalent to a certain number of other whale species. It was clear to numerous observers, be them scientists, government officials, and even the whaling industry, that without some kind of checks, the supply of whales would decline to unsustainable levels.[3]

The decision of the League to enter the fray brought the question of whale conservation before more countries than before. Even nonmembers, such as the United States, took notice. In fact, the United States, alongside New Zealand, had early on pushed for conserving whales. Both had long been involved in whaling, yet neither regarded it as essential to their well-being as was the case for nations like Great Britain and Norway. Under the guidance of Remington Kellogg, a vertebrate paleontologist recently hired by the Smithsonian Institution, delegates from a large number of nations began to work on a draft whaling convention. For a template they relied on a 1929 Norwegian law that required ships flying Norway's flag to log their activities and to have on board a government inspector who would log the catch.[4]

In September 1931, the League opened the Convention for the Regulation of Whaling (CRW) for signature. As little was known about whales at the time, the delegates who endorsed the treaty concurred that they would assemble as much scientific information as they could about those animals and send it to the Bureau of International Whaling Statistics, a body established by Norway in 1929 to track whale catches. The convention prohibited the killing of right whales—which had been popular to hunt because they did not sink when killed and, therefore, had fallen significantly in number—and the mothers and calves of all baleen whales. Finally, while the agreement left indigenous peoples alone as long as they did not use modern technology, it required those persons associated with the modern whaling industry and who used such know-how to get a license from their flag country. To go into effect, the convention required Great Britain, Norway, and six additional nations to ratify it. By early 1932, it had achieved that goal. The United States and even some landlocked countries, including Czechoslovakia and Switzerland, were among those that approved it.[5]

The CRW pleased those who regarded it as a step toward protecting cetaceans as an end in itself. In truth, though, it reflected a desire to conserve a commercially important resource. The Great Depression, which had begun in 1929 in the United States and rapidly spread worldwide, had pushed down the price of whale oil. At the time, there were only a few major national commercial players in the market: the Norwegians and British, for instance, were responsible for nearly all Antarctic kills until 1934, and Unilever controlled the market in whale oil. All accepted the need for some kind of measures to prevent further depletion of the whale population. Even conservationists argued in favor of regulation less out of a belief in the importance of saving whales as the goal and more for economic reasons. Furthermore, the regulations were limited in scope, thereby making the CRW all the more acceptable to the signatories most affected.[6]

Tightening the regulations established by the CRW proved difficult and, ultimately, impossible. One obstacle was the position taken by whaling nations that lacked fleets, among them France and Argentina. These "land-station" countries claimed that they had to rely on individual whales or whale pods that came near their shores, whereas those with high seas fleets had the ability to wipe out those same animals before they had a chance to approach a shoreline. Nevertheless, the pelagic countries had reason to cooperate with those limited to land stations, for the latter could offer places from which to launch rival fleets or flags for whaling companies that might oppose restrictions imposed by their homelands.[7]

More important was the decision by Japan and Germany in the 1930s to join the list of pelagic whaling countries. They had similar reasons for doing so. Both had come under the sway of increasingly militaristic and highly nationalistic governments that did not want to rely on others for their economic well-being. The Japanese, whose whaling industry had been largely local in nature, purchased in 1934 the vessels needed to expand their activities onto the high seas. Germany, seeking to keep as much of its financial resources at home as possible, announced in 1935 its intention to construct its own whaling fleet. Because neither was a party to the CRW, they could hunt at will, further reducing whale stocks that already were in decline. That, in turn, jeopardized the well-being of British and Norwegian whaling companies, which had recently adopted quotas on Antarctic whales. Both Australians and New Zealanders, not wanting to find themselves completely cut out of the lucrative whaling market, began to look into following the lead of Berlin and Tokyo.[8]

With the addition of Germany and Japan jeopardizing the global whaling industry, representatives from ten countries met in London in 1937 to hammer out a new whaling convention. Germany agreed to attend, but Japan did not. One of the most controversial proposals was one that, for the first time, would establish a closed season for whaling. After extensive debate, the delegates decided to permit hunting from December 8, 1937, to March 15, 1938, with every season afterward to close on March 8. The convention contained the same provisions as that of 1931 regarding mothers and calves, and accumulating data. Blue, sperm, humpback, and fin whales had to meet minimum size requirements if they were to be killed, and gray whales joined the list of protected species. Each factory ship had to have an inspector on board. Lastly, the signatories barred whaling in significant portions of the ocean north of 40° south latitude. The convention had a year-long life span, yet it was not until May 1938, when it was about to expire, that it received the fifth ratification required to put it into effect. Though a promising beginning, Japan continued to balk, and whalers refused to accept a quota on their hunt.[9]

Any chance of significantly strengthening the 1937 convention ultimately dissipated. Pelagic and land-station nations quarreled over the responsibility for the overhunting of humpback whales, whose numbers had dwindled to the point of endangering their very existence. After some hard bargaining, the parties to the 1937 pact accepted a protocol in 1938 establishing a two-year ban on the hunting of humpbacks, with the exception of south of 40° latitude, where the hiatus was one year. Japan, however, remained an outlier, and it showed little willingness until August 1939 to join the whaling regime. By then, however, another global military conflict appeared on the horizon. The outbreak of the Second World War brought a halt to any further talk of Japanese accession to regulating its whaling industry or to broader whaling diplomacy.[10]

# Oil pollution

Even less progress took place on another maritime matter, that of oil pollution. During the First World War, a number of the world's navies came to realize that oil offered advantages over coal. It was easier to store, did not require the large number of crewmen to move onboard from storage to the engine, and made it possible to refuel at sea. Even better, oil created less smoke and generated more power—and, in turn, more speed. The faster and less detectable a ship was, the more likely it could elude attack or destroy its intended target. The Italians had first experimented with oil in the late 1800s, but it was the United States and Great Britain that made the greatest strides during the First World War in adopting the requisite technology. Merchant marines followed suit. By 1922, 22 percent of the world's shipping relied on oil for power, an increase of 20 percent since 1914.[11]

The problem with oil is its dirtiness. In this case, it was not the airborne pollution it generated, but that created at sea. Accidents led petroleum to leak into the ocean, but so did the daily cleaning of tanks, from which ships released an oily refuse, or the decision of crews simply to toss used oil over the side of their vessels. Complaints started to come from tourists who traveled to beaches near shipping lanes and left with dark stains on their clothes, from fisherman who said oil pollution placed their trade at risk, and from landowners with shoreline property who worried about taking a loss on their investments because of a dirty ocean. Highlighting the seriousness of the situation to both experts and laypersons was the increasingly large number of deceased or moribund seabirds washing up on the shorelines of the United States and European countries. It was not known at the time that petroleum could kill avifauna, either through ingestion or by damaging the plumage a bird needs to fly or float. That many of these animals lived along major shipping routes and had been "maimed" by petroleum, though, made it clear what the culprit likely was.[12]

It was in Great Britain and the United States where public anger most strongly expressed itself, oftentimes through the voice of NGOs. In the United Kingdom, the Royal Society for the Protection of Birds (RSPB) and the RSPCA led the charge. Joined by women's organizations and the media, as well as members of Parliament, they successfully achieved passage in 1922 of the Oil Pollution Act, prohibiting the dumping of oil in the United Kingdom's three-mile territorial-waters zone. In the United States, the newly formed National Coast Anti-Pollution League, "a mainstream coalition of elected officials and public health advocates," convinced Washington in 1924 to enact a similar law. The furor calmed down in the United States as a result, but the RSPB insisted the Oil Pollution Act was not enough. It pointed out that petroleum could travel far more than three miles, so even if discharged further out at sea, it might still reach British shores. The shipping industry fought back, declaring that the RSPB and its allies imperiled its financial welfare and that of the United Kingdom.[13]

Caught between the environmental NGOs and shipping interests, the British government decided to seek international resolution of the matter by sending representatives to a multination conference held in Washington in 1926. The delegates put together a draft convention that restricted the discharge of oil within fifty miles of a shoreline and required vessels in that zone to keep the oil on board for release at a port facility. However, strong resistance from other participants, such as Germany, prevented further progress. Disappointed, British NGOs intensified their efforts, asking similar organizations worldwide to join them. Not wanting to face accusations of failing to stand up for human welfare, Whitehall again sought to internationalize the issue, this time by asking the League of Nations to put together a convention based on the 1926 draft.[14]

Galvanized, numerous NGOs determined to make their presence known at the League's headquarters in Geneva, Switzerland, including the RSPCA, the American Audubon Society, and the American Humane Association, only to find themselves blocked from participation in the League's oil pollution committee. The state delegates succeeded in writing up a draft convention near the end of 1935. It included the fifty-mile provision of the 1926 proposal and stiff fines for violating the agreement and required "ship masters . . . to enter into the ship's logs all incidents involving the discharge of oil." The draft convention received an enthusiastic response, but, as in the case of whaling, geopolitical tensions entered the picture. Japan's forcible acquisition of the Chinese territory of Manchuria in 1931 had drawn it condemnation by the League, prompting Tokyo to withdraw from the international organization in 1933. Declaring that the League's major powers had rejected its calls for equal treatment on military matters, Germany followed suit that same year. After the international organization imposed economic sanctions on Italy for its invasion of Abyssinia in 1935, Rome in 1937 walked off the League as well. It became obvious that an international conference to formalize the draft convention was out of the question. Both France and Great Britain, therefore, turned to bilateral arrangements with provisions similar to those proposed in the League convention, only to have the Second World War intervene.[15]

# Fisheries

The League's mixed record in finding solutions to whaling and oil pollution reflected that of efforts taken outside its purview to protect fisheries. In 1839, France and Great Britain had reached an agreement dividing up their fishing rights in the English Channel, and in 1882, a number of European nations did the same with regard to fishing in the North Sea. Importantly, none of those agreements restricted overfishing. A growing amount of scientific data, though, pointed to the need for conservation efforts. In 1902, the same nations that signed the 1882 North Sea convention took part in establishing the International Council for the Exploration of the Seas (ICES) to gather such information. The North American Commission for Fishery Research (NACFR) followed suit in 1921. The findings of ICES and NACFR convinced the United States and Canada to seek a resolution to a decades-old dispute between their competing fishing interests. In 1923, the two North American countries signed the Convention for the Preservation of the Halibut Fishery of the Northern Pacific Ocean. It was "the first treaty to be concluded anywhere for the conservation of a depleted deep-sea fishery." The convention established a three-month closed season starting in the middle of November. It also created what became known as the International Fisheries Commission—today, the International Pacific Halibut Commission— to oversee the agreement, with the purpose of looking at the lifecycle of each species in question and making recommendations for conserving those species. In 1929, information provided by ICES convinced Denmark, Germany, Sweden, and Poland to sign the Agreement Regarding the Regulation of Plaice and Flounder Fishing in the Baltic Sea, which imposed a closed season and minimum size requirements for the fish caught.[16]

The accord appearing in Europe and the eastern Pacific did not extend to the western Pacific, where Japan's demands for fish placed it at odds with its neighbors. Historically, the Japanese people have relied heavily on both rice and seafood as food sources, the latter of which is an important source of protein. One species of fish to which Japan desired access was the yellow croaker. Coming in both "large" and "small" versions, it makes its home in the East China, Yellow, and South China seas, and can grow well over two feet in length. During the first three decades of the twentieth century, Chinese fishermen had begun to venture further out to sea to catch croakers as overfishing and, possibly, environmental changes decreased the number closer to the coastline. Adding to the pressures faced by the Chinese was the arrival of Japanese fishing boats. Since the late 1800s, Japan had started to copy Western nations through the acquisition of foreign territory, economic industrialization, and the modernization of its military and civilian technology. It had successfully defeated the Russian navy during the Russo-Japanese War of 1904–05, and acquired from Russia both control over a railway in the Chinese province of Manchuria as well as the southern half of Sakhalin Island. In 1905 as well, it declared Korea a protectorate. In the meantime, modern, steam-powered trawlers began to appear, angering traditional Japanese fishers who complained to the government. To protect those Japanese using older technology, Tokyo ordered the trawlers to ply their trade far away from the coast. These larger vessels, therefore, headed into the East China Sea.[17]

For Chinese fishers whose technology was not much superior to that of their traditional Japanese counterparts, the arrival of the modern fishing vessels was most unwelcome. The number of yellow croaker dwindled further, prompting the Chinese to claim that the Japanese had violated China's territorial waters. Whether this was in fact the case was not clear.

For one, the Japanese denied any such infringement. More important, no international law existed that codified "territorial waters." Since the 1700s, the generally accepted rule was that a country could claim control over water three miles from its shores. The League of Nations had attempted in 1924 and again in 1930 to work out an internationally accepted definition but proved unable to do so.[18]

In the end, there was little China could do. Its noncommunist, Nationalist government was in the midst of a civil war that pitted it against a communist movement. It also faced increasingly tense relations with Japan, where a nationalist-minded military had begun to play a larger role in political affairs, and which viewed China's Nationalist leadership as a threat to its interests. After Japan's seizure of Manchuria in 1931, its boats intensified their hunt for yellow croakers. Chinese fishermen, fearing for their livelihood, did the same. As the number of yellow croaker in the East China and Yellow seas fell precipitously low, the Japanese shifted their focus to the South China Sea, further shrinking the croaker population.[19]

To the north, the Japanese found themselves at odds with the Soviet Union over access to salmon. Referred to as "the divine fish" in Japan, salmon was also among the most popular species consumed by the Japanese. In 1907, Russia and Japan signed an agreement restricting the right of fishing in river mouths and bays to Russian companies while permitting the Japanese to fish off the Russian coast. In addition, Japan had the right to lease facilities on Russian territory to process its catch. It was unclear whether that pact would hold following Russia's Bolshevik Revolution of 1917. Like many of the opponents of China's Nationalist government, the Bolsheviks embraced communism, a form of socialism that called for government control of all economic means of production and the establishment of a classless society. Initially, it appeared that Russia—which in 1922 became part of the Union of Soviet Socialist Republics, or Soviet Union—would stand behind the 1907 convention. There had been from the start of the Bolshevik Revolution an environmental movement in Russia. The brother of the Bolsheviks's leader, Vladimir Lenin, was a biologist and a nature lover. Lenin himself in 1921 had signed a decree providing protections for natural areas (*zapovedniki*) and creating new ones. A 1923 Forest Code called for reforestation of areas targeted for logging. It seemed, therefore, that the Bolsheviks would take the steps required to prevent extirpation of flora and fauna it considered important, including fish. Further evidence came in the form a new Soviet-Japanese convention signed in 1925 that had provisions echoing those of 1907.[20]

For two interrelated reasons, Moscow had a change of heart. First, Lenin had died in 1924, and his successor, Josef Stalin, desired to place his own stamp on the country. For instance, he replaced Lenin's New Economic Policy, which had permitted capitalism (though under state control) with five-year plans that called for far greater state jurisdiction over national production. Second, German philosopher Karl Marx, one of the founders of the communist movement, had written that the achievement of full-fledged communism went through several historical stages, with capitalism being the fourth, socialism the fifth, and communism the sixth and final stage. One prerequisite of that sixth stage was economic self-sufficiency. The Kremlin accordingly began to exploit its resources to their fullest extent, repressing environmentalists and cutting down trees on the *zapovedniki*. It also wanted complete control over its fisheries. The Japanese began to complain, and the adoption in 1928 of another agreement between them failed to resolve their disagreements over access to fish in Soviet waters.[21]

With entry to nearby Soviet salmon fisheries jeopardized, the Japanese began to eye those in the Northeast Pacific. In 1937, Tokyo provided licenses to large factory ships and smaller "catcher boats" to conduct operations in Bristol Bay, near Alaska. Not only did salmon underpin one of the most profitable of North America's fishing industries, but at the time, only Canadian and American fleets had operated in Bristol Bay. The Canadians and Americans not surprisingly considered the arrival of Japanese fishing vessels as unwanted competition, and a threat to the stock itself. These concerns reached the highest levels of the US government, prompting Secretary of State Cordell Hull to issue a protest to Tokyo. Washington heavily financed the construction of salmon hatcheries in the region, he wrote, and so even though those fish swam out to sea well beyond US territorial waters, they deserved special protection to prevent overfishing and safeguard the financial well-being of American salmon fishermen.[22]

On the one hand, Tokyo had reason not to comply. It was still feeling the effects of the Great Depression, and the ability to feed its industry, including its fishing industry, was an important part of its economic recovery. On the other hand, its relationship with the United States had showed signs of souring. Having conquered Manchuria, Japanese military forces invaded China proper in 1937. The conquest of Manchuria had not elicited a US response but that of China had. Viewed in the broader context of German and Italian aggression, President Franklin D. Roosevelt, who officially held firm to a position of neutrality, called the events in China part of an "epidemic of world lawlessness." Later that year, the US gunboat *Panay*, then on China's Yangtze River, fell prey to two Japanese aircraft. Two Americans died, and another thirty suffered wounds. Although the *Panay* crisis quickly passed, Tokyo determined it best not to engage in any other actions that might lead Washington to reconsider its neutral stance. Accordingly, it promised not to send into the Northeast Pacific any more "salmon mothership fleets."[23] There matters stood until after the Second World War.

## The 1933 convention

The anthropocentrism reflected in efforts to protect marine life appeared too in measures to safeguard terrestrial fauna. The number of game reserves

PHOTO 3 Giraffe on Southern game reserve, Kenya colony. Public domain: Edith Matson Photograph Collection. *Credit: Library of Congress.*

increased, but they hid serious flaws. In 1925, the Belgian Congo became the site of Africa's first national park, Parc National Albert (later Virunga National Park). South Africa's Sabi Reserve was incorporated into Kruger National Park a year later, and in 1928, the British founded Hwange National Park in Southern Rhodesia. In combination with existing reserves and parks, these and other new sanctuaries brought the total by 1933 to eighteen in South Africa, five in Nigeria, seventeen in French West Africa, ten in Portuguese-controlled Angola, thirteen in the Belgian Congo, and eight in Italy's African colonies. Yet providing protection to the animals living on them was problematic. Great Britain's Kenya Protectorate—formerly British East Africa—had only two reserves, the Southern and Northern, but in combination, they covered about 48,000 square miles, or approximately the same amount of territory as all of England. To guard both, the colony's Game Department had only seventy-five wardens, with most assigned to the Southern Reserve. In turn, the Northern Reserve remained a prime target for poachers, who sold their acquirements through ports in Italy's Somalia colony. Further complicating matters were the indigenous peoples, who argued the reserves endangered their livelihood. Because of the size of the sanctuaries and the small number of security officials, however, Africans were able to continue subsistence hunting, particularly in the reserves' more isolated areas.[24]

In 1930, the British-based Society for the Preservation of the Fauna of the Empire (SPFE) sent naturalist and explorer Richard Hingston to Africa to look at the impact of the tsetse fly, ivory smuggling, and hunting on the animals of that continent. His discovery was that the 1900 Convention for the Preservation of Wild Animals, Birds and Fish in Africa was performing far less well than hoped. Instead, "Africa fauna is steadily failing before the forces of destruction brought to bear against it." He blamed the slaughter on farmers, whose demand for more land for cultivation brought them in greater contact with wild animals; merchants, who sought ivory and pelts; the indigenous population, which engaged in "methods that are wholesale and indiscriminating in their destructiveness"; and the continued spread of trypanosomiasis by the tsetse fly, which colonists blamed on conservationists determined to protect the animal population. The only solution, concluded Hingston, was to separate humans from wild fauna, with the latter placed on nature parks large enough to provide them true protection.[25]

Using its influential membership to its advantage, the SPFE convinced the British government to look into the creation of permanent animal sanctuaries. Over the next two years, Whitehall brought together diplomatic, economic, plant, and animal experts from within and outside the government, including representatives from the SPFE, Kew Gardens, and the London Zoological Society, who put together two draft reports. So meticulous was their preparatory work that, when delegates from the United Kingdom, France, Spain, Italy, Portugal, Belgium, and several of the colonies met in the British capital in 1933, they signed an agreement very similar to that of the second draft report.[26]

Called the Convention Relative to the Preservation of Flora and Fauna in Their Natural State—or, informally, the London Convention—it covered far more of the continent than that of 1900. The new agreement distinguished between a "national park" and a "strict natural reserve," with the former, as was true with other national parks, open for public enjoyment and the latter to remain entirely untouched. The language left unclear where nature tourism could take place, though the assumption was that such activity was more appropriate for a park than a reserve. In both types of sanctuaries, hunting was strictly prohibited. As for hunting itself, the 1933 agreement offered far more detail than that of 1900 regarding what animals could be killed. The signatories removed the "vermin" list, thereby providing additional protections for those animals, and it offered language that took into account the need of indigenous Africans to engage in subsistence hunting. Finally, the document set forth some ideas regarding the protection of flora, such as "giv[ing] consideration to the desirability of preventing the introduction of exotic trees or plants into national parks or reserves." The convention went into effect in 1936. It guided African conservation efforts until the postwar period, when many of the colonies on that continent gained their independence.[27]

Administering the convention was very difficult. Belgian authorities weakened its provisions on hunting by adding language permitting the continued trade in elephant tusks that weighed "more than five kilograms." British colonial officials sometimes permitted exceptions, particularly for famous visitors. Europeans who broke the law rarely faced prosecution, and the reserves and parks themselves continued to lack staff to enforce the convention's restrictions.[28]

Yet the 1933 convention was important for several reasons. For one, it was an improvement over that of 1900 when it came to protecting fauna. For another, it reflected changing sociopolitical norms in Europe. At the time of the 1900 convention, the focus was primarily on the welfare of a Victorian elite who wanted to preserve animals for sport and commerce. The death of Queen Victoria in 1901 and even more so, the First World War had had a profound impact on Europe, breaking down the German, Ottoman, and Austro-Hungarian empires, and promoting greater democratization—including the right to vote for women in a large number of European countries. (It was, however, a fragile democratization process, one that would come under severe strains as a result of the Great Depression, the rise of nationalism, and other interwar concerns.)

The democratization that took place in much of Europe following the First World War affected the concept of humans' relationship with nature, one codified in the 1933 convention. No longer were animals meant for the enjoyment of the elite; rather, they were for all persons to appreciate. In that respect, the 1933 agreement fostered the development of what later became known as ecotourism. That process was already well underway in the United States. At the turn of the twentieth century, the railroad had allowed ever more Americans to leave the city and head to one of the country's national parks. The automobile industry, which mushroomed after the First World War to the point that by 1929 there was on average nearly one car per household in the United States, made it even easier to experience nature personally. As the train and car became more ubiquitous in Australasia and southern Africa, individuals in those countries and colonies too, including those lower on the socioeconomic ladder, could enjoy their newly created national parks. In this respect, commented one historian, the spread of the concept of the national park from North America and Australia to Africa "presented, at least in theory, an entirely new phase in conservationism."[29]

Finally, the 1933 convention led conservationists to look at adopting similar measures beyond Europe. The SPFE began to insist upon greater effort to protect India's animal life. Bending under the pressure, India passed the UP National Parks Act in 1934. Two years later, Hailey National Park became the first in the colony. Using that momentum, the British sought to extend the 1933 convention elsewhere in Asia and had put together a conference for November 1939 to discuss that very issue. The outbreak of the Second World War in September 1939, though, led to the conference's cancellation.[30] The 1933 convention also inspired conservationists in the Western Hemisphere, particularly those seeking to protect avian life.

## Birds in North America

Just as the British sought to extend the 1933 London Convention beyond Africa, so the United States attempted to widen the scope of the 1916 Convention for the Protection of Migratory Birds signed between it and Canada. Since that agreement, both countries had established a large number of reserves for avian life. In Canada alone, there were fifty-four by 1933. The problem was that many of these birds migrated south of the United States into Mexico, and Central and South America. In 1920, one of Alabama's US senators, John Bankhead, saw passage of a resolution asking for negotiations to expand the 1916 convention throughout the Western Hemisphere.[31]

That was easier said than done. US-Mexican relations had soured since the overthrow of Mexico's leader, Porfirio Díaz, in 1911. Not until the tenure of Mexican president Emilio Portes Gil, who served from 1928 to 1930, did they begin to see improvement. For their part, US presidents Herbert Hoover and his successor, Franklin Roosevelt, wanted to upgrade what had been oftentimes tense relations with Latin America. The atmosphere of good will on both sides of the border permitted the signing in Mexico City of the Convention between the United States of America and the United States of Mexico for the Protection of Migratory Birds and Game Mammals of 1936. It was not much of a step forward insofar as conservation. Modeled on the 1916 convention, its provisions were largely the same, though it prohibited the killing of insectivores year round and the use of planes to hunt avifauna. In some respects it was regressive. It failed to demand year-round protection of birds at risk of extinction and, to please Mexican hunters, it did not nothing, with the exception of ducks, to protect birds during the breeding season.[32] Mexico ratified it in 1936, followed by the United States the following year.

Expanding the coverage of the 1936 convention to the rest of the hemisphere proved more challenging. A couple of months before the exchange of signatures in Mexico's capital, the U.S. State Department, following prodding from the Audubon Society, requested information from all nations in Central and South America regarding their legal statutes to protect avian life. Discovering most had few or even no laws, let alone means of enforcing those on the books, the parties at a meeting at the 1938 International Conference of American States called for a hemisphere-wide convention. Endorsing their effort was an NGO of bird conservationists, the American Committee for International Wildlife Protection. Two years later, the United States, Mexico, and eighteen South and Central American nations signed the Convention on Nature Protection and Wildlife Preservation in the Western Hemisphere.[33]

Unlike the 1936 pact between the United States and Mexico, the 1940 Western Hemisphere Convention had as its model the 1933 London Convention. It defined "migratory birds" as any which "may at any season cross any of the boundaries between the American countries" and asked all signatories to establish nature reserves and national parks. Additionally, it permitted the hunting of birds for food, or for commercial or scientific use, as long as the numbers killed did not threaten the extinction of any species. As promising as the provisions sounded, the convention was weak. It made no requirement for the parties to work with one another to protect birds, leading to a variety of laws among them rather than uniform codes. Moreover, enforcement of the legislation in question oftentimes proved slack. There was more luck insofar as the establishment of national parks and reserves, but the process in many of the nations in question was plodding.[34]

## Transboundary pollution

A year after the Hemisphere Convention, the United States and Canada reached another agreement, this one unrelated to hunting. Just before the turn of the twentieth century, the Canadian Pacific Railway (CPR) purchased a lead and zinc smelter in Trail, British Columbia. In 1905, the smelter and its mines became the Consolidated Mining and Smelting Company (CMS), with the CPR having half ownership. Production at the facility grew to the point that it became the biggest smelting operation within the British Empire. More production meant more pollution. In an attempt to disperse the smoke, CMS in the mid-1920s augmented the height of the stacks to four hundred feet. Although treatment technology captured much of the lead fumes that otherwise would have escaped, the same was not true for sulfur dioxide ($SO_2$), a toxic gas that can harm both plants and humans. $SO_2$ effluvia traveled across the border into Washington State, where it damaged crops. Angry Washington State officials in 1927 turned to the International Joint Commission (IJC). Created in 1909 in the wake of disputes over the allocation of water along the US-Canadian border, it had the right under its Article IX to resolve disagreements involving "the inhabitants of the other."[35]

Given the importance of the operation and the influence of the CPR in Canada, the Canadian government, which now represented itself rather than having the British Foreign Office act as its voice, took notice. Based on evidence provided to it by scientists from both sides of the border, the IJC determined in 1931 that CMS owed $350,000 in damage. American farmers, hurting from not just the ruin they believed the Trail plant had done to their crops but also from the Great Depression, called it far too little. To the CMS, the IJC's award was more than the farmers deserved. Voicing the frustration of Western agriculturalists was a highly influential US senator, William Borah of Idaho, whose support President Roosevelt wanted to get his New Deal domestic program enacted. Roosevelt thus joined the fray, urging all the parties involved to reach some kind of accord. This led to the formation of an ad hoc three-man tribunal that decided in 1938 to limit its award to $78,000 beyond that of the IJC. Furthermore, it required the Trail plant to install technology to abate the release of $SO_2$. Having completed its work, the tribunal disbanded in 1941.[36]

Although it appeared a relatively insignificant international environmental dispute when compared to the multilateral negotiations regarding animal life, the Trail Smelter case was in fact noteworthy. The U.S. Supreme Court in 1907 had ruled that a Tennessee-based company had to pay people in neighboring Georgia because of damage caused by the pollution it generated. The Trail case extended the concept of "polluter pays" to interstate cases.[37] It was an important precedent for the future.


## A World again at war

One reason for the desire of both the United States and Canada to put the Trail case behind them was because of the outbreak of the Second World War, which increased Great Britain's need for zinc and lead.[38] International condemnation of the machinations of Italy, Germany, and Japan had failed to halt their aggression. Instead, Italy joined into a formal alliance with Germany in May 1939, a few months before the German invasion of Poland led to declarations of war on Germany by Great Britain and France. Japan joined Italy and Germany the following year in what became known as the "Axis." The German invasion of the Soviet Union and Japan's attack on the US naval base at Pearl Harbor, Hawaii, in June and December 1941, respectively, drew both Moscow and Washington into the conflict as well.

As in so many wars, the environment affected combat. The Soviet Union's vast expanses demoralized German troops who hoped for a quick victory there. Following Allied landings in Italy in 1943, Rome surrendered, but Germany poured forces into that country that effectively used Italy's terrain to slow the Allied advance. The same was the case with centuries-old hedgerows in France following the Allies' invasion in 1944. Crossing rivers became problematic when bridges were either damaged or destroyed. Caves on the Pacific islands of Peleliu, Iwo Jima, and Okinawa afforded hiding places for Japanese troops. Weather had an impact as well. German soldiers invaded the Soviet Union later than anticipated, and, as a result, ended up fighting in brutal winter conditions without proper clothing or equipment. Conversely, the Germans took advantage of overcast and snow to launch a counterattack against the Allies in 1944 in what became known as the Battle of the Bulge. Rainy conditions and thick rain forests made life difficult for both Allied equipment and soldiers fighting on Guadalcanal in the Solomon Islands, on New Guinea, and in Burma.

Disease added to the misery. As in the First World War, more people died during the planet's second global conflict from combat than disease, but illness still took its toll. The bombing of cities damaged or destroyed sewage lines; the contaminated water became a vessel for the spread of cholera. A shortage of quinine created innumerable difficulties for US troops trying to fend off Japan's invasion of the Philippines in 1942. It is estimated that 90 percent of Allied troops forced to leave the British colony of Burma following Japan's invasion there, also in 1942, were ridden with malaria, though cholera and dysentery were also common. Illness and starvation took the lives of about one-third of those Japanese who fought on Guadalcanal.[39]

Tropical disease did not always appear in the tropics. The Italian island of Sicily, invaded by the Allies in July 1943, offers one example. The craters left from bombs and artillery shells easily filled with water, making them perfect breeding grounds for mosquitoes. Soldiers, who oftentimes had to sleep out in the open, became fodder for those insects and the diseases they carried. Only a few months after they landed in Sicily, 21,000 American and British troops were laid up with malaria, 4,000 more than had been wounded in combat. Treating those servicemen was hard as well, as hospitals, assuming they had not been damaged or destroyed, were oftentimes far from the front. Making sure quinine was available to those at or near the front lines was not always easy. Refugees fleeing the fighting who themselves were infected unknowingly helped transport malaria as mosquitoes drew their blood and then headed for another body.[40]

Not surprisingly, the war's effect on terrestrial life was largely negative. The population of duck and geese in the United States increased, for the rationing of fuel and ammunition on the home front restricted the opportunity for Americans to hunt those birds. Yet the destruction caused by defensive structures, bombs, artillery, and machine gun fire was immense. To protect their European possessions from amphibious attack, the Germans constructed the Atlantic Wall, a system of fortifications from the Franco-Spanish border to the northern part of Norway. Numerous beaches in turn became defaced by concrete- and steel-reinforced bunkers, barbed wire, and mines. Tank warfare in North Africa destroyed sand crusts—living organisms that include lichens, fungi, and algae—that helped stabilize the sand. The region in turn witnessed for decades afterward sandstorms of greater intensity than before the war. E. B. Sledge, an American marine who fought the Japanese on the island of Peleliu, described the devastation he witnessed: "Most green trees and bushes had long since been shattered and pulverized by shell fire. Only the grotesque stumps and branches remained."[41]

As in the First World War, it was not just bombs, artillery shells, or gunfire that wreaked havoc on terrestrial life. So did the need for raw materials and the conflict's effect on international trade. Even before the

United States entered into the war, it had begun a military buildup, which, in combination with ever more civilian conveyance driven by the internal combustion engine, meant greater reliance on domestic and overseas sources of oil. The war intensified that demand for petroleum both in America and among its allies, which had consequences for the environment from where the petroleum came. Americans, who in 1940 consumed as much rubber as the planet's other countries combined, turned to Brazil for that vital military and civilian commodity following Japan's conquest of the British colony of Malaya, which up to then had provided America with over 90 percent of its rubber. In colonial Africa, British authorities found mangrove trees not only made excellent railroad ties but contained high quantities of tannin, a substance used in leather dye.[42]

The Soviet Union, which suffered more deaths in the war than any other country, witnessed widespread destruction to its environment during the war. That attack on the environment was already well underway prior to 1939, as Stalin sought to make the Soviet Union "an unassailable Bolshevik fortress." In addition to the assault on the *zapovedniki*, the Kremlin oversaw numerous construction projects, including new factories and even entirely new cities. Now, facing a Nazi invasion, Stalin stepped up his offensive on the environment. He ordered the construction of highways, mines, and industrial plants to exploit Soviet resources in Siberia. Population centers in the Soviet Union's central and eastern states expanded in size, with new power plants built to provide them electricity. The harvesting of timber grew, as did emissions of pollutants such as sulfur dioxide and nickel. The upshot was widespread deforestation—thereby permitting stronger winds and colder weather—and the devastation of entire ecosystems.[43]

If the war proved more harmful than beneficial to terrestrial life, the opposite seemed the case with marine fauna. An effort by the British in 1944 to set an international quota of whaling in Antarctica to 16,000 BWUs found support from the United States, which had concluded that any multilateral accord required it to play a more active role. Even though the British demarche confronted resistance from whalers, the war proved a boon for whales as whaling vessels were either diverted for wartime use or unable to get onto the high seas. Similarly, fishery stocks grew as Japan's fishing industry took a beating and other countries, such as the United States, had to keep their fishing fleets in port to avoid being sunk by submarines.[44]

But marine life did suffer during the war. The conflict may have dramatically reduced the number of whale hunts, yet sailors using sonar had a difficult time telling the difference between a large whale and an enemy submarine, leading to the depth-charging of the graceful cetaceans. Others died when they encountered mines laid by the belligerents to protect ports, or planes or warships that saw them as useful for target practice. Because of accidents, combat, or poor weather, ships leaked or dumped petroleum into the surrounding water.[45]

Over the longer term, the war had some positive consequences for the environment. City buildings destroyed during the conflict at times were removed and turned into green spaces, and ships sitting at the bottom of the ocean became coral reefs for living creatures. Yet there were many negatives as well. In addition to oil leaking from sunken vessels, ordnance on the sea floor continues to pose a threat to both humans and animal life. Another danger comes from the approximately 65,000 tons of German chemical weapons and agents the Allies dumped into the Baltic Sea. The material in those metal containers, including mustard gas, started to escape in recent years. The same is true with receptacles left behind in China from Japan's biological and chemical warfare program. It is estimated that between the years 1945 and 2000, over 750 people in just China's Jilin Province died from exposure to these substances. A 1997 treaty signed between Beijing and Tokyo to locate and destroy what remains of those buried agents had by early 2017 eliminated many of them. However, at one site, the anticipated completion of the cleanup will not be until 2022, and Beijing has pointed out the dispersal of burial sites makes others difficult to locate.[46]

Chemicals became part of the Allied effort to stop the spread of insect-borne illness. In the interwar period, the language of conflict had entered into discussions over how to control insects that might destroy crops or spread disease. The head of the U.S. Bureau of Entomology, L. O. Howard, commented in 1921 that "the next great world war" would be that "against the class *Insecta*." The years between the wars witnessed the development of new pesticides and means of delivering them, such as crop-dusting aircraft, but many of the concoctions proved lacking, and humans did not enjoy finding themselves in the path of crop dusters. Muddling matters further was the difficulty some companies had breaking into foreign markets. One of them was the Swiss company Geigy. It had developed a product called Gesarol, later called DDT, and which Swiss chemist Paul Müller had discovered was an effective insecticide. Geigy had tried in 1941 to sell Gesarol in the United States, but the company's American subsidiary refused, believing Gerasol could not compete with other products already available.[47]

That changed with the US entrance into the war. In 1942, Geigy provided the U.S. Bureau of Entomology information on Gesarol, demonstrating how its liquid compound killed insects yet was "relatively non-toxic to man and animals." Indeed, it proved a wonder product, one that required only a small dose to eliminate lice and mosquitoes. And it was easy to deliver, whether by plane, truck, or handheld sprayer. Despite early tests that suggested DDT was toxic to animals, the U.S. Army adopted it to control mosquito populations and disease. American military officials used it to halt the spread of typhus in Naples, Italy, and sprayed islands in the Pacific. In the long run, its use had two significant consequences. One was to create mosquitoes resistant to the pesticide, forcing chemical companies to find more powerful alternatives. The other was its accumulation in animal and human tissue,[48] a consequence that would play a part in the development of the modern environmental movement.

# The United Nations

Another player in what would become the modern environmental movement was the United Nations. The League of Nations by the 1930s had proven itself incapable of meeting what had been its prime mission, that of preventing another world war. Italy may have surrendered in September 1943, but it took twenty more months for Germany to follow suit, and another three months after that before Japan called it quits, thus ending the second global conflict of the twentieth century. Left behind were as many as eighty million dead, millions more injured or homeless, and enormous physical destruction not just to the natural environment but to cities, towns, and transportation and industrial infrastructures. Yet the idea that an international organization offered the best means to maintain the peace remained alive. A year before the war came to an end, the United States, Great Britain, and Soviet Union agreed to establish such a body that would replace the League. In April 1945, delegates from fifty countries met in San Francisco to create what became the United Nations (UN). While ostensibly all of them had a say in the UN's composition, it was the "Big Four"—the United States, Soviet Union, Great Britain, and China—that were central to the writing of the UN Charter.

The UN held its first meeting in 1946, the same year the League formally dissolved. On the surface, the new organization appeared very similar to its predecessor. Just as the League had an assembly for all members, so the UN had a general assembly that would act as an international forum for its. The League had a Council on which the world's major powers sat. The UN had a Security Council, consisting of five permanent members—the United States, Soviet Union, Great Britain, China, and France—and six others elected for two-year terms by the League. (In 1966, the number of elected members was increased to ten.) There were key differences, however. The relationship between the League's Assembly and Council was not clear. The UN Charter offered that clarity. The Security Council could veto decisions made by the Assembly, a provision that helped convince the United States to join the new international organization. Furthermore, any decision reached by the Security Council bound members of the Assembly to abide by it, giving the UN greater opportunity to bring political or economic pressure to bear on other countries.

As with the League, collective security might have been the central focus of the UN, but the new body had the potential to address environmental matters. The Charter, which describes the purpose and powers of the various bodies of the UN, established other organizations. One was the Food and Agriculture Organization (FAO). Its prime purpose is to find means to eliminate hunger and boost nutrition through increased agricultural production. But, as stated in the first article of its constitution, a way to reach those goals is through "the conservation of natural resources."[49]

Another was the United Nations Educational, Scientific and Cultural Organization (UNESCO). UNESCO's mandate is to seek international collaboration on educational, scientific, and cultural affairs so as to guarantee support for human rights and the rule of law, as called for by the UN Charter. Its first head, Julian Huxley, was a supporter of conservation who believed "the enjoyment of nature was part of culture, and that preservation of rare and interesting animals and plans was a scientific duty." UNESCO converged with a revival of conservationist movements in Europe following the war. These groups, active in France, Holland, and Great Britain, pointed both to the Second World War's devastation of the natural environment and the importance of making sure environmental considerations entered postwar reconstruction efforts. Taking advantage of this renewed interest in conservation, the Swiss League for the Protection of Nature held a conference in 1946 attended by the continent's chief conservationists. From this meeting came the idea of a new multilateral organization to defend the environment, an initiative endorsed by Huxley. The result was the creation in 1948 of the International Union for the Protection of Nature (IUPN)— later renamed the International Union for the Conservation of Nature (IUCN)—which included representatives from governmental environmental offices and nongovernmental organizations.[50]

The IUPN's full name was a bit of a misnomer, for "protection" did not mean "preservation." Rather, the IUPN, as was the case with many other organizations and the treaties they had endorsed, was conservationist in orientation. Hence, it opposed not the utilization of the planet's flora and fauna for human benefit but its overexploitation or abuse. It believed, however, that the UN would serve as an ally in that endeavor. The IUPN had asked UNESCO to send the former's draft constitution to national governments, thus allowing it to identify itself with the United Nations.[51] By working together, the IUPN might use the UN as the vehicle for defending nature that the League of Nations failed to provide. Once again, though, that hope was short-lived.

# CHAPTER THREE

# Cold war, science, and the environment

On July 16, 1945, the American physicist J. Robert Oppenheimer joined numerous others to witness Trinity, the code name for the testing of the first atomic bomb. Fearful that Nazi Germany might develop such a weapon before the Allies, American and British scientists and military officials had joined forces in what became known as the Manhattan Project. Germany had surrendered two months earlier, but Japan had yet to do so, and the prospect of an invasion of Japan itself hung over President Harry Truman. The A-bomb offered the possibility of ending the war quickly and saving, according to the estimates of the U.S. Joint Chiefs of Staff, approximately 50,000 American lives. Sitting atop a 100-foot tower, the device was detonated at 5:29 that morning. It exploded with a force of fifteen to twenty kilotons, produced a mushroom cloud that lit up the sky and rose 41,000 feet high, and left a crater 1,200 feet across. Oppenheimer recalled that he thought to himself a line from the Hindu scripture Bhagavad Gita: "I am become Death, the destroyer of worlds."[1]

Many of Oppenheimer's contemporaries, both within and outside the scientific community, ignored his implicit warning. Replacing the hot war that ended in 1945 was the Cold War, an ideological, economic, political, and military conflict that pitted the United States and the Soviet Union, alongside their allies, against one another. Numerous individuals believed that in the conflict with communism, science was not mankind's enemy, but its ally, for it allowed Washington and its friends to remain technologically and militarily ahead of the Soviet bloc. In so doing, they could use the threat of nuclear annihilation as part of a broader effort to contain the spread of communism. Maintaining that technical and military advantage became paramount after the Soviets successfully tested their first atomic bomb in

1949. In response, the United States increased the power of its nuclear weapons and the number of atomic tests it conducted. In 1952, the United Kingdom joined the "nuclear club," and by 1958, the world's three nuclear powers had held a total of 231 atmospheric atomic tests.[2]

These two interrelated themes, the Cold War and the emphasis on scientific discovery, had enormous implications for the environment. The United Nations, heralded as an agency that could oversee international efforts to protect the environment, largely focused on what it regarded as more important matters. In the meantime, the United States used its influence to direct decision-making in the West that was largely inimical to the environment. In the name of containment in Asia, particularly following the "loss" of the newly renamed People's Republic of China (PRC) to communism and the onset of the Korean War in 1950, Washington succeeded in expanding Japan's access to fisheries and to whales, causing a decline in fish and whale stocks. Seeing containment tied to a "war" against insects, US officials engaged in spraying pesticides, including DDT, despite warnings of potential harm to fauna and humans. The creation, testing, and disposal of nuclear explosives left behind pollution on land and at sea, and created fallout, all of which imperiled plants, animals, and people.

It would be wrong, however, to place all actions or decisions with environmental consequences solely on the shoulders of the United States. In 1960 France also became a member of the "nuclear club," increasing further the level of radioactivity in the atmosphere. A failure to take precautions led to extensive radioactive contamination in a large region around a Soviet plutonium production complex. Postwar economic recovery in Japan and Western Europe—itself a US Cold War imperative—heightened demand for Middle East petroleum and, along with it, maritime pollution. The United Kingdom assumed the lead in trying to control high seas pollution, with meager results. Meanwhile, a cold war of sorts erupted between the PRC and Soviet Union, with dramatic environmental consequences.

Even if unintentional, the period from the end of the Second World War through the early 1960s had some positive consequences for the environment. Though limited in its effectiveness, the creation in 1946 of the International Whaling Commission offered a possible foundation for conserving whales. The demilitarized zone on the Korean peninsula became an ecological paradise. And nuclear testing generated an international movement to stop such activities. For the most part, however, Cold War imperatives and the faith in science overwhelmed voices calling for defending the environment.


## Containment, fisheries, and whaling

Signs that the Second World War alliance might not last appeared even before that conflict ended. At the Yalta conference held in February 1945, the United States and Great Britain found particularly troublesome the

Soviets' demand to have Poland adopt a communist government. Following the war, Moscow reimposed its will on the Baltic states of Estonia, Latvia, and Lithuania—which it had lost to the Germans during the conflict— refused to budge on Poland, and gradually established dominance over most of Eastern Europe. In Asia, the Kremlin occupied the northern part of the Korean peninsula and oversaw the installation of a communist government there, and sought a role in the occupation of Japan. Meanwhile, communist revolts in Greece, China, and the French colony of Indochina suggested that Soviet premier Josef Stalin had his eyes on spreading his ideology to all corners of the planet.

Viewing these events with alarm, President Harry Truman in 1947 called for the containment of communism worldwide. Reflective of a broader "Cold War consensus" in the United States that Washington had to assume the lead against Soviet-inspired communism, containment took numerous forms. The United States provided military aid to the noncommunist Greek and Chinese governments, and to the French. Believing the devastation wrought by the war had left behind conditions in which communism might thrive, the Truman administration in 1948 approved the Marshall Plan, through which the United States over the next five years furnished the noncommunist (Western) nations of Europe with $13 billion in economic aid. A year later, the United States, Canada, and ten European countries formally created the North Atlantic Treaty Organization (NATO), a military alliance designed to stand up to the Soviet threat. Finally, Washington sought to remain ahead of Moscow in terms of armed might. With the Soviets' acquisition of the atomic bomb, the United States stepped up its efforts to expand both the size and power of its nuclear stockpile. The results of these efforts were mixed. The Greek government succeeded in defeating the communist revolt. The Marshall Plan enhanced Western Europe's well-being by helping restore investment and industrial production in those countries, putting them on the path to recovery and halting the spread of communism. In both China and Indochina, however, US aid proved unable to stop continued advances by communist forces.

The United States had seen China as the bulwark against communism in Asia, but the inability of its Nationalist government to crush the communists convinced Washington that Japan should assume that role. Following the war, Japan was under military occupation, governed ostensibly by an eleven-nation Far Eastern Commission (FEC), the members of which included the United States, the Soviet Union, Great Britain, Australia, and New Zealand. Washington, however, was the key player, as its troops made up the overwhelming majority of those overseeing Japan. The country they occupied lay devastated. Not only had atomic bombs been dropped on two of its cities, but conventional explosives had destroyed large portions of dozens of others. Millions of people were homeless, and a substantial portion of the country's industrial infrastructure had been turned into rubble. General Lucius Clay, who oversaw America's military occupation of Germany, commented in 1946, "There is no choice between becoming a Communist on 1500 calories [a day] and a believer in democracy on 1000."[3] General Douglas MacArthur, the supreme commander for the Allied powers (SCAP) in Japan, agreed. If the Japanese did not receive some form of hope, unrest would spread, leaving him no choice but to use force to maintain order.[4]

There were possibilities for restoring Japan's well-being. During the war, Japan's textile industry had suffered, but it had seen an expansion in both steel and machine-tool production. Hence, there was a foundation of knowledge to which the Japanese could turn as they rebuilt. But none of that would matter if the occupation government was unable to provide even the most basic of necessities, including food. Fish had always been a staple of the Japanese diet, and fishing in distant waters offered a means of providing the Japanese people with sustenance. There were three serious problems, however. One was that much of the country's fishing industry had been hard hit. Japan had lost between 40 and 60 percent of the tonnage of fishing boats it had had in 1940. Numerous ports also had suffered heavy damage and required repair before they could be used. Second, the Soviet Union had taken from Japan the Kurile Islands and the southern part of Sakhalin Island. In turn, the Japanese lost access to the fisheries around those areas. Finally, President Truman showed no intention to permit Japan to engage in distant-water fishing. In late September 1945, just a few weeks after Tokyo's surrender, he issued a proclamation declaring the US government's right "to establish conservation zones" as far out as two hundred nautical miles from the American coastline, a much further distance than the three miles accepted under international law. The president made this announcement to protect Alaskan salmon interests, which did not want to face renewed Japanese competition, and tuna fisheries in the Gulf of Mexico. Tokyo viewed access to distant-water fisheries as vital to its economic recovery. Closure of the Alaska fishery would not have destroyed the Japanese fishing industry, but the possibility of other countries following America's lead worried Japanese fishermen.[5]

At first, and over the objections of other FEC members, MacArthur permitted Japanese fishermen to ply their trade, but only within Japan's coastal waters. To prevent them from doing so, he believed, would imperil an industry important to Japan, require the United States to spend large sums of money to provide food to the Japanese people that they might otherwise get on their own, and push Japan into the arms of communism. As the communists continued to advance in China and the French proved unable to put down the insurgency in Indochina, the Truman administration began to ease those restrictions further. It set aside the president's 1945 proclamation, with the exception of those fisheries that were being scientifically managed and to which Japan had not regularly accessed prior to the war. To ensure Japan's compliance, SCAP and the US government made it clear that Tokyo had to accept such limitations in return for a peace treaty that would officially end both the Second World War and the US occupation. With the signing of that treaty in 1951, and despite complaints from almost everyone in the FEC and the US fishing industry, Japanese trawlers received permission to move into much of the central and western Pacific.[6]

The American change of heart vis-à-vis Japan's access to fisheries extended to whaling. In April 1946, MacArthur informed Washington that he planned to permit Japanese whalers to return to the waters around Antarctica. He sold it as a "one-time-only" initiative rather than a permanent shift in the US position. The State Department offered no opposition to this move, prompting the occupation commander to announce it publicly that August. Although upset, the British government stood behind MacArthur. Not only was it essential to provide the Japanese with fat and oil, Whitehall argued, but if some of that output ended up on the international market, it would benefit numerous countries outside of Japan. Australia and New Zealand were less than pleased, insisting that Japanese whaling endangered not only their economic interests, but that Japan would use whaling ships to collect military intelligence. Neither country, however, had any chance of moving the United States or MacArthur without Britain's help. As it turned out, Japan's access to Antarctic whales continued throughout the US occupation.[7]

Japan's return to whaling was part of broader revitalization of the whaling industry that had taken a hit during the war. The number of blue, fin, and humpback whales killed had fallen dramatically. Nearly 30,300 whales had been caught during the 1939–40 hunting season, versus 2,891 in 1944–45. With the war over, the demand for animal fat, including that from whales, grew. In 1947–48, the number of whales killed reached 28,670. Once again, the specter of extirpation arose, renewing calls for controls over hunting. The question was effectiveness. Western authorities believed that Moscow would flaunt restrictions on whaling. The Japanese felt many of those same officials, too, were likely to cheat, thus undermining any hope of establishing a whaling regime.[8]

Adopting a posture of hostility toward Japan or the Soviet Union, though, was out of the question, for to do so risked undermining any possibility of establishing internationally accepted quotas on whaling. Having decided to assume more of a leadership role than it had in the past, the United States in October 1946 sent invitations to nineteen nations for a conference to take place the following month. To the surprise of the representatives present, the Soviets sent a delegation. The attendees had to find a balance between defending the interests of whalers with ensuring the whales' very existence. In what became the International Convention for the Regulation of Whaling (ICRW), they adopted the 16,000-BWU limit for Antarctic whaling that had been formulated in 1944, agreed that indigenous peoples had the right to hunt whales for their own survival, and permitted the killing "of whales beyond the quota for scientific purposes."[9]

To go into effect, the convention needed the ratification of six countries, of which Holland, Great Britain, the United States, and the Soviet Union had to be part.[10] Those four countries, alongside eleven others—among them

Argentina, France, and Canada—acceded to the convention, thus allowing it to go into effect. Japan, not one of the original signatories, adopted it after it signed the 1951 peace treaty.

The ICRW was simultaneously significant and imperfect. It was one of the first international agreements aimed at protecting whales. Additionally, the convention established the International Whaling Commission (IWC), which became recognized by countries worldwide as the authority on conserving whales. Still, it had its shortcomings. First, its language made reference to the conservation of whales, but it included provisions as well designed to protect the whaling industry. Second, in conserving whales, the expectation was that scientists would play a major role. But those who wanted to protect whales faced numerous hurdles in having their voices heard. One was the concern among IWC members that any attempt to change the regulations on whaling favorable to conservation efforts would cause some nations to leave the Commission. Additionally, the scientists themselves disagreed on such matters as the existing population of whales. Then there was the IWC's structure. The Commission had both a scientific and a technical committee, which seemingly gave scientists a voice in decision-making. Yet the whalers dominated the technical committee, thereby according them the power to prevent any proposals originating from the scientists. The Commission also had limited financial resources, which restricted the amount of money that could be put toward research. Finally, the IWC's chairs from its inception through the 1960s tended to lack expertise or were poor administrators.[11]

The result was a haphazard effort to control whaling. The Antarctic quota held firm at 16,000 BWU through the 1952–53 season, when whalers caught less than 15,000 BWU. Consequently, the IWC, over Dutch resistance, reduced the quota to 15,500 BWU. By the end of the decade, it had been cut by another 1,000 BWU. Yet that number was still greater than scientists favored. Worse, as the West had feared, the Soviets showed no preparedness to abide by those limits. Moreover, the ICRW required two inspectors per whaling ship, but they tended to come from the flag country and got their paycheck from that government. When the IWC in 1959 finally adopted a protocol permitting foreigners on whaling ships, the Soviets, not wanting potential spies on their vessels, refused to accept it. That same year, both Norway and the Netherlands declared their intention to withdraw from the IWC, further hampering efforts to conserve whales.[12] Whale populations continued to decrease, and many whaling states proved unable to reach their quotas.

The survival of the world's largest cetaceans around Antarctica was one reason for the Antarctic Treaty signed in 1959. Antarctica had become by then a potential powder-keg, with seven nations, among them Argentina, Chile, the United Kingdom, France, and Norway, having laid claim to parts of that continent. Although much of this dispute was strategic in nature, whaling entered the picture. The British, Australians, and New Zealanders argued a US Central Intelligence Agency (CIA) report in 1956, and used whaling to justify extending their sovereignty to include Antarctica.[13]

Standing against this climate of competition was the International Geophysical Year (IGY) that began in July 1957 and continued through the end of 1958. It was first proposed by scientists in 1952, who called it an opportunity to break down Cold War tensions through multinational scientific cooperation. Numerous countries participated, including the United States and Soviet Union. Building on the goodwill generated by the IGY, the two superpowers and ten other nations signed the Antarctic Treaty. Covering the continent's land and ice shelves below 60° south latitude, it focused on matters of security: the agreement banned on the continent military operations except those that were peaceful in nature, nuclear testing or the disposal of atomic waste, and the expansion of claims of sovereignty, and encouraged continued scientific endeavors. But it offered also a foundation for environmental protection, as it called for measures that would promote the "preservation and conservation of living resources in Antarctica."[14] The treaty went into force in 1961.

For all of its strengths, the Antarctic Treaty had two significant weaknesses when it came to protecting the environment. For one, establishing a foundation that would protect fauna and flora was not the same as producing a convention that imposed restrictions on the hunting of marine life or destruction of plants. Additionally, and in a further nod to its anthropocentric underpinnings, it specifically excluded the waters and sea ice, meaning seals were not guaranteed protection (and would remain unprotected until 1972).[15]

Protecting marine life entered as well into continued negotiations over oil pollution. In addition to US economic aid, trade, and high seas commerce (including whaling), the postwar recovery of Japan and Western Europe depended on oil, much of which came from the Middle East. By the mid-1950s, Western Europe obtained about two-thirds of its oil from Middle Eastern sources; Japan's dependency on the Middle East's petroleum was even greater. More oil tankers leaving the Middle East meant more ships having to clean their tanks. Once again, complaints began to appear in the United Kingdom of sea birds dying from, and beaches fouled by, blackish, polluted water.[16]

In 1949, the United Nations' Economic and Social Council's Transportation and Communications Commission determined it necessary to do something about oceanic oil pollution. At the end of that year, it issued a report calling for international control. Nongovernmental organizations, which prior to the Second World War had taken charge of that subject, did so again, led by Great Britain's International Committee for Bird Preservation. Accepting the need for action, Whitehall created the Committee on the Prevention of Pollution of the Sea by Oil, which advanced an international prohibition on contaminated water greater than one hundred parts per million (ppm). Using that recommendation as a foundation, London hosted in 1954 a conference attended by forty-two countries, which represented 95 percent of the world's shipping.[17]

The conference from the start faced a crucial stumbling block, that of a lack of interest outside of Western Europe. The United States, once one of the leading advocates for an oil pollution convention, now rejected an international agreement, contending that it had taken unilateral measures to solve the problem. Nor were Soviet bloc or developing countries desirous to sign on either. The end result, called the International Convention for the Prevention of Pollution of the Sea by Oil (OILPOL), looked little different from proposals submitted prior to the Second World War. OILPOL banned discharges above 100 ppm within fifty miles of a shoreline but placed no cap on those taking place outside that zone. New language mandated record-keeping of "all tanker ballasting, cleaning and discharge operations in a newly developed Oil Record Book instead of in the ship's log." Although OILPOL went into force in 1958, the United States did not ratify it until 1961, Japan waited until 1963, and it was another six years after that before the Soviet Union agreed to take part. Furthermore, as with previous agreements, enforcement proved all but impossible. A survey taken in 1962 discovered that only two signatories had taken steps necessary to determine and prosecute violations of the convention. Nor did amendments added in 1962 do much to force compliance.[18]

# Korea

If containment factored into Western policies on fishing, whaling, and oil pollution, it was central to a war that broke out in 1950, one that ended up having unintended long-term environmental consequences. In June of that year, communist North Korea launched an attack on the noncommunist South, with the goal of trying to unify the entire peninsula under communist rule. The invasion came on the heels of several events that unnerved the West: the Soviet atomic bomb test in August 1949, the communist victory in the Chinese civil war in October, the retreat of China's noncommunist leadership to the island of Taiwan that same month, and the signing in January 1950 of a treaty of friendship between the Soviet Union and the PRC. To US officials, Pyongyang had acted as part of a broader effort by the Kremlin to spread its ideology worldwide. With the Soviet Union boycotting the United Nations because of the US refusal to permit the PRC to represent China in that body rather than Taiwan, the Security Council passed a resolution calling on its members to assist Seoul. Soon, sixteen nations had troops on the way to South Korea.

The Korean War had important diplomatic and military ramifications for not just the peninsula but the region. It stimulated an already-ongoing process to sign what became the 1951 peace treaty with Japan and contributed to that country's economic revitalization. It also raised the specter of another world war, particularly after the PRC's decision in November 1950 to intervene. The question was whether the now-nuclear Soviet Union might follow suit. Moscow decided against a full-scale intervention—it did provide military aid to both Beijing and Pyongyang—but the help it gave, alongside China's invasion, served to stalemate the conflict. Not until July 1953 did UN and communist negotiators reach an armistice, establishing a 2.5-mile wide demilitarized zone (DMZ) that largely followed the old North Korean-South Korean border.

As in the world wars, the fighting in Korea affected and was affected by the environment. The Chinese used the mountains in the North to hide their movements prior to their attack. Shortly after the PRC entered the conflict, UN and communist troops spent two weeks fighting in brutally cold weather in what became known as the Battle of Chosin Reservoir. Forests in both the North and South, already depleted during Japan's occupation of the peninsula from 1910 to 1945, underwent further despoilment as Koreans turned to trees for firewood. US bombers inflicted enormous physical damage, destroying most of the North's heavy industry and flooding towns and portions of the countryside by targeting dams. Animals, both wild and domesticated, suffered from fighting or from being hunted and trapped for food or to be sold. In the years following the armistice, though, the DMZ became, in the words of one author, "a nearly complete set of Korean ecosystems within its boundaries, ranging from wetlands to grasslands to mountainous highlands, all of them largely untouched by human activities since the end of the war." The biodiversity on this "accidental nature preserve" includes numerous types of fish, birds, plants, insects, and mammals. Many of them are considered endangered, and some at one point were thought to have disappeared altogether.[19]

## Science, nature, and the cold war

Despite the successful effort at stopping the communists' attempt to spread their ideology to South Korea, the threat posed by the Soviet Union and its allies elsewhere remained omnipresent. Consequently, the United States retained a military presence in South Korea, tightened its relationship with Taiwan and Japan, intensified ongoing initiatives to split the Sino-Soviet alliance, increased military aid to the French fighting in Indochina, used the CIA to undermine "communist" regimes in Iran and Guatemala, and bolstered its support for NATO. US scientists and military officials also looked into, in the words of one author, "arming mother nature."[20]

The idea of turning the environment into a weapon emerged from a long-standing faith that science could open the doors to a world of discovery and accomplishment. Human ingenuity since the late 1800s had created

**PHOTO 4** Looking across the DMZ, Korea. *Credit: Dreamstime.*

new and faster means of travel, including the automobile and the airplane. Modern methods of communication, among them the telephone, radio, and motion picture, had appeared. The possibilities for the future seemed endless, as reflected in the 1939 World's Fair. Held in New York City, it was the first world's fair to emphasize the future, with science acting as the medium. Many visitors could remember a time when electricity was a novel concept, so General Electric's "Electric Home" display drew a lot of attention. Borden Inc. foresaw the "Dairy World of Tomorrow," with the "rotolactor" simultaneously milking dozens of satisfied cows, while "Rocket Port" envisioned a "rocket gun" shooting ships into space.[21]

The discoveries of the Second World War, among them improvements in rocketry, radar, sonar, and, most importantly, the creation of the atomic bomb, magnified humans' faith in science. Inventions and medical breakthroughs in subsequent years appeared to confirm that sentiment. The new medium of entertainment and information transfer, television, witnessed a dramatic increase in owners and viewers in the United States, United Kingdom, and Soviet Union.[22] Computers, though far more massive and slower than modern models, came into greater use, and Xerox Corporation introduced the photocopier. Scientists discovered the structure of human DNA. Due to medical advances, among them a vaccine for polio, life expectancy in industrialized countries rose.

If science could conquer airspace, send messages through television signals, and cure disease, could it not master nature itself? US officials, imbued with a Wilsonian ideology that the spread of democracy would benefit the entire planet, asked themselves that very question, wondering if they might use the natural environment to foster containment. They had all the more reason to raise that query, for it was likely their counterparts in the Kremlin were thinking the same thing, but in the name of fostering communism. Thus, American military and political officials, alongside scientists, looked into modifying the weather to help other countries or to use it as a weapon against enemies. They began to learn all they could about the vulnerability of flora, fauna, and humans to natural killers should a war with the Soviets break out. They considered the possibility of trying to spread any number of pathogens among an enemy's population, ranging from bubonic plague to anthrax and melioidosis. To see if it might be possible to target another country's foodstuffs, the Army's Chemical Corps discovered during tests on the US Virgin Island of St. Thomas and in New York State that it was possible to use pigeons or even just their feathers to spread a fungal disease called cereal rust among oat crops. Scientists also tried weaponizing insects. The Second World War's devastation and disruption of trade routes forced nations in Western Europe to rely heavily on imports, including food. It was not uncommon for alien insects to ride along, and, if they survived their new home, to have an effect on the food chain. Finland in the years after the war had to contend with the Mediterranean mill moth. Great Britain witnessed the introduction of about 150 beetle species from 1942 to 1947. If insects accidentally brought into a country could wreak havoc on crops, then those dropped on or sent purposely to an enemy could have the same impact.[23]

These conclusions reflected the growing influence of ecology on scientific— and, in this case, military—thinking. The concept of an interconnectedness between living organisms had existed since at least the 1800s. In both the United States and Great Britain, zoologists, botanists, biologists, and other scientists had realized intersections existed among their fields of study and began to share their findings, creating the new field of ecological studies. It was those two nations, the United States and the United Kingdom, that well into the twentieth century were centers of ecological research, for they had the financial resources to fund the universities and programs the new discipline required. They formed professional societies, starting with the British Ecological Society in 1913 and the Ecological Society of America a year later. One of the individuals who became a president of the British Ecological Society was Charles Elton, a native of Manchester, England, who received a degree in zoology from Oxford University in 1922. In 1958, he authored *Ecology of Invasions*, demonstrating how invasive species destroyed ecosystems, causing nations billions of dollars in damage.[24] Such findings convinced US officials of the possibility of weaponizing ecology, using the introduction of pathogens, insects, or animals to destroy a wide spectrum of organisms in the name of defeating communism.

If introducing natural pests into communist nations offered one means of containment, so did exterminating them outside of the communist bloc.

The American weekly magazine, *Time*, reported less than three weeks after the dropping of the second atom bomb on Japan that DDT had become available for civilian use. Using the language of armed conflict, it declared a "war against winged pests was under way." Winning that war would enhance food production, which Lucius Clay had insisted was an essential component of containment. Commented one official in the U.S. Department of Agriculture before Congress in 1951, "As a weapon for defense, food and fiber may not be as spectacular as atomic bombs and guided missiles. But gentlemen, it is not a matter of which is more important to the defense of the Nation, food or weapons. They are equally important."[25]

As US industry had come out of the war unscathed, it fell upon American companies to take the lead in developing those ever-more-effective pesticides. There was, in fact, a dual purpose to this research. In addition to guarding foodstuffs produced in the United States and allied countries, the new chemicals would allow America to "keep ahead" of the Soviets' own chemical and biological weapons programs. Entomologists and university researchers joined the effort. New chlorinated hydrocarbons, the family of compounds that included DDT, appeared. Organophosphates, derived from phosphoric acid, entered the market in 1946. It was clear that organophosphates were harmful to humans, but some insects had become resistant to DDT, others were immune to DDT to start with, and these new compounds killed those pests faster than previous ones.[26]

None of this is to suggest that DDT was on the outs. It continued to remain a wonder product. In the United States, ranchers argued that spraying it on cattle increased beef production, and potato farmers credited it with higher yields. There were warnings about its effects. "If, for example, insects are eliminated from a large area," wrote two officials from the U.S. Bureau of Entomology, "young birds may subsequently starve as a result."[27] Claims regarding DDT's usefulness in containing communism, though, meant such implorations went unheeded.

In fact, pesticides did more than protect crops. They also prevented the spread of disease, which too would assist anti-communist efforts. In the 1950s, US officials argued that attacking malaria in Mexico was essential to containment, for otherwise the Soviets might try to draw Mexico into their orbit by offering "grants and promises of development." Similar considerations applied to the Italian island of Sardinia. In the immediate aftermath of the Second World War, the United States sent billions of dollars in assistance to Italy, not only to halt the spread of illness but to rebuild the Italian economy and preempt "an outburst of revolutionary activity fueled by social distress." Joining this endeavor was the Rockefeller Foundation, an American organization founded in 1913 with the mission of "promoting the well-being of humanity throughout the world," and the Ente Regionale per la Lotta Anti-Anofelica di Sardegna (ERLAAS), a special organization made up of thousands of men whose job it was to use jeeps and planes to destroy every last mosquito there. With the endorsement of the Foundation,

Shell Petroleum Company in 1948 sent a film crew to record those efforts. From their work emerged between 1949 and 1950 three short films: *The Sardinian Project*, *Battaglie di Pace* (*Battles of Peace*), and *Adventure in Sardinia*. As seen elsewhere, the language of war appeared in this public relations campaign. Aside from the title *Battles of Peace*, the narrator in *The Sardinian Project* spoke of an "all-out campaign" against insects. ERLAAS's publications depicted men with spray guns shooting down flying mosquitoes, not unlike the troops who had manned antiaircraft guns during the Second World War.[28]

The United States had worked in conjunction with the United Nations Relief and Rehabilitation Administration (UNRRA) in combating mosquitoes in Sardinia, and the UN joined other measures against pests. Under the auspices of the United Nations Food and Agriculture Organization twenty-nine countries signed in 1951 the International Plant Protection Convention. Its parties agreed to cooperate with each other through regional organizations, engage in research, and conduct surveillance to prevent the introduction of foreign insects and flora. Soviet bloc nations in 1959 signed a similar pact, the Cooperation in the Quarantine of Plants and Their Protection against Pests and Diseases. These agreements, though, faced—and still confront—numerous challenges, among them the expansion of urban areas, the need for more agricultural land, and the purposeful or accidental transfer of plants and animals.[29]

## The Great Leap Forward

The question of pests, even if indirectly, also entered into an emerging cold war between China and the Soviet Union. Despite rhetoric that suggested otherwise, US officials from the point China turned to communism never assumed a monolithic Sino-Soviet bloc. Yugoslavia, itself a communist nation, had publicly broken with the Kremlin in 1948, and the assumption was that similar tensions existed between Moscow and Beijing. Even before the Chinese Communist Party (CCP) declared the PRC's founding, American officials presumed that it might be possible to drive a wedge between the Soviet Union and China.[30]

By 1953, the CIA had reached the conclusion that disagreements did indeed exist in the Sino-Soviet relationship, and events over the next few years confirmed that finding. Following the death of Josef Stalin, Nikita Khrushchev had emerged as the Soviet Union premier. The Kremlin's new leadership spoke of "peaceful coexistence" with the West—that is, communism would emerge victorious in its worldwide conflict with capitalism, but through means that would avoid the risk of nuclear war. Khrushchev also denounced Stalin for his brutality. These actions displeased Chinese leader Mao Zedong. In his mind, "peaceful coexistence" was irreconcilable with communism's call for violence. Having looked up to Stalin, he took Khrushchev's condemnation of the former Soviet leader as a personal affront. By 1958, the two communist countries were at loggerheads, with Kremlin officials charging their Chinese counterparts with "bellicosity," and the CCP's leaders arguing that Moscow was led by "revisionists" rather than true communists.[31]

Neither the Soviet Union nor the PRC believed it had completed the stages of history proffered by Karl Marx and achieved full-borne communism. With the two countries now at odds, whichever achieved that goal first would endow it with the title of leader of the communist world. Therefore, in 1958 Mao announced the start of the Great Leap Forward, a plan to mobilize the Chinese population, and achieve both communism and self-sufficiency. "As much as we may brag about our large population and our thousands of years of history and culture," a somber Mao commented, "our country is no better than Belgium." To achieve self-sufficiency, he called for eliminating the "four pests": flies, sparrows, rats, and mosquitoes, for all posed a danger to humans or China's agriculture. Simultaneously, he wanted to expand the industrial capacity of his largely agricultural nation, so that within fifteen years, the PRC's industrial output would reach parity with that of Great Britain.[32]

Even if they never admitted it, there was a similarity between communist and capitalist thinkers, that of an assumption that human know-how could conquer any impediment, including that posed by nature itself, to the achievement of one's economic, political, or ideological goals. In the case of China, it led Mao to forcibly crack down on anyone who resisted his plans. One example was Ma Yinchu, an economist who had been inspired by the English scholar Thomas Malthus. In 1798, Malthus had written the highly influential *An Essay on the Principle of Population*, in which he contended that food production could not keep up with population growth. Unless humans instituted measures to control the number of births, mass starvation would result. Ma agreed with that theory and warned the PRC's rapidly growing population threatened its economic well-being. Marxism disproved such thinking, argued Mao, and China would have no trouble feeding its people. Furthermore, a large population was militarily important. Despite the fact that the United States had nuclear weapons, Mao declared, China's vast size and numerous people made it impossible for America to conquer the PRC. Another person purged was hydraulic engineer Huang Wanli, who rejected a proposal to build the Sanmenxia Dam across the Yellow River to provide hydroelectric power. He insisted that sediment would build up in the dam and prevent it from functioning properly. But to Mao, giant projects like the Sanmenxia represented what communist states could accomplish.[33]

The result of the Great Leap Forward was an economic, demographic, and environmental disaster. As many as ninety million people, many of them former agricultural workers, were sent to smelt iron into steel in what was largely backyard furnaces. The steel produced was of such low quality that much of it was unusable. Despite calls for producing more food, mobilizing such a large number of people for industrial production meant fewer were able to tend to the country's crops, leaving what was supposed to have been a bumper harvest to rot. To fuel their backyard furnaces, Chinese cut down numerous trees—the country lost about 10 percent of its forests within just a few months of the Leap's commencement—thereby allowing for erosion, siltation of waterways, and even changes to the microclimate. Construction of the Sanmenxia Dam starting in 1957 required displacing 280,000 people, many of them farmers, and flooding nearly 125,000 acres of farmland. The dam, as Huang had warned, repeatedly silted up, so much so that it required reconstruction numerous times to release the silt. Those changes to the dam also substantially reduced the amount of power it produced. The killing of sparrows allowed the insect population to grow, which then began eating the country's foodstuffs. Famine spread. By 1959, Mao realized the mistake of the anti-sparrow campaign and declared bedbugs, not sparrows, as the fourth pest. Yet the Great Leap did not come to an end until 1962, and only after as many as twenty-six million Chinese perished.[34]

# The atomic arms race

How destructive human know-how could be on the environment, and to humankind itself, became apparent as well via the atomic arms race, which was well underway by the late 1950s. The determination to build more and improved weapons meant oftentimes putting aside consideration for persons or other living organisms that resided at or near the production facilities. Two examples are the Mayak Chemical Combine, located close to the city of Ozersk, Russia, and the Hanford Site, situated near the town of Hanford, Washington. During forty years of operating, these two facilities produced twice as much radioactivity as that emitted by the Chernobyl nuclear accident of 1986.[35]

A closer examination reveals the environmental damage caused by these facilities. Placed within a complex called Chelyabinsk-65, the Mayak Chemical Combine provided the radioactive material the Soviet Union used for its 1949 atomic bomb test. Authorities at Chelyabinsk dumped radioactive waste into the Techa River, a 150-mile long waterway that flows into the Tobol River. The Tobol itself intersects with the Irtysh, which drains into the Arctic Ocean. About 28,000 people lived along the Techa alone, relying on it for drinking water. Another 100,000 made their homes at or near the Tobol and Irtysh. Between 1953 and 1961, Moscow had to resettle over 12,000 people along the Techa. In the meantime, Chelyabinsk shifted its dumping operations to Lake Karachay, contaminating it with various fission products. Among them was cesium-137, a radioactive isotope that is easily absorbed by plants and the animals that feed off of them. In 1957, an explosion at a storage facility at Chelyabinsk sent radioactive waste over a large area, forcing the evacuation of nearly 11,000 people. To the present, Chelyabinsk remains one of Earth's most highly radioactive areas. Because of its location and the high level of radiation there, Ozersk to this day remains cordoned off. Fenced off as well is the highly contaminated Techa, though farmers still reportedly cut through those cordons to water their animals.[36]

The Hanford Site was one of the facilities involved in the Manhattan Project. During the Cold War, it produced plutonium for thousands of America's atomic weapons. Radiation released from the site, both in the air and from leaky storage tanks, exposed people and animals to various isotopes, including iodine-131, a short-lived radionuclide that can cause thyroid cancer. In the 1960s, acknowledgment by the US government of the radiation released by Hanford created a public relations uproar and a series of lawsuits, the last of which was not settled until 2015.[37]

Not all of this waste ended up on land or in rivers and lakes. A good portion of it was dumped on the high seas. In 1946, the United States had started discarding a portion of its nuclear detritus in the Atlantic and Pacific Oceans, assuming that their deep waters had "dead zones" where that material would sit and, over time, dissipate. The United Kingdom—which lacked large, unpopulated areas like the United States—the Soviet Union, and France followed suit. By the late 1950s, it became clear to American, Soviet, French, and Japanese scientists that water circulated even at the deepest depths, meaning that the radioactive materials dropped there, could pollute large areas and harm marine life, if not humans. Notwithstanding the destruction caused by their own dumping policies, the Soviets engaged in a propaganda campaign against the United States and the United Kingdom, accusing them of endangering the oceans.[38]

Although the United Kingdom insisted on continuing to dump at sea, the United States by 1962 had stopped doing so. Since 1946, it had deposited 86,000 containers laden with radioactive materials into the oceans. The political costs, however, became too great. The Soviet propaganda campaign had put Washington on the defensive, and it was difficult for the United States or its allies to prove that the highly secretive Kremlin had engaged in hypocrisy. There was also strong opposition within America to dumping radioactive waste near US shores. That a barrel laden with such material ended up in 1960 in a fishing net just off the coast of Massachusetts added to the domestic uproar.[39] Finally, the reaction to dumping detritus offshore was part of a broader international movement aimed at curbing, if not halting, the danger posed by radioactivity, including fallout.

The atomic bombings of Japan had demonstrated not just the explosive power of the atom but the danger posed by the radiation it released. Therefore, one of the requirements for choosing where to conduct nuclear tests (or "shots") was for them to take place far from human habitation so that neither the blast itself nor the radioactive fallout produced by the explosion affected people. Another prerequisite was that those tests had to occur where it was possible to keep secret preparations for each of them. From 1946 to 1962, the United States conducted over one hundred shots in the Pacific Ocean's Proving Grounds. The islands selected for the tests were remote and had few, if any, people on them. The blasts took place without the consent of the native populations who resided on or used the islands. Oftentimes involuntarily, those who lived in or near the affected locations were moved elsewhere. Starting in 1951, the US government conducted hundreds of additional tests at the Nevada Proving Ground. Renamed the Nevada Testing Site,[40] it was situated approximately sixty-five miles north of the city of Las Vegas. The Soviet Union carried out most of its tests in a remote area of Kazakhstan called Semipalatinsk. Great Britain held its shots in Australia and in the Central Pacific, while France conducted its tests in Algeria and later French Polynesia.

Prior to 1963, most of these tests took place above ground. A look at three carried out by the United States offers indications of the impact they had on the environment. The first two were the Operation Crossroads shots of 1946 at Bikini Atoll in the Marshall Islands. Less than 2.5 square miles, Bikini had a small number of residents—who were transported to another, smaller island 125 miles away—and was far from human settlements, fishing grounds, and shipping lanes. Designed to examine the impact of nuclear explosives on warships, the United States placed dozens of those vessels, some of them taken from Germany and Japan, around the atoll. The first of the Crossroads tests, called Able, exploded with a force of twenty-three kilotons just over five hundred feet above the assembled fleet. The Baker device, placed ninety feet underwater, released the same explosive power as Able. The third shot, Ivy Mike, took place at Enewetak, also in the Marshalls and about the same size as Bikini, in 1951. Like Bikini, Enewetak's residents had no option but to relocate. What made Ivy Mike different, though, was the device itself. Both Able and Baker employed fission, in which an atom is split apart, releasing energy. Ivy Mike was the world's first fusion, or thermonuclear, explosive, by which atoms are forced together. The result is a far more powerful blast. Indeed, Ivy Mike exploded with a force of just over 10 megatons, or over 215 times the size of Able and Baker combined.

The most obvious impact of these tests was topographical. Ivy Mike blasted about eighty million tons of dirt into the air, and left a crater on Enewetak that was 160 feet deep and over a mile in width. Because of where Able and Baker occurred, their physical effect was less obvious. However, those were only two of nearly two dozen tests that took place in the air, on the ground, and underwater at Bikini, which produced underwater craters and obliterated three of the atoll's twenty-five islets. Likewise, forty-nine blasts occurred at Enewetak, turning 8 percent of it to dust and leaving half of what remained unsafe for human habitation.[41]

These tests also affected animal and plant life. Baker heated the water beyond the boiling point in a few seconds, killing off fish in the lagoon.

Tests conducted in 1947 and since then found high levels of radioactivity among the marine biota, including cesium-137. On Enewetak, the removal of humans permitted the local bird and crab populations to increase. As the number of birds grew, so did the amount of fish they ate in the waters around the atoll. Fewer fish allowed the algae upon which the fish fed to spread. In 1980, the people of Enewetak were allowed to return after over 100,000 cubic yards of contaminated soil were placed under a concrete dome, resulting in a decline of the bird and crab populations and an increase in the number of fish.[42]

What was less clear at the time was the impact of these tests on humans. It had been known since 1927 that X-rays could generate mutations in the human body, and the effects around the immediate vicinity of the atomic bombs dropped on Japan had received widespread publicity through photographs, film, and the accounts of various authors, including the Pulitzer Prize–winning reporter John Hersey. Undetermined was whether radioactive debris falling far away from the blast site posed any harm. After a rainstorm in Troy, New York, in 1953, physicists from Rensselaer Polytechnic Institute (RPI) detected an increase in strontium-90 ($Sr^{90}$), a radioactive isotope with a twenty-eight-year half-life that can cause cancer. Following further research, the scientists at RPI traced the fallout to explosions at the Nevada Test Site. Other specialists, however, disagreed, contending that strontium would remain in the atmosphere. The result was to leave both scientists and the wider public unsure about the seriousness of the threat to human health.[43]

That uncertainty dissipated for many after the United States in March 1954 tested a fifteen megaton bomb at Bikini. Not only was the blast twice as big as scientists had anticipated, but a change in wind direction blew radioactive fallout to the east. About two hundred people living on the island of Kwajalein, some 175 miles from Bikini, suffered radiation sickness. More ominously, the twenty-three crewmen aboard a Japanese fishing vessel *Fukuryu Maru*, which was eighty-five miles from the test, also were exposed to the fallout, one of whom passed away a few months afterward. The US press reported on the fate of those on the *Fukuryu Maru*, anti-American protests took place in Japan, and Indian prime minister Jawaharlal Nehru asked that all nuclear testing cease.[44]

Strontium-90 emerged as the focal point of the debate over testing. Willard Libby, a physical chemist and member of the U.S. Atomic Energy Commission (AEC), insisted that despite what had happened near Bikini, nuclear testing was safe. Yes, he said, $Sr^{90}$ was a product of such tests, but it took about a decade for it to fall from the atmosphere to the planet's surface. Furthermore, as it went through the food chain from plants to animals to humans, filtering occurred, so that by the time it entered a human body, it was virtually harmless. Another physical chemist, Linus Pauling, strongly demurred. Appearing on national television in the United States in 1955, he pointed out that radiation caused cancer. In April 1957, a month before the United Kingdom held its first test of a hydrogen bomb, he warned that the radiation created by earlier atomic blasts would cause 10,000 people to die from leukemia. Britain's test, he added, would kill another thousand "for every megaton of explosive power released."[45] It was such appraisals, in combination with the arms race, that convinced activists in Great Britain to form in 1958 the Campaign for Nuclear Disarmament. By the end of the following year, it had branches in Canada, the Republic of Ireland, and New Zealand.

These fears entered the realm of popular culture. One common theme was that nuclear explosions mutated insects, animals, or humans, thereby placing humankind at risk. In the 1953 US film *The Beast from 20,000 Fathoms*, atomic blasts unfroze a giant dinosaur that then attacked New York City. Similar movies appeared in America as the decade continued, among them *Them!* (1954), *Tarantula* (1955), *The Beginning of the End* (1957), and *The Amazing Colossal Man* (1957). Japan, the only nation to have atomic bombs used on it in wartime, joined the fray in 1954 with *Godzilla*, the first of a series of films featuring what was to become a cultural icon. Other motion pictures, though, depicted the horrific aftereffects of nuclear testing or warfare on the human race, including the American productions *Five* (1951), *Red Alert* (1958), and *The World, the Flesh and the Devil* (1959), and the British movie *The Day the Earth Caught Fire* (1961). Novels echoed the doomsday motif, such as *Ape and Essence* (1948) by British writer Aldous Huxley, American author Judith Merril's *Shadow of the Hearth* (1950), and the powerful *On the Beach* (1957), penned by British emigré Nevil Shute. The trepidation that the arms race was a Pandora's box that jeopardized humankind continued throughout the Cold War.

Nikita Khrushchev, who became the Soviet Union's premier following Stalin's death in 1953, took advantage of the growing international pressure to end nuclear testing by announcing in March 1958 a unilateral suspension of Soviet shots. Aside from winning his nation a public relations coup, he hoped that his declaration would force the United States to halt an upcoming series of tests called Hardtack. If Washington refused to follow Moscow's lead on testing, then Khrushchev could defend a resumption of his own tests. A month later, Pauling, who already had alerted the public to the perils posed by $Sr^{90}$, brought attention to another isotope created by nuclear blasts, carbon-14 ($C^{14}$). At an international science convention, he warned that $C^{14}$ posed up to 200 times as much a threat to the human body as strontium. Shortly thereafter, the *New York Times* reported his findings to a broad audience. The AEC declared Pauling's conclusions baseless, yet was unable to find any proof to substantiate that conclusion.[46]

The American president, Dwight D. Eisenhower, found himself in a tough spot. Two-thirds of Americans favored him halting testing, and a majority of them agreed that radioactive fallout constituted a "real danger" to humans. Edward Teller, a physicist who had championed development of America's thermonuclear bomb, urged Eisenhower not to give in to public pressure, insisting that the Kremlin would "find methods to cheat."[47]

Despite the warnings from individuals such as Teller regarding Soviet untrustworthiness, and his own concerns about US security, Eisenhower began to lean in favor of an agreement banning testing. Solidifying his decision were the findings of both atomic physicist Hans Beth and the president's own science adviser, James Killian, who believed that it was possible to establish a system capable of detecting any test less than two kilotons, which would account for approximately 90 percent of all atomic blasts. With those assurances, Eisenhower announced both to Khrushchev and the world his preparedness to join in a cessation of tests in anticipation of a formal treaty. Shortly thereafter, the United States, Soviet Union, and Great Britain began preliminary negotiations in Geneva to determine if a treaty banning nuclear blasts was feasible.[48]

A willingness to suspend tests, though, did not equal actually ending them. On the one hand, Eisenhower faced intense resistance from the heads of America's military branches and the AEC. On the other hand, he had to consider an August report from the delegates at Geneva, who concluded that by using 160-170 control stations placed around the planet, it was possible to detect an atomic blast as small as five kilotons. That was enough to make up the president's mind. Later that month, he announced publicly a willingness to accept a one-year moratorium that could be extended on an annual basis if the Soviets withheld resuming tests of their own, and to initiate negotiations aimed at a test ban treaty. Khrushchev accepted the proposal, and the discussions opened that October.[49]

## From moratorium to test ban

The moratorium put a halt to military tests. Simultaneously, the representatives at Geneva slowly made headway on a formal treaty. Deciding it was impossible to achieve a comprehensive ban that would end all nuclear shots, the US and British delegations agreed the best move was a phased approach, starting with atmospheric blasts, as they were the greatest creators of radioactive fallout; a halt to all tests greater than five kilotons; and annual on-site inspections. The Soviets accepted these suggestions, though the delegates had yet to determine the total number of inspections. Nor had they reached agreement insofar as the duration of the ban.[50]

Any hope of further progress evaporated in August 1961, when the Soviets announced their intention to resume testing. As part of their test series, the Soviet Union exploded the fifty megaton Tsar Bomba, the most powerful manmade weapon ever detonated. The United States conducted dozens of atmospheric shots in the Pacific and at the Nevada Test Site. All the while, the Geneva talks remained stalled, largely over the issue of on-site inspections, which the Soviets charged would permit Western espionage. It appeared the fight to stop the release of dangerous fallout had been lost.

An international crisis changed that pessimistic outlook. On October 14, 1962, an American U-2 spy plane flying over Cuba took photographs that showed the Soviet Union was placing medium and intermediate-range nuclear missiles on that island. Determined to prevent the installation of additional missiles and pressure Khrushchev to withdraw those already on Cuba, President John F. Kennedy publicly announced on October 22 the imposition of a naval blockade around the island and warned that any missiles launched from Cuba against any country in the Western Hemisphere would lead to retaliation by the United States. For the next week, people worldwide waited, worrying that the next day might be their last. They breathed a sigh of relief when cool heads prevailed. In exchange for a promise by the Kennedy administration not to invade Cuba, the Soviets removed the missiles.

The Cuban Missile Crisis led to a warming of relations between the United States and the Soviet Union. Kennedy and Khrushchev sent numerous messages back and forth, with some of them mentioning arms control. Joined by British prime minister Harold Macmillan, the three leaders began to make headway on a test ban treaty. To evade the stumbling block presented by on-site inspections, the three countries accepted an earlier draft treaty submitted by Washington and London that would allow only underground tests. As such shots released shock waves detectable by seismic equipment, there would be no need for officials to make on-site assessments.[51] After several more weeks of bargaining, the three nations signed the Limited Test Ban Treaty (LTBT), which prohibited all aboveground and underwater nuclear blasts.

# Victory for the environmentalists?

The LTBT is generally viewed within the context of arms control, but it arguably was also an international environmental agreement, as it was a major step forward in protecting fauna, flora, and humans from the dangers of radioactivity, particularly from atmospheric nuclear tests. It was by no means perfect. The LTBT did not include France, which already had a nuclear weapons program, and China, which was in the process of developing one. Furthermore, it permitted underground testing. While on their face tests performed underground stood a good chance of trapping any radioactivity released, there was no guarantee of that. Additionally, the LTBT's language was vague. Aside from atmospheric and underground tests, it prohibited shots where the "explosion causes radioactive debris to be present outside the territorial limits of the State under whose jurisdiction or control such explosion is conducted." What constituted "to be present" was unclear. Did it mean any amount of radioactivity, or only an amount detectable by monitoring equipment? For those who favored continued testing, the latter definition made the most sense. In turn, they could argue there was nothing wrong with underground shots that released radioactivity into the atmosphere, as long as it was small enough that no one knew it was there.[52]

The determination to give priority to humans' economic, geopolitical, or security concerns over those of the environment appeared elsewhere. In the name of economic well-being or containment (or both), the number of parties engaged in fishing and whaling in the Pacific expanded. The ICRW, albeit a significant step forward, had to confront parties that, on the grounds of national interest, threatened to leave or showed no willingness to abide by its provisions. The IWC's enforcement of the ICRW was unsystematic. The United Kingdom sought to continue dumping radioactive waste. Meanwhile, China's determination to reach full-fledged communism ahead of the Soviet Union created an environmental and demographic disaster.

Throughout, the United Nations, which environmentalists had hoped would join their cause, remained largely on the sidelines. Given its mandate, this is not surprising. Those who established the UN saw its main purpose as addressing the weaknesses of the League of Nations in promoting peace and prosperity, and in protecting human rights. The UN Charter itself has no language regarding the environment.[53] Hence, the United Nations participated in pest-control efforts, but like the League of Nations, it devoted the majority of its attention to what it considered more pressing matters, among them international crises, including the Korean War, conflicts in the Middle East, and the Cuban Missile Crisis; nuclear testing, which the organization repeatedly called for halting; and a debate over whether the PRC or Taiwan should represent China.

But by the time the LTBT achieved fruition, there were clear indications that the environment was about to receive far more attention than in the past. In 1961, sixteen of the world's most famous conservationists, including British biologist Sir Julian Huxley, US aviator Godfrey Rockefeller, and Sir Peter Scott, the vice president of the International Union for the Conservation of Nature, founded the World Wildlife Fund to raise and provide money to conservation organizations globally. It acquired $5 million during its first decade in existence and would become the planet's biggest conservation organization.[54] Europe's empires had started to collapse, bringing into the international community a large number of new countries, many of which had priorities different from those of the noncommunist countries of the West or the communist nations of the East. Finally, a book had appeared which, building on the existing fears of fallout, was to bring heightened attention to environmental protection.

# CHAPTER FOUR

# *Silent Spring*, Stockholm, and the North-South divide

"At long last, the battle has ended! And thus, Ghana, your beloved country is free forever!" So declared Kwame Nkrumah in 1957,[1] when Ghana became the first sub-Saharan European colony to achieve its independence. Numerous other colonies, both within and outside Africa, were to follow. By 1970, the United Nations had 127 members, 92 more than it had at the time of its founding in 1945. Largely made up of former colonies, these new states of the "South"—a reference to LDCs—tended to have nonwhite populations, faced economic problems because of their colonial past, were suspicious of governmental structures similar to the countries that once controlled them, and wanted to see decolonization continue.

Simultaneous with the rapid growth in the number of countries on the planet was a new wave of environmentalism in the DCs of the "North." There had existed by the time of Nkrumah's speech increasingly strident calls for protecting the environment, particularly from the perils of radioactive fallout. Yet those voices had faced powerful challenges from others who argued that science would lead the world down the path to a better day. The publication of Rachel Carson's book *Silent Spring* in 1962 turned that faith in science in the noncommunist West on its head. Those in the scientific community who had pooh-poohed voices of caution now found themselves on the defensive in the face of heightened awareness of what humans were doing to the planet.

The interests of the countries of the South and North were likely to clash on environmental matters, and did so. For LDCs seeking to escape their previous economic dependence on others, protection of the environment was of less importance than economic self-sufficiency. For more advanced nations, such thinking risked damage to the environment. Countries in the South replied that the North's criticisms constituted a new form of imperialism and a violation of national sovereignty.

None of this is to suggest that during the period from the early 1960s through the mid-1970s, environmental disputes fell solely along a North-South axis. Advanced nations continued to argue among themselves or engaged in policies that aroused domestic opposition on environmental grounds. The Cold War entered into both rhetorical and policy disputes between the noncommunist West and communist East. But the North-South divide became an overarching theme as the 1960s turned into the 1970s, and witnessed a growing involvement by the United Nations, best exemplified by the 1972 UN Conference on the Human Environment. Although that meeting successfully resolved some environmental matters that placed DCs at odds with each other or with LDCs, it failed to find a solution to others.

# The new environmentalism

The new wave of environmentalism that appeared in the North in the 1960s did not emerge from a vacuum. There was already a foundation for such a movement that included warnings about DDT and the increasingly widespread opposition to nuclear testing. It was also the case that pollution in the developed world had been on the rise. During the 1950s, Los Angeles acquired the moniker "smog capital of America." In December 1952, pollutants in London, combined with weather conditions, produced the "Great Smog" that severely reduced visibility, killed thousands of Londoners, and made many others ill. Voices of caution, though, were largely stymied. The United States and Great Britain passed legislation in the 1950s to combat air pollution, which helped to reduce some of the pressure on those countries' capitals to do more to protect the environment. Faith in the ability of science to provide for the needs of humans remained potent, as did a lack of understanding that persisted among laypersons as to what pesticides could do. As for fallout, by the time the LTBT went into force in October 1963, it had over one hundred parties. One of the non-signatories was France, but the fact that so many countries, including the majority of the world's nuclear powers, had accepted its provisions was taken as a positive step forward toward curtailing atmospheric radiation.

By then, however, a powerful environmental movement had developed in the United States and began to spread throughout the North. Looking back, it is understandable why the United States became the locus of this new wave of environmentalism. There had been an interest in protecting nature in that country for nearly a century. It was highly populated and had the world's largest industrial infrastructure. Finally, it was the home of the planet's largest community of scientists, meaning that any threats to the natural environment were likely to receive extensive attention.[2]

The person who was at the heart of this postwar environmental movement was an American marine biologist, Rachel Carson, who in 1962 published

**PHOTO 5** Rachel Carson. *Credit: U.S. Fish and Wildlife Service.*

the groundbreaking work *Silent Spring*. If the warnings about pesticides and nuclear testing had provided the substructure for the modern environmental movement, *Silent Spring* built the edifice on it. In what became one of the most, if not *the* most, important works of that movement, Carson argued that about five hundred synthetic chemicals had entered the marketplace since the Second World War. Desirous to apply those chemicals in the name of maximizing profit, both producers and users failed to understand the ecological damage they caused. In graphic detail, she described the violent deaths suffered by animals in areas sprayed with dieldrin, an organochloride discovered in 1948 that was fifty times as strong as DDT. She also pointed to the spraying of DDT conducted by the US government without regard for the welfare of the people in the targeted areas. Indeed, the use of pesticides made a bad situation worse, for the insects humans sought to destroy became resistant, while the predators that ate those insects disappeared, increasing the number of crop-destroying pests. Although Carson did not call for abandoning the use of pesticides, she urged more judicious application of them, and for giving more attention to "biological control and insect sterilization" as alternatives to chemicals. The decision of the US magazine *The New Yorker* to publish installments from *Silent Spring*, and efforts by chemical companies to discredit Carson by charging she was a communist dupe only helped drive interest in her findings. For thirty-one weeks, *Silent Spring* was on the US bestseller list. Within short order it was available in sixteen nations on both sides of the Atlantic and in translation in nearly two dozen languages.[3]

"Not since the appearance of John Maynard Keynes' *General Theory of Employment, Interest and Money*—which was published in England in

1937," commented one scholar, "did a single book have such a dramatic and simultaneous impact on public opinion, scientific research, and state policy" as did *Silent Spring*. Other factors served to enhance Carson's message as the 1960s progressed. One was a number of environmental disasters. In 1967, the 975-foot oil tanker *Torrey Canyon* ran aground off the British coast. All 117,000 tons of crude in its hull spilled into the water and eventually washed up along the Cornish coastline, with some of it also ending up on the French coast. An estimated 30,000 birds died; puffins, razorbills, and murres saw their population fall by 80 percent or more. A year later, the Japanese government traced so-called Itai Itai disease in the Toyama prefecture to pollution created by cadmium mines. In 1969, the highly polluted Cuyahoga River in the US state of Ohio caught fire, and that same year, a blow-out on an oil platform off the California coast led as much as 100,000 barrels of petroleum to wash up on that state's coastline.[4]

Such disasters tied to a second reason why Carson's message resonated, which was modern technology. News, whether broadcast in print form or through television, brought home daily events taking place around the globe, including environmental disasters such as the *Torrey Canyon* or the Cuyahoga fire. Indeed, wrote one observer in the early 1970s, the last time the US media had given as much attention to a single public issue was Japan's surprise attack on Pearl Harbor. The "earthrise" photo taken in 1968 by US astronauts floating over the moon, which shows Earth as a tiny blue orb in the distance, became an international symbol of just how tiny and environmentally fragile the planet was.[5]

Finally, a growing number of people in advanced nations had reached the conclusion that a good life meant not just the material wealth they had come to enjoy but also a clean environment. Most famous on this score was the counterculture movement of the 1960s. Rejecting societal "norms," it first appeared in the United States and the United Kingdom, and soon spread into other parts of Europe. Some members of the counterculture took the position that the only way to defend "earthly values" was to adopt a communal lifestyle in harmony with nature. It may be no coincidence that Yale University professor Charles Reich, who became a hero to American counterculturalists, entitled his best-selling 1970 book *The Greening of America*.[6] In less than a generation, many elements of the counterculture, including its call for treating nature with respect, had become part of the mainstream in developed states.

It is hard to understate the multifarious impact of this environmental movement in the North. Nonfiction on both sides of the Atlantic favoring conservation received widespread notice. In a famous paper published in 1968 entitled "The Tragedy of the Commons," American biologist Garrett Hardin wrote that the planet's resources were owned by all people. In the absence of international regulation those resources risked overexploitation. That same year, US entomologist Paul Ehrlich published *The Population Bomb*. In this book, which sold more copies than *Silent Spring*, Ehrlich echoed Thomas Malthus's warning regarding population growth. Two works published in 1972, *The Limits to Growth*, an international bestseller put together by the Italian-based global think tank Club of Rome, and *A Blueprint for Survival*, written by two editors of the British environmental journal *The Ecologist*, offered a similar exhortation. The Club of Rome, which had used computer modeling on an unprecedented scale to reach its findings, added that even with technological improvements, by the year 2100 the planet would not be able to sustain humankind's population and its economic needs.[7] The themes of environmental degradation or dystopia also became more commonplace in popular culture, as seen in the novels *Earthworks*, by Brian Aldiss (1965), and J. G. Ballard's *The Drought* (1966), Dr. Seuss's children's book, *The Lorax* (1971), the US film *Soylent Green* (1973), and the Japanese movie *Godzilla v. Hedorah* (1971).

Influenced by what they saw, heard, and read, hundreds of thousands, if not millions, of people joined the environmental movement. In West Germany, the "alternative movements," which had in the 1960s emphasized the promotion of social justice and curbing the nuclear arms race, had by the end of that decade also come to address environmental matters. In Great Britain, the environmental movement by the early 1980s had three million members, where it became "the largest mass movement in British history." The number of environmental lobbyists in the US capital exploded, from two to eighty-eight between 1970 and 1985.[8]

Similar to other movements of the time, such as those that emphasized civil rights, students' rights, and women's rights, elements of the environmental movement began to adopt a more confrontational tone. Such could be seen in new environmentally interested INGOs that appeared in the late 1960s and early 1970s. These groups believed their earlier counterparts, such as the Sierra Club and World Wildlife Fund, were neither activist nor political enough to stop humankind's destruction of the environment. One was Friends of the Earth (FoE), founded in 1969 by David Brower, who formerly had served as executive director of the Sierra Club. FoE rapidly developed chapters in Western Europe, and in 1971 became part of Friends of the Earth International. To FoE, existing environmental NGOs were too moderate and had tended to ignore such issues as nuclear power and industrial pollution. It was time, FoE argued, for those wishing to protect nature to take a more aggressive stance, one that was willing to criticize industry and to engage in civil disobedience (and sometimes violence) to draw widespread attention. Another was Greenpeace. Founded in 1971 by Canadian and American environmentalists, it got its name from environmentalism (Green) and opposition to nuclear weapons testing (peace). It called for engaging in civil disobedience, hoping that its activities would receive notice from the press and, in turn, put pressure on those who threatened the planet's welfare.[9]

Finally, the environmental movement gave credence to what became known as the "precautionary principle," the idea that even if the threat to the planet's welfare had yet to be confirmed, it was best to take action now than wait until it was too late. That principle influenced at both the national and international level to a flurry of new laws, new government bodies, and efforts to codify chemicals that could pose a danger to humans. By the early 1970s, the US government had signed into law the Clean Air Act (1963), the Motor Vehicle Pollution Control Act (1965), and the National Environmental Policy Act (1970), and had banned the use of DDT and imposed restrictions on chemicals used in pesticides. It created in 1970 the Environmental Protection Agency (EPA). In 1972, it adopted the Marine Mammal Protection Act to protect all such creatures (cetaceans, polar bears, seals, sea lions, and walruses) in US waters, and to prohibit the import, export, or sale of marine mammals. In 1970, Canada passed the Arctic Waters Pollution Prevention Act to protect those waters from pollution by the oil industry. In 1971, both the Netherlands and France established environmental ministries, while Canada passed its own Clean Air Act and created a federal Department of the Environment. Japan, which after the Second World War had focused on industrialization, had generated pollution so serious as to lead to the so-called Pollution Diet of 1970, during which that country's parliament passed a series of antipollution laws. A year later, Tokyo established a federal environment agency. Whereas in 1972 fifteen countries in the North had governmental bodies to provide protection for the environment, that number a decade later had reached thirty-four.[10]

Agreements by, or those established new, international bodies reflected this emphasis on environmental protection. The 1,250-kilometer-long Rhine River in Europe had become so polluted that it received the moniker as the continent's "romantic sewer." Therefore, in 1963, the International Commission for the Protection of the Rhine (ICPR), an organization founded thirteen years earlier by West Germany, the Netherlands, France, and Luxembourg to monitor and find means of combating the river's defilement, signed the Convention on the International Commission for the Protection of the Rhine against Pollution. Also known as the Berne Convention, this agreement detailed the duties of the ICPR as that organization sought to clean up the Rhine. The European Union, an economic and political association of European nations founded in 1958, passed in 1967 its first environmental decree, requiring its members to adopt similar procedures for labeling and classifying dangerous chemicals. In 1968, the UN Food and Agriculture Organization (FAO), alongside the World Health Organization (WHO), established the Codex Alimentarius Commission to determine safe levels of pesticides in various types of food and worked to convince countries to adopt the commission's findings. Two years later, the Organization for Economic Co-operation and Development (OECD), an economic organization founded in 1960 and, in 1970, made up of nearly two dozen advanced nations in North America, Europe, and Asia, established a ministerial-level Environmental Committee to find means of incorporating environmental concerns into the OECD member states' trade and economic policies.[11]

# Vietnam and the environment

It was in the United States that the modern environmental movement first emerged, and, not surprisingly, environmental considerations had an impact on US foreign policy. The Vietnam War was one example. Having lost their Indochina colony to Japan during the Second World War, the French sought afterward to reassert their control. They faced, however, resistance in the form of the Viet Minh and its communist leader, Ho Chi Minh. Using guerrilla-warfare tactics, including hit-and-run strikes and booby traps, the Viet Minh proved a highly capable foe to French troops, who had been trained to fight a conventional war similar to the Second World War. In the name of containing communism, the United States pumped millions of dollars of aid to the French. It proved not enough. In 1954, having suffered more than 75,000 dead, the French withdrew from their colony. The attendees at a conference held in Geneva later that year—including the United States, France, Great Britain, the Soviet Union, the People's Republic of China, and the Viet Minh—agreed to divide Indochina into three independent countries: Vietnam, Laos, and Cambodia. Vietnam itself was split into a noncommunist South and a communist North, with elections to take place in 1956 to reunify that country. Significantly, of the conference parties, only the United States did not sign the accords.

Afterward, US officials increased their commitment to South Vietnam, furnishing economic and military aid and standing behind Saigon's refusal to hold the planned elections. The rejection of the Geneva Accords convinced the North Vietnamese to provide aid to a growing insurgent movement in the South that became known as the National Liberation Front (NLF). The NLF's military arm, the Viet Cong (VC), used guerrilla tactics against a conventionally trained and poorly led South Vietnamese army tarnished by corruption and a high desertion rate. In response, the United States sent more aid as well as military advisers to help Saigon. In 1965, supported by the overwhelming majority of Americans, President Lyndon B. Johnson increased that commitment by sending 3,500 American combat troops to South Vietnam. By early 1967, there were over 500,000 members of the U.S. Armed Forces engaged in combating the VC on the ground and using aircraft to bomb North Vietnam.

Like the French and South Vietnamese army, most of those in the U.S. Armed Forces had been trained to fight a conventional war. They were not prepared for the VC's tactics, which proved particularly effective in a country where 70 percent of the land consisted of marshes or thick jungle. To get rid of the trees and brush to expose VC bases or troop movements,

President John F. Kennedy in 1961 gave the go-ahead to Operation Ranch Hand, which called for using aircraft to drop herbicides, the most famous of which was known as Agent Orange. Developed in the 1940s in the United States and Great Britain, it combined two herbicides, 2,4-D and 2,4,5,-T, and had been used domestically to control weeds. The British found it helpful as well in an ultimately successful military campaign in the 1950s against rebels in Malaya who, like the VC, adopted guerrilla tactics. What the Kennedy administration failed to realize was that there were significant differences between Malaya and Vietnam. Most of the insurgents in Malaya were ethnic Chinese whom the Malayan people loathed, while the VC had found widespread backing among the Vietnamese. Furthermore, the Malayan rebels lacked the large stocks of rice that were readily available in Vietnam.[12]

The escalation of the war under President Johnson prompted an expansion of Ranch Hand. A vicious circle ensued. Following military action against the VC, herbicides were used to uncover the area and, hopefully, prevent a return of enemy forces. The VC moved to an untreated area, forcing the use of Agent Orange there, and so forth. Ultimately, about 12 percent of South Vietnam suffered the effects of spraying. Because herbicides did not distinguish between friend and foe, civilians themselves could (and did) end up covered with poison. In fact, well over half of the Agent Orange used was known by the late 1960s to contain a deadly form of dioxin called 2,3,7,8-tetrachlorod-ibenzo-p-dioxin. That defoliants killed not just forest cover but the crops on which the Vietnamese relied further hurt the American cause. Locals might blame the NLF's presence as the cause of the herbicide campaign, but they knew who conducted the spraying that put their lives in jeopardy.[13]

Opposition to America's involvement in Vietnam had existed prior to the introduction of US combat troops, but it escalated parallel to the war. A wartime draft and President Johnson's attempts to avoid a debate about the conflict had by the mid-1960s created a "credibility gap" within the United States as Americans questioned the president's justifications for continued military action. Marches against the war grew in both size and fervor. The Cold War consensus broke apart as defenders of the US effort called it necessary to contain communism and a test of America's preparedness to stand behind its allies, whereas opponents charged the administration with engaging in an imperialist endeavor that took resources away from more important problems at home.

But there was also an environmental argument against the war. Rachel Carson had warned about overuse of herbicides, and in light of Ranch Hand, her words appeared prophetic. In March 1963, not long after Ranch Hand began, Representative Robert Kastenmeier, a Democrat from Wisconsin, raised a red flag about the use of herbicides, pointing out that the United States had not employed such weapons against Japan during the Second World War. More significant was an editorial that appeared in a mainstream

US political journal, the *New Republic*, not long after Kastenmeier sent his letter. The military had claimed the herbicides it used were safe, the *New Republic* noted, but that was "only true if one postulates an essential difference between something poisonous and something highly toxic." It was true that herbicides were applied within the United States, the magazine's editors continued, but "they are hardly ever used in the concentrations and over the wide areas in which [American] aircraft spray them over the Vietnamese countryside."[14]

Following the *New Republic*'s commentary, the American Association for the Advancement of Science (AAAS), prodded by members who said scientists had to do more to stop "American militarism" and promote "human welfare," decided in 1965 that it had to devote more attention to events in Vietnam. Three years later, it passed a resolution calling for a field study of Ranch Hand and its effects. The Sierra Club and student activists, many of the latter angered by the draft and assistance to US military operations from university administrations, cheered on the scientists, seeing them as allies against an increasingly unpopular war.[15]

In 1968, two AAAS members, wildlife biologist Bert Pfeiffer and zoologist Gordon Orians, traveled to Vietnam. In the report they submitted upon their return home, they stated they were unable to determine for certain whether Agent Orange was harmful to animals. What they did discover, though, was that large areas of Vietnam had suffered from herbicides. Mangrove forests had vanished, along with the animals that had lived in them. Moreover, they learned that flora outside of the targeted area was affected, indicating that when sprayed, the herbicides had a tendency to drift. Their conclusion was that the long-term damage of Ranch Hand was "*very* severe."[16]

Dispelling any uncertainties about Agent Orange was another *New Republic* article, published in 1970. One its authors was a biology graduate student, William Haseltine, who in 1969 had received information that three years earlier, a research laboratory had discovered that even small doses of Agent Orange caused birth defects. Makers of Agent Orange, including Dow Chemical Company, rejected the findings, but the fact of that matter was that critics of herbicidal warfare, and of the war itself, had gained the upper hand. In 1968, Richard Nixon had won the presidential election, in part because he promised to extricate the United States from Vietnam. Now, facing a backlash because of the cover-up involving Agent Orange, the Defense Department suspended its use.[17]

In the meantime, Nixon and his national security adviser, Henry Kissinger, sought improved ties (or detente) with both the Soviet Union and communist China. The once-friendly relationship between the two communist powers had disintegrated to the point that in 1969 they had engaged in skirmishes along their border. Detente, Kissinger and Nixon believed, would permit the United States to further widen the Sino-Soviet gulf. Furthermore, the Nixon administration knew that Moscow and Beijing offered military support to

Hanoi. As the price of better relations with Washington, the White House intended to demand that each communist power stop providing help to North Vietnam. In so doing, Nixon could more easily withdraw America's armed forces from Southeast Asia.

But detente also had an environmental component to it. Joining the criticism of the war were even some of America's closest allies. Great Britain, for example, had refused to offer anything more than moral support for the US effort. Many of those who denounced what Washington was doing in Vietnam wanted to see more done for the environment. The president's chairman of the Council on Environmental Quality, Russell Train, a champion of the environment who had founded the African Wildlife Leadership Foundation to help West African countries protect their local ecology, saw an opportunity. President Nixon was not an avid proponent of environmental protection, but he knew that the subject had become important to an ever-growing number of Americans. He had already taken some actions, such as establishing the EPA, to appeal to environmentally minded voters. Train realized that if the Soviets joined in the effort to protect the world's flora and fauna, it would not only enhance the president's reputation as an environmentalist, but it would offer a means of encouraging detente. Convinced, Nixon instructed Kissinger to include the environment in his demarches to the Soviet Union.[18]

Moscow's premier, Leonid Brezhnev, responded positively. He too favored detente. For one, it would enhance his country's prestige. By 1970, the Soviet Union had achieved nuclear parity with the United States. Meanwhile, Nixon had reached out to Moscow not just on Vietnam but on measures to curb the atomic arms race. To the Kremlin, these overtures were proof that the White House viewed the Soviet Union as an equal. Furthermore, while Brezhnev did not believe detente meant cooperating with the United States on all matters—for instance, he had no intention of ending Soviet support for communist nations or groups elsewhere—a preparedness to work with America could serve Moscow's diplomatic goals. It might draw Washington away from Beijing. It would also further enhance Soviet prestige if the Kremlin championed itself as a defender of the environment at the same time Washington was being denounced for environmental destruction in Vietnam. Lastly, cooperating with the Nixon administration on environmental matters could assist Moscow's need to address its own serious environmental problems. By the early 1970s, the Soviet Union was losing $12 billion a year combating water pollution and soil erosion, and nearly two-thirds of that country's land had suffered environmental damage. Therefore, in May 1972, the United States and the Soviet Union signed the US-USSR Agreement on Cooperation in the Field of Environmental Protection. Included in it were a series of joint projects and studies designed to address air and water pollution, conservation of animals, and pesticides.[19]

Whether the environmental component of detente extended to herbicidal warfare was another matter. To augment his reputation as a man of peace and a believer in detente, Nixon early in his first term in office called for the United States to sign the 1925 Geneva Protocol, which prohibited weapons that hurt or killed people. Furthermore, he made clear he wanted to prevent the proliferation of CBW—chemical and biological weapons. Driving his position on CBW was a desire to be seen as a leader who favored arms control, not that herbicides violated the protocol. In truth, he saw no inconsistency between the Geneva compact and the use of Agent Orange, a position rejected by many in the international and US scientific communities. Indeed, as early as 1966, Hungary had charged Ranch Hand–violated Geneva. That accusation generated a years-long debate in the United Nations, culminating in a 1969 General Assembly resolution that largely echoed Hungary. That the resolution passed 80-3, with thirty-six abstentions, demonstrated the lacking endorsement for the Nixon administration's stance on herbicidal warfare. Within the United States, scientists continued to rail against Ranch Hand. One of them was an American botanist, Arthur Galston. A coauthor of Haseltine's *New Republic* article, Galston at a February 1970 conference used the term "ecocide" to describe the destruction caused to Vietnam. Nixon, though, refused to back down from his restricted interpretation of the Geneva Protocol, leading US senators to refuse to ratify it. Not until 1975, following the withdrawal of US forces from Vietnam and Nixon's resignation as a result of the Watergate scandal, did the Senate change its mind. Afterward, the United States sent its remaining Agent Orange to an island in the Pacific, where it was destroyed.[20]

# Marine life

As opposition to the war in Vietnam intensified, so it did with regard to whaling. The inability of whaling nations to meet their quotas convinced the Netherlands and United Kingdom to give up on that trade in 1963. Norway by 1967 was well on its way to following suit, leaving Japan and the Soviet Union as the two major whaling countries to continue hunting around the globe's most southern continent. Although the International Whaling Commission (IWC) banned the killing of humpback and blue whales in Antarctic seas in 1963 and 1967, respectively, the Japanese continued to purchase whaling ships and the quotas of other nations. The Soviet government not only refused to abide by restrictions to their whaling activities but encouraged overexploitation by offering annual bonuses for catches that exceeded quotas, requiring whalers to kill more whales each year to receive those bonuses, refusing to rehire whale-hunters who did not meet quotas, and under-reporting the number of kills. That the inspectors required by the International Convention for the Regulation of Whaling were appointed by the state made it even easier for Moscow to circumvent IWC regulations. Enforcing the rules became all the more difficult when

New Zealand in 1968 joined the list of countries to withdraw from the Commission. By 1969, only fourteen countries claimed IWC membership.[21]

There were, however, indications that the whales' fortunes might soon change. The environmental movement, in conjunction with the civil rights and antiwar movements, fed a growing eagerness to protect not just humans but animal life. Aiding the conservationist cause were television programs like Mutual of Omaha's *Wild Kingdom*, which started airing in the United States in 1963. Some of this attention focused specifically on whales. In 1970, Capitol Records produced a record of whale songs. In 1972, the British Broadcasting Corporation aired a program on the planet's largest cetaceans, and that same year, the American magazine *Reader's Digest* included an excerpt from *A Whale for the Killing*, a book by Farley Mowat about a fisherman who tortured one of the giant mammals caught in a cove in Newfoundland, Canada. Whales increasingly were portrayed as intelligent and graceful creatures. Consequently, the pictures, video, and literature regarding whale hunts came to be seen among many people as tantamount to murder.[22]

The "Save the Whales" movement, as it became known, had wide-ranging implications. Whale-watching became big business during the 1970s. The US government in 1970 banned whaling. The following year it adopted the Pelly Amendment to the 1967 Fishermen's Protective Act, which permitted the president to ban or curtail the importation of seafood from countries that threatened international fisheries. More important, it helped drive a desire in some corners to impose a moratorium on whaling. As early as 1963, the International Union for the Conservation of Nature (IUCN) had proposed such a measure, only to have it go nowhere. Now, in 1971, FoE made a similar proposal to the IWC. Nixon administration officials could not agree whether to endorse it. The Interior Department favored a moratorium, but the State Department countered that doing so risked pushing the United States into a corner and even the destruction of the IWC.[23] Yet the idea was on the table, and it was soon to reappear.

Overexploitation of the planet's marine life intersected with the Cold War and Soviet fishing policy. Embracing the communist doctrine that self-sufficiency necessitated conquering nature, Moscow after the Second World War planned to develop a domestic program of aquaculture that would rely on reservoirs—many of them manmade—to meet the nation's demand for fish. This initiative failed in many respects. A lack of understanding that the water in which each species of fish lives has to meet certain thermal and chemical requirements killed off enormous numbers of the animals. In still other cases, the reservoirs destroyed what had been spawning areas. Experts in forestry pointed to the hundreds of thousands of acres of forest lost, and large swaths of prime farmland that ended up underwater. Industrial pollution, a widespread problem in the Soviet Union, complicated efforts to save fish stocks. So did the desire for water to irrigate crops considered important to Soviet planners. The Aral Sea, once one of the world's largest lakes at 26,000 square miles, began to disappear as its waters went toward cotton farms. Less water and greater salinity of what did exist killed off fish in the Aral. Poor enforcement of fishing laws and subsequent overfishing where stocks existed further compounded the Kremlin's difficulties to provide for its own needs through domestic aquaculture.[24]

Moscow, therefore, turned to pelagic fishing. Using modern technology, including radar and sonar, and large nets, as well as improvements in the vessels themselves—such as freezer refrigerator trawlers (BMRTs) that had on board a factory to process fish and, later, "supertrawlers" that could remain at sea for as long as a year—the Soviets began to exploit fisheries on the high seas, with vessels appearing throughout the northern Pacific and Atlantic oceans. By 1960, over 80 percent of all fish caught by the Soviets was pelagic. In 1969, the Soviet fishing fleet at Murmansk, located in northwestern Russia on the Barents Sea, had 180 BMRTs, another three hundred smaller ships, and caught 7 million tons of fish.[25] In combination with other Soviet flotillas and those of other countries, pelagic fish stocks risked depletion, if not extermination.

The impact of pollution on the high seas and the species living in them also continued to draw attention, particularly in the West. The *Torrey Canyon* disaster led later that year to two multinational agreements. One was the International Convention on Civil Liability for Oil Pollution Damage, which made a ship owner financially responsible for any pollution resulting from the escape of petroleum from that vessel. The second, the International Convention Relating to Intervention on the High Seas in Case of Oil Pollution Casualties, permits nations, in cases of potential or actual oil pollution, to take action outside their territorial waters so as to protect their coastlines.[26]

The Canadian government regarded these two 1969 conventions as not strong enough, leading it to enact the Arctic Waters Pollution Prevention Act (AWPPA). The law's broad provisions give Canada the right to oversee the Arctic Sea, whether iced over or not, one hundred miles from Canadian land. Within that zone, Canada prohibits the dumping of "waste" and reserves the right to search and even seize the cargo of ships it believes are in violation of the act. Not surprisingly, the AWPPA has drawn opprobrium from other countries, including the United States, which contend that it is a violation of the doctrine of freedom of the seas and could be used by other nations to undertake similar measures.[27]


## Decolonization and the North-South divide

As environmental considerations entered into US Cold War policy, and environmental negotiations or disputes took place within the industrialized North—or, in the case of the Soviet Union, were ignored—the number of countries voicing their own concerns increased rapidly as a result of decolonization. During the Second World War, Europe's imperial powers retained much of their control over Africa, but Japan seized many of their Asian holdings, including the Dutch East Indies, French Indochina, and the British colonies of Malaya, Singapore, and Burma. Losing their colonies battered the prestige of those colonies' parent countries (or metropoles) and intensified the desire among their colonial subjects for freedom. Financially, prewar military preparations and the conflict itself had taken billions of dollars out of European treasuries. In 1936, France devoted 14 billion francs to defense, the equivalent of US$17.2 billion in 2017. During the conflict, Great Britain alone spent US$120 billion (US$1.56 trillion in 2017). Aerial bombing and fighting on the ground had caused billions of additional dollars in destruction. Belgium, the Netherlands, and France each had about 20 percent of their homes damaged or destroyed. That number reached 30 percent for Great Britain. Around thirty million Europeans were homeless, and 70 percent of Europe's industrial infrastructure had been obliterated.[28] Repairing that damage would take untold sums out of the metropoles' coffers. Confronted with colonial resistance and financial shortfalls, Europe's colonial powers began to relinquish their colonies, though some, including Kuwait and South Yemen, had to wait until the 1960s to receive independence.

The rapid pace of decolonization in Asia reverberated in Africa, where nationalists pressed for a greater say in their local social, political, and economic affairs. How peaceful or turbulent the process of independence was depended largely on the preparedness of the metropole to accept the burdens, be them financial or otherwise, to retain its imperial possessions. Thus, whereas independence in Ghana and Uganda took place peacefully, freedom for Kenya, Algeria, Angola, and Mozambique came only after bloody wars. Then there was the Belgian Congo, where the metropole, facing widespread nationalist sentiment, suddenly declared its colony independent, leaving behind a new nation, Zaire, wracked by political instability. Not until 1977, when France granted Djibouti its independence, did the last vestige of European colonialism in Africa disappear.

These new nations faced numerous challenges, at least two of which had implications for the environment. One was a rate of population growth far higher than in the developed world, driven by poverty, a lack of contraception, and poor education. The other was finding a means of providing for these populations, where many lived off the land. For LDCs, the answers were economic growth, which meant tearing down trees and grasslands to make way for homes or crops, and modern technological and scientific knowledge. An application of that modern know-how came in the form of the so-called Green Revolution of the 1960s. The wider use of fertilizer, in combination with new scientific advances in agriculture—among them improved pesticides as well as high-yield, and drought- and disease-resistant varieties of wheat and rice—made it possible to increase the yield of crops produced per acre. The resulting prosperity, it was believed, would "trickle down" the socioeconomic ladder, benefiting everyone.[29] As the 1960s came to a close, the Green Revolution was well underway in the South.

The South's emphasis on economics and modern technology clashed with the environmentalism that had found a large audience in the North. More DCs took the position that it was a mistake to exploit the planet's flora and fauna without considering its effect on nature's beauty or, as was more often the case, on humans' well-being, and urged LDCs not to commit such mistakes. The countries of the South viewed the situation far differently. Having lived under oftentimes exploitative imperialist governments, any effort by developed nations to tell those living in LDCs how to run their affairs was simply another form of imperialism, one designed to continue their dependence on industrialized nations.[30] In an effort to defend their interests and give themselves as powerful a voice as possible within the United Nations, states in the South formed in 1964 a coalition called the Group of 77 (G-77), getting its name from its seventy-seven original members. Today it has over 130 parties, but it has retained its moniker as a tribute to its founders.

# LDCs and the environment

An early example of LDCs' desire to chart their own course vis-à-vis the environment was the 1968 African Convention on the Conservation of Nature and Natural Resources. The process leading up to this agreement began in 1953, when Belgium called for what became the Third International Conference for the Protection of Flora and Fauna in Africa. Held in Bakavu in the Belgian Congo, the purpose of the meeting was to update the 1933 London Convention. Representatives from all of the nations with colonies in Africa, as well as the United States, Denmark, and the Anglo-Egyptian Sudan, revised the lists of animals deserving protection. Most important, though, the attendees realized that existing measures to protect the continent's flora and fauna, as well as the national parks in existence or planned, did not do enough to conserve the environment. Rather, it was time for a new convention, one that expanded the concept of conservation of the environment to include "natural vegetation, soil, water, and natural resources," and which took into account the needs of local African populations. It was a conclusion that recognized the increasingly vocal demands in the less developed world to give more attention to development as a means of combating poverty.[31]

The collapse of European imperialism in Africa starting in the late 1950s gave the UN, INGOs, and the people of that continent the opportunity to take the Bakavu conference's call for doing more for Africans and put it into motion. In 1960, the IUCN declared during a meeting of the

UN General Assembly the importance of encouraging African leaders to engage in environmental protection. The following year, the FAO and the UN's Educational, Scientific, and Cultural Organization cosponsored in Tanganyika the Pan-African Symposium on the Conservation of Nature and Natural Resources in Modern African States. What emerged from this meeting was an anthropocentric, conservationist approach to the environment. Julius Nyerere, who served as Tangyanika's prime minister and as the first president of an independent Tanzania, established that very theme in his keynote address. "The survival of our wildlife is a matter of grave concern to all of us in Africa," he declared. However, he continued, "these wild creatures amid the wild places they inhabit are not only important as a source of wonder and inspiration but are an integral part of our natural resources and of our future livelihood and well-being."[32]

Endorsed by thirty-eight African countries, and supported by the IUCN, the UN, and the Organization of African Unity, the Convention on the Conservation of Nature and Natural Resources called for managing wildlife, soil, and water "'in accordance with scientific principles' and 'with due regard for the best interests of the people.'" The pact entered into force in 1969 and was revised in 2003. As with other international environmental agreements, the African convention's effectiveness remains in question. It has been praised for its comprehensiveness and for encouraging conservation measures in some African nations. Only thirty African nations have ratified it, though, and it failed to establish both a formal administrative structure and means of ensuring compliance with its provisions.[33]

Conservationist principles applied as well to the 1971 Convention on Wetlands of International Importance. Taking note of the danger posed to wetlands by pollution or drainage and to wetland birds because of hunting, shortly after the Second World War ended, the International Council for Bird Preservation (ICBP)—an international nongovernmental organization founded in 1922 and today known as BirdLife International—submitted a proposal to protect both. It also established the International Wildfowl Research Bureau (IWRB) to gather more information on the subject. The ICBP's initiative, which became known as Project MAR, found favor from the IUCN. In 1962, the ICBP, IWRB, and IUCN hosted the MAR conference. Relying on ornithological data, they identified approximately two hundred sites worthy of protection. The MAR conference also expressed a need for an international convention on wetlands, prompting the IWRB to send memoranda to thirty-five nations, offering specific topics such a meeting might address.[34]

In 1971, delegates from eighteen nations met at Ramsar, Iran, where they adopted the Convention on Wetlands of International Importance, better known as the Ramsar Convention. Under its provisions, the signatories had to encourage "wise use" of their wetlands and to encourage wetlands research. They also had to provide to the IUCN details on any wetlands of international importance, which would be put onto a list maintained by the

IUCN and IWRB. It went into effect in 1975,[35] and by 2016 it had been adopted by nearly 170 countries.

As with so many other international environmental conventions, Ramsar has its pros and cons. It has a large number of parties, and it currently covers over 2200 wetlands encompassing over 2 million square kilometers. Furthermore, the involvement of the IUCN and IWRB, which are more concerned with wetlands conservation than national interest, has helped to encourage compliance with its provisions. While it does not make a large number of legal demands on signatories, that has been cited as a reason why so many countries have joined it. And the language regarding the protection of wetlands of "international importance" imposes a moral responsibility on the parties to abide by that provision. There are weaknesses, however. A moral compulsion to protect wetlands of "international importance" is not the same as a legal one. Furthermore, in what became one of their key complaints, LDCs charged that a lack of guaranteed funding from the world's wealthier countries made it difficult for them to fulfill the convention's obligations. That charge to the present is cited as a reason for the reluctance of some countries to partake in the Ramsar agreement.[36] This demand by LDCs for more help from DCs was one of many issues raised in one of the most important environmental conferences of the twentieth century, held in Stockholm, Sweden, three years before the Ramsar Convention went into effect.

# Stockholm

The meeting at Stockholm may never had occurred had it not been for another environmental issue, that of acid rain. Scottish chemist Robert Angus Smith had invented the term in 1872, basing his findings on a high level of sulfuric acid in Manchester, England, emitted by the burning of coal. Troublesome as well was sulfur dioxide in the air that had come from the smokestacks of local alkali factories. To address local pollution, the British, followed by other West European countries, mandated taller smokestacks, some of them six times as high as before. Although this succeeded in curbing pollution in the immediate vicinity of the plants in question, it also served to disperse it more widely, including to other countries. One of those recipient nations was Sweden, where researchers traced sulfur dioxide pumped from outside Swedish borders to a heightened acidity in the rain that fell on Sweden.[37]

The Swedes could have called for a meeting to focus solely on transnational air pollution. Instead, influenced by the global environmental movement, Sweden's representative to the United Nations in May 1968 called on that body's secretary-general to look into holding a broader "international conference on the problems of human environment." The United Nations Economic and Social Council took up the proposal, passing a resolution at the end of July endorsing it. The General Assembly followed suit that December. A year later, the General Assembly voted for another resolution, establishing a committee to prepare for the meeting. News of these moves excited nongovernmental organizations, among them the International Council of Scientific Unions (ICSU) and the IUCN, which sought to help shape the meeting agenda.[38]

During the preparatory phase for what would be the first UN-themed conference, LDCs suspected that DCs would ignore their desire to develop economically and instead emphasize protecting the environment. But as the conference got underway, LDCs, with the help of some four hundred NGOs, made their voices heard. Taking advantage of the 1,000 reporters present, they pressured the delegates from the 113 UN Member States in attendance to adopt a middle ground between developed and lesser developed nations. They expressed concern with population growth in the South but identified a need for the North to offer "a significant redistribution of the world's resources in favor of the developing countries."[39]

The deliberations themselves at times were testy. As anticipated, LDCs insisted that economic growth had to come before environmental protection, a position strengthened by the presence of a delegation from communist China. The United States, which had been among the strongest champions of the conference, resisted a proposal to stop atomic weapons tests and took offense when several countries (representing both LDCs and DCs) challenged its activities in Vietnam. Neither it nor Great Britain appeared willing to do much when charged with emitting acid rain beyond their borders. Still, what emerged from the negotiations were twenty-six guiding principles and an action plan. The principles fell into five broad categories: protecting and conserving natural resources, and the sharing of nonrenewable resources; promoting simultaneously economic development and the environment's welfare, with countries in the North helping those in the South; permitting each nation the right to develop its own standards of development and environmental management, as long as they did not threaten the well-being of other states; restricting pollution; and using science and technology to encourage protection of the environment.[40] Additionally, the delegates established procedures to achieve the UN's new mandate, most notably the creation of the UN Environment Programme (UNEP).

In formulating the principles and action plan, LDCs indeed had been heard, and used their voting power to include principles of importance to them. NGOs, among them the IUCN and the World Wildlife Fund, had helped shape the conference agenda and used the gathering to meet one another, discuss common goals, and, thanks to the presence of so many reporters, to air their concerns to a broad public. The end result was still anthropocentric. But there were three key differences between what came before Stockholm and what emerged from the 1972 summit. First, prior to the meeting in Sweden, the overwhelming majority of environmental meetings and agreements had focused on conservation of natural resources or protection of flora and fauna. Now, it had become clear that humans had to think more about properly managing the entire biosphere. Second, those earlier conventions had oftentimes been regional or continental in nature as opposed to global.[41]

Finally, Stockholm served as a milestone for the concept of "sustainable development." A year before the conference, Maurice Strong, who had been named the executive director of the 1972 meeting, asked experts on so-called alternative development to meet at Founex, Switzerland, to address matters of interest to developing nations in the hopes of convincing them to send delegates to Sweden. The Founex panelists concluded that whereas environmental harm in the North originated from pollution, its causes in the South were multifold: poor housing, water quality, nutrition, and medical care, as well as a greater likelihood of suffering from natural disasters. They concluded that economic development offered the best means of addressing poverty, which it turn would allow developing countries to tackle environmental matters. Conversely, permitting environmental protections to usurp development would cause more damage to LDCs. Simply put, the right of a nation to pursue its own economic initiatives outweighed other considerations.[42]

What concerned LDCs was the possibility that their counterparts in the North would ignore the Founex report and instead try to slow industrialization in the South so as to keep the latter in a continued state of dependency. At Stockholm, communist China charged the "imperialistic superpowers" as the main cause of the planet's pollution. Along similar lines, Indian prime minister Indira Gandhi proclaimed that "sheer ruthlessness, undisturbed by feelings of compassion or by abstract theories of freedom, equality or justice" had made the globe's advanced countries as rich as they were. The question, therefore, was whether it was possible to find a means of balancing LDCs' desire to modernize and expand their economies with that of developed nations to devote greater attention to the environment. What came out of Stockholm was a repeat of the finding that economic development could be conducive to a better environment. A more advanced economy, driven by more highly educated people, would improve standards of living, curb population growth, and reduce pressure on both the environment and national resources. So would newer forms of technology (like nuclear power and substitutes for DDT). LDCs, however, complained that they lacked such technology or the financial resources to adopt or produce it. Therefore, Principles 8 and 9 at Stockholm called for economic development to promote a better environment, and for the North to transfer "substantial quantities of financial and technological assistance as a supplement to the domestic effort" of nations in the South.[43]

Beneath the optimism, however, was a warning sign, one witnessed in the debate over "sustainable development," and one that since has challenged any effort to create an international regime: finding a balance between convincing states to adhere to the regime and each nation's desire to protect its sovereignty. No state is likely to join an international regime if it undermines its self-interest. Nothing better represented this difficult balancing act than Stockholm's Principle 21, which granted each country the right to decide how it used its resources. Although that principle includes the caveat that such activities "do not cause damage to the environment of other States or of areas beyond the limits of national jurisdiction," the nod to national self-interest is quite apparent.[44]

## Stockholm's legacy

"The Stockholm Conference marked the start of the modern era of global environmental cooperation," stated one scholar. Indeed, the meeting generated a momentum to do more to promote the planet's environmental well-being. Before Stockholm, most nations in the North ignored the link between economic growth in LDCs and the environment; that changed following the gathering in Sweden. More INGOs appeared, among them the Cousteau Foundation, founded in 1973, and in 1974, the WILD Foundation, Biodiversity International, and the European Environmental Bureau (EEB). The Cousteau Foundation focuses on marine life, the WILD Foundation's mandate is wilderness protection, and Bioversity International promotes agricultural biological diversity. The EEB, for its part, provides NGOs with access to the European Community (EC), which had begun developing environmental action plans. National Green parties, which devote heavy emphasis to defending the natural environment, first appeared in 1972 in New Zealand, followed by Great Britain 1973 and, shortly thereafter, by France.[45]

The advent of Green parties in Western Europe and portions of Oceania reflected the extent to which the momentum that led to and followed Stockholm heightened determination to do more for environment nationally and regionally. West Germany revised its laws in 1972 to bolster the federal government's ability to defend flora and fauna. A year later, Holland passed the Land and Regional Planning Acts, and the Act for the Protection of the Environment. The EC's Council of Ministers adopted that organization's first environmental action plan in 1972, calling for harmonization of its members nations' economic policies to take into account the environment. Among its specifics, the program, using language similar to the Trail Smelter case, called for polluters to pay for any environmental damage they caused, and for the EC to endorse international programs that addressed environmental problems that could not be handled at a national or regional level. The EC's second action plan, dated 1977, reiterated these goals. In 1976, the signatories to the Bonn Convention for the Protection of the Rhine against Pollution from Chlorides addressed the release of salts from chemical fertilizers by promising to hold steady or reduce the amount of salt they allowed into the Rhine River. In 1975, the OECD, which now included Australia and New Zealand, reorganized its work to more thoroughly incorporate environmental concerns. In so doing, it placed a new emphasis on preventing environmental degradation rather than addressing that which had already taken place.[46]

Stockholm created impetus as well for reinvigorating detente. The US-Soviet Strategic Arms Limitations Treaty (SALT), which was signed a month before the Stockholm meeting and restricted the number of land- and sea-based intercontinental ballistic missiles held by each superpower, symbolized detente's success. Within a few years, however, detente began to show signs of weakness. The United States criticized Moscow for violating the human rights of the Soviet people and for supporting communists fighting in a civil war in Angola. The Kremlin responded that Washington had no right to interfere in its internal affairs, and that its assistance to communists abroad was no different than the aid the United States provided to noncommunist countries and movements.

In 1975, the United States, Soviet Union, and more than thirty other nations met at a summit in Helsinki, Finland, to formalize agreements reached at the Conference on Security and Cooperation in Europe (CSCE). Although the Axis had surrendered thirty years earlier, the Second World War had never formally ended in Europe. During that period, a number of national boundaries on that continent had changed, and the Soviet Union had come to dominate that Europe's eastern half. The CSCE's Final Act, formalized in July 1975, addressed these matters and others through a series of "baskets" that confirmed the existing borders in Europe and called for international cooperation on a variety of subjects, including the environment.

To the Soviets, a high-level meeting with Western officials to discuss the environment offered two interrelated benefits. One was that it would keep the spirit of detente alive. Human rights had recently become a hot-button topic in the West, particularly in the United States, yet any attempt to find a resolution to that matter was likely to fail because of the Kremlin's stance on it. Nor were additional talks regarding arms control likely to make headway. The environment, though, remained of keen importance in the West, and a preparedness to hold talks on that matter was likely to find favor among both government officials and the broader public in Western Europe and North America. Moreover, Soviet studies concluded that the deposition of acid rain in the European portion of the Soviet Union was far more likely a product of West European industry than acid rain falling west of the Soviet Union was likely to come from Soviet factories. The Kremlin estimated that the damage caused by acid rain to Soviet agriculture was about $150 million a year.[47] A convention that controlled air pollution and, in turn, lessened acid rain would ease this financial burden on Moscow.

It was up to the UN Economic Commission for Europe (ECE) to decide exactly what that proposed gathering would address. Established in 1947, the ECE's members were virtually the same as those that had met at the

CSCE. After considering a number of possible environmental topics to discuss, the ECE concluded that air pollution made the most sense, as it was the most likely to find favor in the Soviet bloc.[48]

It was not clear how the West would respond. On the one hand were countries such as Sweden, Norway, and Canada. Like their Scandinavian counterparts, Canadian scientists had discovered a decline in fish stocks in lakes in Ontario and, using the evidence coming out of Sweden, traced it to acid rain coming from the United States. Indeed, US laws passed to curb pollution, such as the Clean Air Act, had, as was the case in Europe, encouraged industry to build higher smokestacks, which spread their emissions further afield. Media reports about the cause and effect of acid rain had by the second half of the 1970s led Canadian public opinion to demand its government take action. On the other hand were Western European countries outside of Scandinavia. The British denied having any problems of their own with acid rain and questioned Sweden's findings. West Germany, for its part, did not favor the prospect of the ECE telling it how to run its affairs. Both insisted that if required to force their industries to install pollution-reducing technology, such as stack scrubbers, it would hurt their economies. It was only after the Nordic states gave up their insistence that the proposed convention require cuts in sulfur emissions that a final agreement became possible.[49]

The result was the Convention on Long-Range Transboundary Air Pollution (LRTAP). Signed by thirty-five nations, including the United States, Soviet Union, and Canada, it established no definitive targets for curbing emissions. Rather, it called upon the parties to do their best to restrict them, to undertake new research to address transboundary pollution, and to share information. Despite its weaknesses, the LRTAP offered opportunity. By 1979, detente had weakened further. The United States and the Soviet Union continued to throw barbs at one another over human rights, Washington expressed growing anger at Moscow's activities in other parts of the world, and a SALT II agreement, though signed between the superpowers, looked unlikely to receive ratification by the U.S. Senate. The LRTAP thus represented one possible realm of continued cooperation between the Kremlin and the White House. Additionally, the LRTAP set a foundation for future protocols that could strengthen its provisions. Finally, the call for curbing acid rain gave rise to arrangements similar to the LRTAP. Most notably, in 1978, the U.S. Congress authorized negotiations with Canada that led to a 1980 Memorandum of Intent on Transboundary Air Pollution, in which the two nations committed themselves to reaching a formal agreement.[50]

The determination to curb pollution that emerged from Stockholm extended to the seas and oceans. One of the principles of the Stockholm Convention was to put a halt to pollution that endangered the oceans, which encouraged Great Britain to host a conference in November to write up a convention on that score. What the British had not anticipated was the demand that any such agreement include radioactive waste. London relied heavily on the oceans to dump its atomic detritus, and it wanted to continue to do so. By the time of Stockholm, though, it found itself isolated. The United States had stopped such activity in the 1960s but had not explicitly condemned other countries for doing it; now, in the 1970s, it did. Thus, when opened for signature in December 1972, the London Convention on the Prevention of Marine Pollution by Dumping of Wastes and Other Matter focused on radioactive detritus in the list of materials it regulated. It went into effect three years later.[51]

In 1973, the Intergovernmental Maritime Consultative Organization, a UN agency that regulates shipping—and today known as the International Maritime Organization—brokered the International Convention of Pollution from Ships (MARPOL), which expanded the 1954 Pollution of the Seas by Oil Convention. Amended in 1978 and entering into force five years later, MARPOL covers pollution caused not just by oil, but by dangerous liquids or other substances carried on board as well as the garbage and human excrement generated by crews. It also established particularly strict controls in enclosed or largely enclosed seas that, by their nature, were more susceptible to pollution, such as the Black, Red, Baltic, and Mediterranean.[52]

In fact, Mediterranean nations had already taken steps to restrict pollution via the Mediterranean Action Plan (MAP). Much of the Mediterranean's water comes through the thin Strait of Gibraltar, meaning it lacks the tides or outlets needed to disperse pollutants. The Mediterranean itself is surrounded by dozens of cities with populations of more than 100,000 as well as heavy industry. A large number of these people and factories are in LDCs that lack effective means of removing or treating sewage. Instead, much of the human waste is sent directly into the water. The garbage from ships, dredging operations, and runoff from chemicals and fertilizers used on crops added pollutants of their own. Fishermen argued that so much contamination affected their trade, with some in Corsica rioting in response to waste dumped from an Italian chemical company into the water. Tourists complained about dirty coasts, some contracted diseases, and a number of beaches were closed for a time due to health concerns. Local economies suffered as potential visitors went elsewhere. In response, a number of countries bordering the Mediterranean called in the early 1970s for a regional pact to address the pollution problem.[53]

Negotiating the MAP was not easy. LDCs did not want efforts to reduce pollution to divert resources away from economic development. They and DCs disagreed over how quickly to implement pollution control measures and how strong those measures would be. UNEP sought to cut through these differences by calling on the help of scientists and specialized international bodies. Among the latter were the FAO, WHO, and the International Oceanographic Commission. Nongovernmental organizations, among them the IUCN and the ICSU, tendered assistance as well. Additionally, UNEP sought compromises that would encourage participation. It established six Regional Activity Centers to oversee projects related to Mediterranean pollution, with five situated in Europe and one in northern Africa. Major laboratories were placed in advanced and lesser developed nations. Lastly, UNEP set up a series of networks to share information, taking into account political differences. For instance, none of the networks required Arabs and Israelis to work together because of their long history of animosity.[54]

UNEP's efforts bore fruit in February 1975, when sixteen nations adopted the MAP. Its provisions called for "integrated planning of the development and management of the resources of the Mediterranean Basin," a coordinated effort to control pollution, a convention to protect the environment of the Mediterranean, and providing financial and institutional mechanisms to oversee the plan. Soon thereafter, research got underway, which discovered that most of the pollutants that entered the Mediterranean came from rivers that emptied into it, meaning that any cleanup efforts would need to take place not just along the coast of the countries involved, but inland. In 1976, twelve countries signed the Convention for the Protection of the Mediterranean Sea against Pollution, otherwise known as the Barcelona Convention, as well as two protocols. One requires signatories to prohibit the dumping of certain substances from aircraft and ships into the Mediterranean; less dangerous effluents necessitate a permit. The other protocol states that the parties must alert one another in the case of an oil spill and to coordinate cleanup efforts. It took another four years for Mediterranean nations to adopt a protocol focused on land-based sources of pollution. Most difficult of all were the financial arrangements. In 1979, a trust fund was established. Each state's contribution was based on how much it gave to the UN, meaning nearly half of the trust fund came from France. But the trust continues to face the challenge of having all contributing members pay their pledged contributions on time.[55]

In addition to controlling pollution, Stockholm reinvigorated demands for international treaties to protect flora and fauna. One result was the 1973 Convention on the International Trade in Endangered Species (CITES). The idea of controlling commerce in parts of, or products made from, endangered animals was not new. As early as 1911, Swiss conservationist Paul Sarasin had urged the international community to restrict the trade in bird feathers. The growth in the number of newly independent nations in the developing world, in combination with their desire to acquire capital, had during the 1950s and 1960s seen a dramatic increase in the commercial shipment in the number of endangered species. As examples, Kenya by the end of the 1960s exported 150 tons a year of ivory. The United States itself by that same time was importing almost 130,000 ocelot skins annually. Such numbers infuriated the IUCN, which called for a multilateral convention to restrict such commerce. The United States, joined by others at Stockholm, called for writing up a convention "on export, import and transit of certain species of wild animals and wild plants."[56]

Relying on a conservationist classification system based on the precedent set by the 1900 London Convention, CITES focuses not on ecosystems but on individual species. Nor does it eliminate the trade in endangered animals. Rather, it regulates it by dividing those species into three appendices, with each based on the determination of CITES's parties as to how endangered the species is. Appendix I includes those most in danger of becoming extinct and strictly regulates their trade to protect them from extirpation. Appendix II seeks to protect those that are not threatened but could become so without rigorous control over their use or trade. Included in Appendix III are those which any party to the convention believes deserves protection "within its jurisdiction." Among the first species placed in the CITES appendices were the black pine tree, five species of tiger, the ruffed lemur, the Chinese pangolin, the cheetah, and the grey-crowned crane. In 1977, the African elephant joined the list of animals on Appendix II,[57] as did the American bobcat and the Canadian lynx.

By then, CITES had intersected with the fight against whaling. At Stockholm, the United States suggested that lower quotas were not enough to conserve whale populations. To Japan, what the United States favored was a moratorium. In 1972, by a 53-0 vote, with Japan, Portugal, and South Africa abstaining, the participants passed a nonbinding moratorium. The Soviet Union, though not present at Stockholm, also rejected any suspension.[58] The very fact that a moratorium, even if nonbinding, had passed was an indication of the growing strength of those opposed to whaling.

As the 1970s came to a close it appeared a binding moratorium was only a matter of time. The continued decline in some whale populations and the Save the Whales Movement kept the world community aware of the cetaceans' fate. Backing the whales' cause were numerous NGOs, none of which drew more notoriety than Greenpeace. In 1975 Greenpeace activists made international news when they used small boats to try to shield sperm whales from a Soviet whaler, only to have the Soviets fire their harpoons anyway. Not only did the Soviets put the activists' lives at risk, but one of the Greenpeace protestors recorded several of the harpoon shots. International resolve stiffened. By 1977, CITES included all blue, bowhead, humpback, right, and gray whales, as well as most species of sei and fin whales. In 1979, New Zealand, which under public pressure had recently rejoined the IWC, and Great Britain added themselves the list of those countries favoring a moratorium. Even Australia began to change its position. Malcolm Fraser, elected prime minister in 1977, too faced calls to save the cetaceans, and instructed Justice Sydney Frost to head a committee of inquiry to recommend Canberra's stance. A year later, Frost called for an end to Australian whaling and a suspension of international whaling.[59]

Just as whales are migratory animals, so are many species of bird. It was that realization that led the United States in 1972 to sign with Japan the Convention for the Protection of Migratory Birds and Birds in Danger of Extinction, and Their Environment. Four years later, in what was another symbol of detente, the United States joined with the Soviet Union in a similar treaty. Japan followed suit by signing its own bilateral conventions with both Australia and the Soviet Union. The problem with these and earlier treaties, such as the 1916 Migratory Birds treaty and the 1940 Convention on Nature Protection and Wildlife Preservation in the Western Hemisphere, was that they were limited insofar as the number of signatories and their geographic scope. To address that shortcoming, recommendation 32 of the Stockholm Conference's Action Plan called for a global convention. West Germany, supported by an agreement drafted by the IUCN, hosted a conference that included all migratory animals. One outcome of that meeting was the Convention on the Conservation of Migratory Species of Wild Animals (also known as the CMS or Bonn Convention). This pact supplemented CITES by calling on signatories to "endeavor" to protect fauna listed in two separate appendices. Appendix I included animals that required "immediate protection," while those in Appendix II had "an unfavorable conservation status" and required new international agreements to provide them necessary protections.[60] Still the only global treaty designed to protect migratory animals, it was signed by twenty-eight nations, went into force four years later, and currently has 124 parties.

# Omens

By 1980, then, an international environment movement had begun to form. It would be wrong to call it a coordinated movement, for the interests of those involved in it did not necessarily coalesce. But what had occurred was growing awareness among industrialized nations of the North, and even within some LDCs in the South, of the harm befalling on flora, fauna, and humans. This movement also served as a bridge between East and West, even as detente began to weaken. From it had come not only the Stockholm Conference but numerous bilateral and multinational conventions aimed at providing protections to particular species. Yet as before, these agreements tended to be anthropocentric in nature, and their language, such as that found in the Ramsar Convention, the LRTAP, and the CMS, could be weak, focusing on goals or moral obligations as opposed to precise targets or legal requirements. The tug-of-war between creating an international environmental regime and protecting national sovereignty served as a stumbling block. So did the unwillingness of DCs to provide the levels of assistance sought by LDCs.[61]

Coming to grips with these challenges was likely to become even more daunting. Building on Malthus, US conservationist Fairfield Osborn in the early 1950s tied environmental degradation to the concepts of war and security, commenting that "one of the principal causes of the aggressive attitudes of individual nations and of much of the present discord among groups of nations is traceable to diminishing productive land and to increasing population pressures." That notion became more commonplace in the 1970s in the writings of international law professor Richard Falk and two prominent scholars of international environmental studies, Margaret and Harold Sprout.[62] The language of security also entered into a debate over what, by the end of the twentieth century, had become a focal point for scientists and politicians around the globe: climate change.

# CHAPTER FIVE

# Creating regimes

In 1980, the UN General Assembly passed a resolution calling for the UNEP to host a meeting in 1982 to determine the impact of the 1972 Stockholm Conference on the environment. Meeting at UNEP's headquarters in Nairobi, Kenya, in 1982, the attendees offered a rather bleak assessment. "The Action Plan," they commented, "has only been partially implemented and the results cannot be considered as satisfactory." Those areas that had seen the most progress included environmental monitoring and research, and exchanges of information—none of which required national governments to alter policymaking or administration.[1]

Stockholm in fact had not resolved a number of issues regarding humans' attitude toward the environment, but at the heart of them were continued differences between the LDCs of the South and the DCs in the North. DCs believed LDCs were too insistent on giving priority to economic development at the expense of the environment. Less developed nations charged more advanced countries infringed on their national sovereignty and failed to provide them the financial or technological assistance they needed as a precondition for stricter environmental regulations. The desire of multinational financial institutions to encourage economic development further opened the door to environmental degradation, particularly in LDCs. In the meantime, the election of politically and economically conservative governments in the United States and Great Britain served to downgrade the importance of environmental protections, at least among the leaders of those two countries.

None of this is to suggest that conservation or even preservation of the planet's flora and fauna disappeared. This was particularly the case in the North, where public opinion exhibited a preparedness to do more to protect the environment. Environmental NGOs remained active or grew in size. Whereas only two international environmental NGOs existed in 1953, forty years later that number had grown to ninety. By 1982 alone, the total number of environmental NGOs worldwide that had registered with UNEP was 15,000.[2] Green parties appeared or became more influential. In Brazil, locals fought efforts to destroy trees in the name of development. An even broader movement, one that included government officials, appeared among LDCs to resist the dumping in their countries of hazardous waste from the North. Both developed and lesser developed nations came together in 1982 to impose a moratorium on whaling. In 1984, nearly two dozen countries agreed to tighten restrictions on emissions that contributed to acid rain.

It was in the second half of the 1980s, however, that yet another wave of environmentalism swept through both the North and South. There were several reasons for this. One was the revival of detente between the United States and the Soviet Union, which reduced international worries about the nuclear arms race and the possibility of an atomic exchange between the superpowers. In turn, other subjects, many of them environmental, began to draw media and public notice. Humans began more than ever to discern a link between carbon dioxide emissions and climate change. Confirmation in 1985 of a hole in the ozone layer led to warnings about an increase in cancer and genetic mutations. The Chernobyl nuclear accident of 1986 cast a pall over nuclear power, brought heightened attention to the horrific environmental conditions within the Soviet bloc, and played a part in bringing down communist governments in that part of the word. Two years later, the fate of the merchant ship *Karin B.* drew international attention to the hazardous waste trade.[3]

In addition to assisting the collapse of communism in Europe, the renewed awareness of what humans were doing to their planet led to the Single European Act and the Montreal Protocol of 1987, the 1988 Basel Convention, the Bamako Convention of 1991, and the Rio Convention of 1992. In combination, these agreements created international regimes designed to combat pollution, protect the ozone layer, halt dangerous changes to the Earth's climate, and stop the trade in hazardous waste. As was the case with previous agreements, the well-being of humans received priority over that of the environment. That anthropocentrism, which appeared in the form of North-South divisions and the desire of national governments to protect their sovereignty, dictated the effectiveness of these regimes.

## Stockholm: A legacy lacking

The momentum that came out of Stockholm had indeed borne fruit, be it in the form of the CITES, bilateral treaties to protect avian life, and the Bonn Convention. Yet much was left unaccomplished or even undone. For example, not every country signed the Bonn agreement. The bilateral conventions did not stop the drainage of wetlands to make room for construction projects or farmland. By 1980, about 117 million acres of wetlands in the continental United States had been lost, leaving less than 50 percent of the 221 million acres that had existed two hundred years earlier. Wetlands shrunk as well in Canada and Mexico. The 1972 London Convention failed to ban all hazardous waste. Rather, it divided that detritus into two lists. Those on the "black" list could only be dumped in small amounts; "grey"-list items, however, could be dropped into the oceans as long as the party in question had a permit and took "special care" to make sure it would not harm the marine environment.[4]

Another attack on the natural environment came in the response to a worldwide food crisis in the first half of the 1970s. Although the Green Revolution of the 1960s had generated an increase in food production in the South, it was not uniform: India, for example, saw its yields of crops rise far more than was the case in sub-Saharan Africa. Worldwide, the demand for food outpaced its availability in numerous LDCs. Higher oil prices caused by instability in the Middle East, as well as an increase in the cost of fertilizer, hit developing nations' economies particularly hard. Finally, climatic anomalies, some of them related to an El Niño of 1972–73—a period of approximately one to two years during which temperatures over the central and east-central Pacific increase—contributed to poor global harvests in 1972 and 1974, putting further pressure on food supplies.[5]

Countries in the North and South agreed that one of the ways to combat the food shortage was to make sure what was available did not end up in the mouths of insects. That, in turn, meant putting aside reservations about pesticides, as became clear at a UN World Food Conference held in Rome in 1974. The attendees there said nothing about the risks of pesticide use, focusing instead on the need to increase the number of chemicals reaching farms in LDCs. Afterward, the Council of Europe's Parliamentary Assembly passed a resolution calling on all industrialized countries to augment their output of both pesticides and fertilizers to encourage larger harvests in developing nations.[6]

National sovereignty further complicated the effort to create international regimes to protect the environment. Deforestation in Brazil had been taking place at the start of the twentieth century, but it expanded rapidly after the Second World War. Logging and road-building in Brazil starting in 1960 destroyed 10 percent of forests in the Amazon within a generation. Deforestation of that region averaged about 21,800 kilometers annually. Eighty-five percent of what had been forest became farmland, leaving the soil vulnerable to erosion. Mexico insisted on exploiting its coal reserves to provide for its energy needs, and Japan refused to adopt restrictions on whaling. The Soviet Union appeared to champion the environment and even adopted in 1977 a constitution calling for the "scientific, rational use of the land and its mineral and water resources, and the plant and animal kingdoms, to preserve the purity of air and water, ensure reproduction of natural wealth, and improve the human environment." Yet it continued to kill whales and fish in large numbers,[7] and to adopt land policies inimical to the environment's well-being.

IFIs shared responsibility following the Stockholm meeting for the failure to do more for the environment. The World Bank, the International Monetary Fund (IMF), and the Inter-American Development Bank (IADB) encouraged the countries that received their help to devote their energies primarily to economic growth. The first two bodies were created at the 1944 Bretton Woods Conference, a gathering of the Allied countries of the Second World War to improve trade and loan money to countries to improve their economic well-being. Created fifteen years later, the IADB's very name indicated its focus. Among the initiatives these IFIs funded in 1970s and 1980s were the colonization of rain forests in Indonesia and Brazil, tobacco-farming in Africa, and cattle-ranching in Latin America.[8]

There were environmental and human costs to LDCs' focus on economic development. For a decade starting in 1976, the World Bank loaned Indonesia's government about $500 million. Part of that money went toward resettling millions of poor from that country's densely populated inner islands to the outer ones. Few people—most of them members of indigenous tribes—lived on those outer islands, but they were home to about 10 percent of the world's rain forests. The rest of the money was supposed to be put toward helping the newcomers grow crops, including coffee and cacao. That help never came. Accordingly, the settlers turned to clearing rain forests to make way for subsistence agriculture. Similarly, the World Bank gave Brazil $443 million from 1981 to 1983 to build a new highway that would connect a number of rural towns and attract settlers. Lacking money or land titles, the settlers destroyed rain forests to grow crops. They also brought with them diseases against which the indigenous peoples of the forest had no immunity, with some tribes losing as many as 50 percent of their children. India regarded coal as the key to providing electric power for its growing population and received World Bank funding to develop that sector of its economy. The heightened pollution that resulted took a heavy toll on that country's populous.[9]

Furthermore, the emphasis on economic development created a dangerous cycle of events. Financially, the recipient nations faced the new burden of paying back both the principal and interest on those loans. So, many countries in Latin America owing creditors that much of that region fell into a debt crisis in the early 1980s. In Africa, the belief that industrialization would eliminate poverty, in combination with precarious governments and the aftereffects of a colonial system that had emphasized exports to the motherland rather than the economic diversification of the colonies themselves, placed them in unstable financial waters. Owing ever more money, they and other countries in the South had to restructure their economies to get further assistance from the IFIs. They also sought means of raising more capital, which meant development projects that required international financial support—thereby putting the recipients further into debt—and causing still more harm to the environment.[10]

It was the desire of LDCs to encourage development that, with the exception of fertilizers and pesticides, continued to place them at odds with their industrialized counterparts. More than anything else, it was that North-South dispute that placed a pall over the Stockholm Conference's ambitious Guiding Principles and Action Plan. Principle 16, for instance, encouraged governments to take steps to control "the rate of population growth or excessive population concentrations [that] are likely to have adverse effects on the environment of the human environment and impede development." At a 1974 population conference in Bucharest, Romania, delegates from developed nations in the West argued that curbing the number of births was vitally important to prevent the outcome warned about in works such as *The Population Bomb*. The Soviet Union took a different point of view, regarding itself as "underpopulated." But the strongest reaction came from less developed states, which took the position of DCs as imperialistic. China argued that its population was an internal affair. Brazil and India were even more hostile. The former, which had called the Stockholm meeting "a sinister conspiracy to prevent the developing world from developing further," declared at Bucharest that population "growth is . . . necessary for economic development and for national security." Pointing to his country's priorities, India's delegate commented, "Development is the best contraceptive." The final document that emerged from Bucharest gave primacy to national sovereignty in determining population policy; called for making sure that those persons who wished to have children had access to the "information, education, and means to do so"; and emphasized that a relationship existed between population and economic development. At a follow-up conference in 1985 in Mexico City, LDCs took a slightly more pragmatic position, arguing that "contraception is the best contraceptive."[11] The rub was turning that prescription into policy.

The question of overpopulation was tied to yet another matter that split DCs and LDCs: desertification. A term coined in the 1920s, it is difficult to define. The 1992 UN Conference on Environment and Development—to be discussed later in this chapter—described it as "land degradation in arid, half arid and dry sub-humid areas resulting from various factors including climatic variations and human activities." UNEP and experts in the field use a similar explanation, though they state desertification "result[s] mainly from adverse human impact." Either definition is problematic. The word "desertification" itself implies something natural, namely, that deserts, such as the Sahara in Africa, were (and are) rapidly expanding onto what had once been arable land. Yet both descriptions, particularly that of UNEP, refer to the human element.[12]

The Sahel of Africa, the semiarid region of the continent just below the Sahara Desert, explains why this lack of clarity in definition proved troublesome. Africa's newly independent countries engaged in programs to develop their economies, including exporting food and digging wells for cattle ranchers. Cattle themselves were regarded by many living in the region as a means to wealth, and the more cattle one had, the better. As a result, by 1971, as many as twenty-five million head of cattle lived in the

**PHOTO 6** Desertification caused by overgrazing. *Credit: Dreamstime.*

Sahel, far more than the region could maintain. A drought had taken hold in the region and, with the exception of a brief respite in the mid-1970s, persisted into the 1980s. Between 1968 and 1983, the yearly flow of rivers into the Sahel fell by one-quarter. The vegetation on which the cattle fed died from lack of water or from being pummeled under the animals' hooves as they clustered around wells for sustenance. What once had been grazing lands turned into desert. In the meantime, governments in the affected nations continued to sell food abroad to raise funds rather than provide it to their citizens, leaving their people ever more reliant on humanitarian aid. That help was not enough to prevent 100,000 to 200,000 people and approximately 1.2 million cattle from dying by 1973.[13]

Was this calamity human-bred or the result of meteorological conditions over which humans had no control? That question split the delegates at a 1977 conference on desertification held in Nairobi. Sponsored by UNEP and the UN Development Programme—a body founded in 1965 to assist

LDCs—some of the representatives of the ninety-four nations attending considered desertification primarily an African problem that did not deserve the same attention as more global environmental matters like whaling or acid rain. Furthermore, the delegates split along North-South lines over what, if anything, to do about it. For African states, it was important to tackle desertification as quickly as possible. The way to do so was to end poverty, which required financial assistance from countries in the North. More advanced nations were unwilling to offer such aid, for even if meteorological conditions (such as cycles in the climate) were partly to blame, the degradation of the land appeared largely human-induced: overpopulation, poor government planning, and poor land use. Why offer monetary assistance, asked DCs, if it could do nothing to alter nature itself or might be wasted by the governments that received it? Consequently, the conference attendees agreed to a "plan of action" to address the problem but omitted requirements for funding.[14]

## The Anglo-American shift

By the end of the 1970s, countries in the North that had devoted at least some attention to the environment began to push it even more to the wayside. This was particularly the case for the United States and Great Britain. Jimmy Carter, who had assumed the US presidency in 1977, had repeatedly referenced in his speeches his belief in conservation of the environment,[15] but that commitment was overwhelmed by other priorities. At home, he confronted a growing conservative backlash, an energy shortage, and a weak economy. Abroad, he faced a number of crises, among them the fourteen-month-long Iran hostage crisis that began in November 1979—in which Iran held dozens of Americans against their will—and, a month later, the Soviet invasion of Afghanistan. In 1980, an angry American electorate turned away from Carter and to his Republican rival, Ronald Reagan.

At the time of Reagan's election, detente was on life support. Following the invasion of Afghanistan, Carter had announced an arms buildup, imposed an embargo on grain shipments to the Soviet Union, and threatened to use force if the Soviets tried to take over the Persian Gulf. Reagan showed little preparedness to reverse this course of events. He initiated the largest peacetime expansion of the US military in its history up to that point, went ahead with a plan developed in 1979 to put nuclear missiles in Western Europe, dubbed the Soviet Union the "evil empire," promised to support "freedom fighters" combating communism, and called for the construction of an anti-ballistic missile system named the Strategic Defense Initiative. Fears grew in both the United States and Western Europe that the superpowers were heading toward an atomic exchange. The reintensifiction of the Cold War served to push environmental matters down the list of priorities. Yet even had detente been alive and well, Reagan had no intention to champion the environment. What mattered to him was reducing federal regulations, including environmental ones, that interfered with the ability of the business sector to conduct its affairs nationally and internationally.[16]

The political conservativism that had taken hold in the United States extended to Great Britain. A weakening economy had served to turn voters there against the incumbent Labour Party and toward the Conservatives. In 1979, a year before Reagan's election, Margaret Thatcher assumed the prime ministership. Like Reagan, she considered governmental regulations, including those on the environment, as an unnecessary drag on the economy.[17] Following his accession to the US presidency, Reagan became one of her closest personal and political allies.

There were countervailing forces. Protecting the environment might have been demoted in the White House and Whitehall, but it was by no means forgotten. In the United States, the Sierra Club had about 180,000 members when the 1980s began. It had nearly doubled that number by 1982. The National Audubon Society and other environmental organizations witnessed an expansion in membership as well, thereby allowing them to raise more funds to generate awareness of their causes. A new organization, Earth First!, appeared in 1980, using direct action and even sabotage (or "ecotage," as its members called it) in the name of defending the environment. Despite Thatcher's antagonism toward the environmental movement, it retained influence in Europe. Between 1980 and 1983, Green parties were founded in Finland, Sweden, Austria, the Republic of Ireland, and the Netherlands. In 1983, West Germany's Green Party, which was only four years old, captured twenty-seven seats in that country's parliament. That same year, the European Community (EC) approved a new action program, reaffirming its commitment to environmental protections nationally and internationally.[18]

## Marine life

The determination to do more for the planet's flora and fauna expressed itself in other ways as the 1970s turned into the 1980s. The moratorium on whaling gained momentum. Anti-whaling NGOs expanded their presence at IWC meetings. Because there were no restrictions on the Commission's membership, countries lacking a vested interest in the subject could join. Oman, Costa Rica, Jamaica, India, the Philippines, Kenya, Egypt, Belize, and Monaco were among those that became Commission members between 1980 and 1982. Their rationales varied. Costa Rica and Kenya, which relied heavily on ecotourism, evidently concluded that appearing pro-whale would draw more visitors. Others may have believed that a seat on the IWC would make them seem "modern, responsible countries." Still others, particularly developing nations, understood that the recent conservationist bent in the United States and Great Britain was not favored elsewhere in the North, and probably concluded that being pro-whale would play well among similarly minded developed countries. That could pay off dividends, whether it be in the form of aid or support for the LDCs' position at the third UN Conference on the Law of the Sea (UNCLOS III), which had begun in 1973. Further contributing to the moratorium's momentum was the decision of Canada, a whaling nation that had grown upset with the trend of events on the IWC, to leave.[19]

The year 1982 became the key. By then, there were more than three dozen countries, many of them non-whaling, that had seats on the IWC. The result was to weaken the power of those that continued to hunt the mighty mammals. Norway and Japan both threatened to leave the Commission if the moratorium passed. In a last-ditch effort to protect its interests, Japan sent foreign aid to other Commission states in the hope of swaying their vote. Tokyo's bid failed. In July, the IWC voted, 25-7, with five abstentions, to phase out whaling by 1985 and ban it altogether from 1986 to 1990. Both the United States and Great Britain were among those in favor, as neither engaged in whaling and had come under intense domestic pressure to endorse the suspension. The Japanese, for their part, resisted, but yielded under the threat of American sanctions.[20]

As restrictions on whaling intensified, so did those related to fishing. International law declared that a coastal nation's territorial claims extended three miles into the sea. By the late 1970s, the attendees at UNCLOS III had agreed to expand that claim to twelve miles. More significant, however, was the "enclosure movement." As early as 1945, US president Harry Truman had announced the United States had a right to a "conservation zone" that, by its definition, could extend two hundred miles from its coasts, well beyond the internationally accepted three miles. The Truman administration never acted on that proclamation, yet the idea of creating 200-mile-wide "exclusive economic zones" (EEZs) gained momentum over the next several decades. If accepted as part of international law, EEZs would grant control of all resources within that zone, including fish, to each country claiming them. By the 1970s, a large number of states, including the United States and the Soviet Union, had declared the creation of such EEZs.[21] In 1982, as UNCLOS III came to a close, the attendees adopted the concept of the 200-mile-wide EEZ as part of the Convention of the Law of the Sea (though that agreement did not go into effect for another twelve years).

EEZs had an impact on the Soviet and Japanese distant-water fishing industries. The Soviets found a way around such restrictions by expanding their harvests globally. Japan took a much harder hit. Since the Second World War, it had successfully reached agreements with a number of countries, including the United States, Soviet Union, and China, granting it access to fish in the central and western Pacific Ocean, and the Yellow and East China seas. In 1975, Japanese trawlers had caught 10.5 million tons of fish, 150 percent more than in 1962. By the time UNCLOS III adjourned, though, ninety-one nations had made claims of 200-mile-wide EEZs, meaning Japan had to negotiate with each to get entry to its fisheries. Tokyo's access to Soviet fisheries was cut by 50 percent, the United States replaced Japan as the largest exporter of fishery products, and Japan became dependent on imported seafood.[22]

## Acid rain and the climate conundrum

By then, nations in the North had taken additional steps to combat acid rain. As of 1983, when the 1979 Convention on Long-Range Transboundary Air Pollution (LRTAP) went into effect, new scientific evidence had demonstrated even more convincingly than before that acid rain had a deleterious effect on forests and buildings. Therefore, Norway, Finland, and Sweden proposed that by 1993, the convention's signatories pledge to curb sulfur dioxide ($SO_2$) emissions by 30 percent relative to pre-1980 emissions. West Germany, France, and Italy, which had resisted any specific commitments in the LRTAP, signed on: West Germany's forests showed clear signs of damage from acid rain, and both France and Italy had begun to turn more to hydroelectric and nuclear power for their energy needs. A year later, at a meeting in Canada, ten nations formed the so-called Thirty Percent Club when they signed on to the 30 percent reduction, applying it not just to $SO_2$ but other gaseous pollutants. In 1985, twenty-one nations signed the LRTAP's Protocol on the Reduction of Sulfur Emissions or Their Transboundary Fluxes by at least 30 percent, or for short, the Helsinki Protocol.[23]

There were several important holdouts, however. In Europe, Great Britain, Poland, and Spain refused to participate. At the time of the LRTAP's signing, they relied heavily on coal for power, emitted nearly one-quarter of that continent's $SO_2$, and were upwind from the discharges they produced. Nor did the United States become a party, despite repeated requests from Canada that it join into the agreement. Not until 1991 did the two nations sign the US-Canada Air Quality Agreement, in which they pledged curbs in emissions of $SO_2$ and nitrogen oxides, the latter which is a product of automobiles and power plants. The agreement significantly reduced the amount of cross-border pollution. However, emissions from US plants continued to play a factor in the air quality in eastern Canada.[24]

At the time of the US-Canadian agreement, the world community was in a heated debate over humans' responsibility for another atmospheric phenomenon: climate change. It already had been well established that natural processes, among them dust and gaseous emissions from volcanic eruptions, could disrupt sunlight penetration to the Earth, creating fluctuations in the planet's atmospheric air quality and temperature. Whether humans could do the same was another matter. In 1824, French physicist and mathematician Jean-Baptiste Joseph Fourier speculated that the atmosphere could retain heat and make the planet hotter than would be the case without an atmosphere or if the atmosphere lacked carbon dioxide ($CO_2$). He referred to this as a "hothouse," which years later became known as the "greenhouse effect." Early the next century, Swedish chemist Svante Arrhenius found evidence to support Fourier's thesis. At the time, the United States and Europe were both in the middle of the Second Industrial Revolution. Oil and coal production, and their use, both expanded exponentially to provide fuel to a burgeoning manufacturing sector. Smokestacks sprung up in numerous cities, spewing particles and gases such as carbon and sulfur into the atmosphere. Once ejected, water and oxygen in the atmosphere reacted with the carbon and sulfur to produce $CO_2$ and nitrous oxide. Arrhenius determined in 1903 that the burning of fossil fuels contributed to an increase in atmospheric $CO_2$. Others demurred. One of them, British physicist Sir Gilbert Walker, insisted that climatic disasters were due less to human influence and more to natural atmospheric conditions.[25]

For the next fifty years, the question of climate change received only fleeting attention. In the late 1950s, though, an American chemist, Charles Keeling, relying on findings he collected at Mauna Loa volcano in Hawaii, proclaimed that there was very likely a correlation between a greater concentration of atmospheric $CO_2$ and higher air temperature. Still, doubt persisted. The *New York Times* in 1959 commented that while the amount of ice in the Arctic Ocean had fallen by 50 percent over the previous century, "the warming trend is not considered either alarming or steep."[26]

The emergence of the modern environmental movement in the 1960s coincided with the growing attention to human modification of the atmosphere. Keeling was again a key mover, proving in 1961 an increase in $CO_2$. Two years later, he and other specialists warned that if, as anticipated, the amount of $CO_2$ over the next century doubled, global temperatures could increase by more than 4°C (over 6°F). Should that happen, glaciers would melt faster, sea levels would rise, and coastal communities would be subject to flooding. Joining them was American glaciologist John Mercer, who declared that even a small hike in global temperatures could cause the West Antarctic Ice Sheet to melt and generate a rise in sea levels of up to five meters (sixteen feet). Therefore, in 1971, with financial assistance from both private and public sources, specialists from over a dozen nations met in Stockholm, where they accepted the possibility of "serious changes" to the Earth's climate if humans failed to reduce gaseous emissions.[27]

## The ozone quandary

Two years after the Stockholm meeting came another warning about humankind's effects on the atmosphere, specifically, the ozone layer. That term, "ozone layer" is a misnomer, for it suggests that it is entirely made up of ozone ($O_3$), a pungent-smelling, blue-colored gas. In fact, ozone makes up only a small portion of the Earth's upper atmosphere. However, the gas itself is an essential component, for it absorbs dangerous ultraviolent radiation from the sun that, if allowed to reach the Earth's surface in high doses, would induce genetic modifications to crops, animals, and humans. In extreme cases, biological life could be eradicated from the planet.

The charge that humans had put the ozone layer in jeopardy came in 1973 from two chemists, Mario Molina of Mexico and an American, Sherwood Rowland. The cause, they said, was chlorofluorocarbons (CFCs). First invented in 1928 by two US-based companies, DuPont and General Motors, CFCs are a class of halogenated gases that at the time were cheap to produce, and were "nonflammable, nontoxic, and noncorrosive." Industry found uses for them in numerous products, including plastic foam and aerosol cans, and as a replacement for ammonia in refrigerators. By 1974, CFC production had reached 800,000 metric tons, more than five times what it was in 1960. It was assumed that CFCs also were environmentally safe, but the opposite proved the case. Because they were a gas, they rose into the atmosphere. Because they were highly stable, they could remain there for hundreds of years. More ominously, in the stratosphere, they reacted with the sun's ultraviolet rays and destroyed $O_3$. The more CFCs reacted with the atmosphere, the greater the probability of cancer among humans and genetic mutations among animals and plants. Joining Molina and Rowland was ocean scientist Veerabhadran Ramanathan of the US National Aeronautics and Space Administration (NASA). Bringing climate change into the mix, Ramanathan pointed out in 1975 that CFCs were greenhouse gases that easily reacted with the sun's radiation and increased the Earth's temperature.[28]

Not surprisingly, CFC manufacturers, as well as some scientists, fought back. But political officials in the United States, Canada, Sweden, Finland, and Norway stood behind the conclusions reached by Molina, Rowland, and Ramanathan. All of these nations had adopted leading roles in combating pollution and defending the environment. In 1978, the U.S. Congress banned the two most common CFCs, numbers 11 (trichlorofluoromethane) and 12 (dichlorofluoromethane). Two years later, the members of the EC followed suit by restricting CFC production and use; Sweden and Norway curbed the use of CFCs by as much as 98 percent by banning them except for "essential" purposes; and Canada eliminated their presence from popular products, including deodorant and hair spray, which checked the use of CFCs in that country by 80 percent.[29]

Matters heated up in 1982 when Joseph Farman, a British geophysicist interested in meteorology, discovered a hole in the ozone layer. He realized the significance and ramifications of his discovery for the longevity of carbon-based lifeforms on the planet. Further research with two colleagues confirmed his revelation. In 1985, they published their conclusions in the journal *Nature*,[30] thus bringing their discovery to an international audience.

The growing evidence that CFCs damaged the environment convinced UNEP to create a working group to develop a "framework convention" aimed at protecting the ozone layer. The working group met over the next four years, during which the evidence accumulated of an atmosphere under threat. The same year as Farman and his colleagues published their article in *Nature*, a team led by Ramanathan examined about thirty "infrared-absorbing gases" and determined that in combination, they could produce climate change at a pace equal to that of $CO_2$. The indication, therefore, was that the planet could heat up twice as quickly as originally assumed.[31]

Scientific warnings, however, ran into economic considerations. At the center of what became intense international wrangling over how far to proceed with eliminating CFCs was the EC. As UNEP's working group hammered out the framework convention, the US government, having come under pressure to expand the domestic regulations on CFCs to international commerce, joined in 1983 a working group established that year in Toronto made up of Canada, Switzerland, Finland, Sweden, and Norway. The "Toronto Group" sought to write a protocol aimed at prohibiting "'nonessential' uses of CFCs in spray cans," proclaiming such a move "would at one stroke reduce global CFC emissions by about one-third." The EC resisted. Although the EC had cut back on the use of CFCs, it had not eliminated them entirely. Indeed, claimed many Europeans, production of chlorofluorocarbons was important to a number of their industries. For instance, French perfume makers contended the alternatives to CFCs were unsuitable to them. Furthermore, the Community maintained that what consisted of "nonessential" use varied from nation to nation. The EC, therefore, proposed its own protocol, one that would forbid expansion of the existing production of CFCs. The result was a stalemate, with the "Toronto Group" calling for the ban, and the EC standing firmly against one. Complicating matters further were developing countries. To them, access to cheap CFCs was part of their broader effort to develop their economies.[32]

With such disparate points of view, it appeared a plenipotentiary meeting hosted by UNEP and another UN agency, the World Meteorological Organization (WMO), in Vienna, Austria, in 1985 was doomed to fail. How fruitful that gathering turned out to be depended on one's point of view. On the one hand, representatives from twenty countries signed the Vienna Convention for the Protection of the Ozone Layer, calling for continued research and the sharing of scientific information. Furthermore, they asked UNEP to continue working on an ozone protocol, with the plan of having it ready by 1987. In that respect, the agreement set a potential foundation for a more significant international pact. On the other hand, these provisions favored those who wanted to do the minimum required to control production and use of CFCs. In December of the following year, negotiations for an ozone protocol got underway in Geneva.[33]

# Chernobyl

Overshadowing preparations for the Geneva conference was an environmental disaster that took place in the Soviet Union at the Chernobyl Nuclear Power Plant. On April 26, 1986, workers conducting a safety test in one of the reactors shut down both the power-regulating and emergency systems, allowing for a chain of events that caused an explosion powerful enough to blow off the reactor's steel roof and release more radioactivity into the atmosphere than that of the two atomic bombs dropped on Japan. Thirty-two people died from the explosion, and firefighters needed five hours to put out the flames. In the meantime, people in the nearby city Pripyat began to fall ill, prompting what became its permanent evacuation. Although some radioactivity ended up in Western Europe, most of it fell on the Soviet states of Russia, Belarus, and Ukraine. Deformities in both animals and humans saw a noticeable increase for several years following the disaster. The number of Soviet nationals who died from cancer caused by Chernobyl will never be known, but it is certainly in the thousands.[34]

PHOTO 7 The ghost city of Pripyat. *Credit: Dreamstime.*

Mikhail Gorbachev, who had assumed the Soviet premiership a year earlier, tried to keep the disaster quiet. Doing so proved impossible. On April 28, Geiger counters in Sweden recorded unusually high levels of wind-driven radioactivity coming from the direction of the Soviet Union, prompting it to demand an explanation. It was only at this point that the Kremlin admitted to the accident.

The immediate effects of Chernobyl were twofold. The first came in the form of panic and protection. Knowing that their populations feared the possibility of falling ill or dying from radiation poisoning, West German authorities encouraged their constituents to avoid consuming certain foods, European border guards used Geiger counters to check incoming foodstuffs, and caribou herders in northern Finland were told not to eat meat from those animals. The second was passage of two international agreements signed in Vienna, Austria, in September 1986. One was the Convention on Early Notification of a Nuclear Accident. Signed by sixty-nine countries, it went into force a month later. In the case of a nuclear accident that poses a threat to other countries, it requires the nation where the accident took place to report when and where it occurred, and how much radiation was released, so that those affected have the opportunity to take countermeasures. The other, the Convention on Assistance in the Case of a Nuclear Accident or Radiological Emergency, had sixty-eight signatories and went into effect in February 1987. Under its provisions, nations agree to provide assistance to the country where a nuclear accident took place.[35]

The Chernobyl disaster, though, had longer range consequences for the environment. It invigorated the Green movement, with Green parties expanding the number of seats they held in both West Germany and the European Parliament. It also played a part in convincing the EC to address its environmental policy. Since the 1970s, the EC had begun incorporating environmental concerns into its policymaking, but some members did not take Community mandates and turn them into law, and others failed to enforce the measures passed. Additionally, the EC's treaties lacked language that referred specifically to the environment. By the mid-1980s, it had become apparent to EC member states that they needed a single environmental policy. The Chernobyl disaster provided the final impetus. In 1987 the EC adopted the Single European Act (SEA), the first significant revision to the Treaty of Rome that had created the Community thirty years earlier. Although the SEA's main purpose was to institute a "Single European Market," it had environmental provisions. It called for preventive measures to protect the environment and adopted the principle of "polluter pays," that is, the creator of the pollution should be responsible for the environmental damage caused. Moreover, to meet the concern of member states who feared adopting EC-approved legislation would require them to relax national laws, it permitted tighter restrictions, as long as they did not promote economic protectionism.[36]

Maybe most impressive was Chernobyl's reverberations in the Soviet bloc. Those who had led the Soviet Union and its satellite states had vivid memories of the Second World War. They had come of age or entered positions of power when Josef Stalin was Soviet leader and had accepted the concept that a state-run communist system was superior to a capitalist one. Under their leadership, the environmental conditions within the Soviet bloc had worsened. By the 1980s, every river system in the Soviet Union was polluted because of the use of fertilizers and pesticides, including DDT. Sixty percent of the Soviet population lived "in ecologically bad conditions." Two-thirds of Europe's sulfur dioxide emissions came out of Eastern Europe, causing acid rain that destroyed large areas of forest in those satellite nations and numerous health problems for humans. The pollution in Krakow, Poland, was reported to be ten times as bad as in the West, and 10 percent of the city's children suffered from bronchitis. Ufa, a city in the Soviet Union with a population of more than one million people, was declared in 1987 by the state newspaper *Pravda* as unsuitable for humans.[37]

Gorbachev had sought to keep Chernobyl quiet, but he also had seen to it to permit unprecedented economic and political freedoms in the Soviet Union and its satellites. In so doing, he strengthened the voice of a burgeoning environmental movement there. This is not to say environmentalism had been nonexistent beforehand. There had been an effort during the Stalinist era to create *zapovedniki*—nature preserves that would be untouched by human hands. Those behind the *zapovedniki*, though, could not overcome a communist ideology that called for exploitation of nature for human benefit.[38] The Stockholm Conference created, at least educationally, a shift in Soviet policy. Although Moscow sent no delegation to that 1972 meeting, the conference led the communist bloc to teach more about the environment. In turn, those who came of age in the 1970s and 1980s received far greater exposure to environmental science than had their predecessors, and passed that knowledge down to the next generation.[39]

The combination of the Chernobyl disaster, pollution, Gorbachev's political reforms, and a more environmentally aware population weakened communism's hold in Eastern Europe and the Soviet Union. Just as environmentalists found a home in the US antiwar movement of the 1960s and 1970s, so protecting the environment became a cause célèbre of those in the Soviet bloc who wanted to see greater democracy. Furious with communist leaders who had stifled basic freedoms and encouraged economic growth above all else, including human health, protests erupted in favor of a more open political and economic system that would permit greater freedoms and do more to protect flora, fauna, and people. The intensity of the anger forced the Soviet Union to cancel about a dozen nuclear power plants, the Ukraine outlawed atomic energy, and Yugoslavia announced it would suspend the construction of atomic power plants for twenty years. When pro-democracy activists in 1989 successfully breached the Berlin Wall—the symbol of Europe's division into communist and noncommunist halves—without facing retaliation, it invigorated similarly minded individuals elsewhere in the communist bloc, who eventually brought down the governments of Eastern Europe and, in 1991, that of the Soviet Union.[40]

## The Persian Gulf War

Concurrent with the rising tide of democracy in the Soviet bloc was a warming of US-Soviet relations, which had a direct impact on yet another war. In 1988, Iran and Iraq declared an end to eight years of military combat that had left 400,000 people dead. Iraq's leader, Saddam Hussein, sought to recoup his financial losses by selling oil. However, his neighbor to the south, Kuwait, had increased petroleum production, thus pushing down the price of that commodity on the world market. Furious at the money Kuwait was costing him, and seeking to offset growing discontent at home, Hussein ordered the invasion of Kuwait in August 1990. Not only did Hussein now find himself with control over an even greater proportion of the world's known oil reserves, but he appeared prepared to invade Saudi Arabia, itself a large petroleum producer. Determined to protect the Saudis, the United Nations Security Council, including the Soviet Union—which at one time had been an Iraqi ally but now sought Western economic aid—approved a resolution giving Hussein until January 16, 1991, to withdraw from Kuwait. Meanwhile, the United States led the establishment of a military coalition of forty-eight nations to protect Saudi Arabia from possible attack. When Hussein refused to meet the UN deadline, the coalition struck, starting with a month-long aerial assault on Iraqi military forces, and industrial and communication facilities, followed by a ground assault. In less than two weeks, Iraq's military had been forced out of Kuwait and a cease-fire established.

Unlike Vietnam, the terrain in Kuwait and Iraq proved ideal for a conventional-style military campaign involving airstrikes and rapid movement by motorized ground forces. Like Vietnam, however, the war had consequences for the environment. In what some refer to as another example of "ecocide," the Iraqis, as they retreated, set fire to over six hundred oil wells in Kuwait, spilling up to thirty million barrels of oil on land and another six to eight million barrels into the Persian Gulf, and sending twelve thousand tons of particulates into the atmosphere. Black rain fell as far away as Turkey, Iran, and the Himalayas, and black snow was reported in Pakistan and India. Yet surprisingly, the evidence points to limited long-term damage to the local ecosystem. Coral reefs, birds, fish, and crustaceans exhibited no significant effects. How extensive the damage was to flora and fauna remains unclear. There is evidence that some plants suffered harm, likely because salt water was used to combat the oil fires, thus causing salination to some areas. In 1996, after a multiyear assessment, the United Nations awarded Kuwait $610 billion for Iraq's environmental damage, making Iraq the only nation ever to face such a charge.[41]

# Addressing ozone

As the world community confronted the fallout, literally and figuratively, of the Chernobyl meltdown and the enormous amount of soot deposited in the atmosphere following the Persian Gulf War, the debate over CFCs' complicity in ozone depletion continued. A report by the WMO and UNEP concluded that chlorofluorocarbons "were thousands of times more powerful than carbon dioxide in their heat-trapping capability." Still, uncertainty persisted. NASA used satellite imaging to *suggest* that if CFC emissions grew by just 3 percent, the ozone layer would suffer a 10 percent loss by 2050. The World Resources Institute, an NGO that promoted sustainable development and favored regulating chlorofluorocarbons rather than banning them, took a more definitive position, declaring that "proof of changes in natural ozone levels and the primary role of CFCs is still lacking."[42]

Companies in the EC used this uncertainty to proclaim that the "scare" over CFCs was just that. If anything, they insisted, the push to eliminate chlorofluorocarbons was part of a conspiracy by US corporations. The pressure they had faced within the United States to find substitutes for CFCs had led American companies to do just that. To their delight, they discovered those substitutes were cheaper to produce than CFCs. The result was role reversal: US firms, which had produced about 46 percent of CFCs 11 and 12 sold worldwide in the mid-1970s—about 8 percent more than companies in the EC—made about 28 percent of them by 1985, versus 45 percent for the EC. To industrialists in the EC, what the Americans wanted to do was to move those numbers back in America's favor by using the chlorofluorocarbon "scare" to convince consumers to buy aerosols manufactured with CFC substitutes. Joining West Europeans were the Soviet Union and Japan, each of which by this time manufactured about 10 percent of all CFCs. To the Soviets, chlorofluorocarbons were vital to refrigeration and air conditioning in their southern states. To the Japanese, they were essential to electronics manufacturing, the keystone of their national economy.[43]

These disparate points of view cast a pall over the next international meeting on the ozone layer, held in Montreal in 1987. Yet what appeared to be another meeting that had only a small chance of success turned out to be another step forward. Part of the credit went to UNEP executive director Mostafa Tolba and the head of UNEP's Environmental Law and Institutions Unit, Iwona Rummel-Bulska, who encouraged the delegates to meet informally in closed session, away from the scrutiny of prying eyes. At those meetings, US representatives brought pressure to bear on their colleagues. President Reagan joined the cause. Environmentalists, Congress, and the chemical industry urged him to adopt further measures, and he understood that doing so gave him a chance "to demonstrate U.S. global leadership." Additionally, the EC exhibited growing signs of disunity. Countries such as West Germany, Denmark, and Belgium leaned in favor of tougher regulations. Of them, only West Germany was a significant producer of CFCs, but it was the home of an increasingly influential Green Party that favored environmental protection. The presence of numerous NGOs helped as well, for they brought with them expertise to which the national delegations could turn. Those same NGOs, along with the reporters present, publicized the events taking place in Montreal, thereby bringing international opinion into the mix of considerations facing those in the meeting rooms.[44]

Inspired by the "precautionary principle" and signed by thirty-one nations, the Montreal Protocol on Substances That Deplete the Ozone Layer called for cutting production of CFCs by one-half of 1986 levels by the end of the century. But for all of its promise, the Montreal Protocol had its weaknesses. The scientific community asserted that halting ozone depletion required curbing CFC use by 85 percent globally; the Protocol would reduce it by half that number. It did not prohibit the production of other chemicals that could destroy ozone and offered no punishments for those nations that failed to comply with the restrictions on production or consumption of chlorofluorocarbons. Reflecting the continued North-South divide, developing countries angrily pointed out that the decisions reached at Montreal offered them no financial help from the developed world so they could offset the higher spending they would incur from using alternatives to CFCs. Indeed, to get developing countries to sign on, the Protocol allowed them to increase their use of CFCs over the next 10 years. Even that, however, was not enough for all LDCs, as Brazil, China, and India rejected the Montreal agreement.[45]

The resistance to creating a regime designed to protect the ozone layer convinced environmentalists to redouble their efforts. With the assistance from the US-based NGO Friends of the Earth International, environmentalists in Europe encouraged worldwide boycotts of goods with CFCs in them. This tactic convinced McDonald's and other fast-food chains in the United States to eliminate CFCs in their packaging, as did the Foodservice and Packaging Institute, which was the fast-food industry's trade association. The West German leadership declared its intention to reduce CFC use by 95 percent and to achieve by 1995 the 85 percent reduction called for at Montreal, and the EC Council announced it would ratify the protocol signed there. Yet even then, a group of British scientists concluded that the agreements reached in Canada would not do enough to prevent continued destruction of the ozone layer.[46]

# Hazardous waste

The year after the Montreal Protocol, the world learned of the *Karin B.*, a ship laden with 2,100 tons of toxic waste. It had picked up its cargo in Italy and dropped it off in the town of Koko, Nigeria, where a local farmer had agreed to have it dumped on his land in return for $100 in rent per month—a handsome sum for that nation. The farmer had been told that inside the barrels was fertilizer, when in fact it was industrial waste that included asbestos and polychlorinated biphenyls, both of which were known to have harmful effects on humans. Exposed to the elements, the containers ruptured. Some locals took the barrels, emptied the contents, and used them for drinking water, after which they became sick. When Nigerians learned the truth, indignation swept through the local population and environmental NGOs, and international news outlets picked up the story. The Nigerian government forced Italy to remove the waste at the end of July and reload on the *Karin B*. After several European nations refused the ship entry, it returned to Italy, where the detritus was unloaded for treatment.[47]

The *Karin B*. and its cargo drew attention to the toxic waste industry, which by the 1970s had become quite extensive. Approximately three hundred to four hundred million tons of toxic waste was produced annually in the 1980s, the overwhelming majority of it in Western Europe and the United States. Some estimates suggested that more than half of all of the toxic waste manufactured by the DCs that made up the OECD went to non-OECD states. At times, this waste purposely was mislabeled to make it harder to trace, particularly for the LDCs that received it.[48]

There were several interrelated reasons for the development of the hazardous waste trade. One was the publicity generated when dangerous materials affected residents in the countries where it was created. In 1976, an industrial accident in Seveso, Italy, exposed residents in the surrounding area to dioxin and left some with injuries. A few years later, cleanup of the site began. During the process, over three dozen barrels of waste disappeared, only to be located in an abandoned slaughterhouse in a village in northern France. Two years later, a reporter discovered an inordinately large number of birth defects in Love Canal, a neighborhood of the US city of Niagara Falls, New York. Subsequent investigation discovered that numerous houses there had been built on top of a dump previously used by Hooker Chemical Company. Residents were forced to give up their homes, which were subsequently destroyed, and the American government passed legislation to clean up Love Canal and similar sites. Not surprisingly, the companies from which the wastes came faced a public relations backlash from those who declared "NIMBY": not in my backyard.[49]

This backlash led to a second cause for commerce in hazardous waste, that of cost. Events like that at Love Canal led to the passage of new, expensive regulations. In the United States, the dumping of hazardous materials in landfills rose from an average of $15 per ton in 1980 to $250 per ton eight years later. Concurrent with more costly controls at home were improvements in transportation that made it cheaper to ship waste elsewhere.[50]

Transportation tied into a final reason for the waste trade, the existence of willing recipients, particularly within the developing world. Some were in Latin America and the South Pacific, but it was Africa that became the prime target of the waste industry. The countries on that continent had lax environmental statutes and little control over the officials who oversaw imports. Additionally, many African nations were impoverished and desperate for income. As such, they were not about to pass on an industry that in the late 1980s was valued at some $3 billion and could bring them a financial windfall. The detritus these nations accepted oftentimes was put into substandard containers and buried where the hazardous material could leach into the soil and groundwater. The *Karin B.* was one of the most famous instances. Less advertised was a shipment disguised with labels declaring it "dry cleaning fluid and solvents," that ended up in Zimbabwe in 1984. Later that decade, a US company dumped fly ash on an island near the capital of the nation of Guinea. Described as material for building bricks, it killed off trees and created a smell the locals found intolerable. Only after an investigation discovered the truth was the waste removed and returned to the United States, where it was put into a landfill.[51]

By then, an international effort to tackle the waste trade was underway. Negotiations began in 1981 at a conference in Montevideo, Uruguay, and proceeded for the remainder of the decade. As with desertification and climate change, North-South differences entered the deliberations over hazardous waste. During the 1980s DCs, such as members of the EC, had taken steps to curb the transshipment of dangerous materials among their members, but they had not addressed commerce with LDCs, which was where most of such trade took place. Companies that produced and shipped toxic materials adopted a laissez faire stance, one that called for no regulations over their activities. The Western nations where those corporations had their headquarters were willing to accept some restrictions. In particular, they favored what became known as the principle of prior informed consent (PIC), in which an exporter had to inform an importer of the material being shipped and for the latter to agree to accept it. UNEP too leaned in favor of regulation on the grounds that it might be safer to send a developed country's waste elsewhere, but with the caveat that such materials should not be transported to LDCs. For numerous nations in the South, particularly those in Africa, regulation was not enough. What they favored was a ban. They were helped by NGOs, especially Greenpeace, that were able to bring with them expertise that representatives at international conventions oftentimes lacked.[52]

These differences came to the fore when over one hundred countries, as well as members of the EC, met at Basel, Switzerland, in 1989. What emerged from that meeting, the Basel Convention on the Control of

Transboundary Movements of Hazardous Wastes and Their Disposal—or, Basel Convention, for short—was a form of PIC. Those who wished to ship hazardous materials had to apprise the receiving nation ahead of time. If the recipient accepted the shipment, and if could be disposed of safely, then the transaction could move forward. Signatories were to curtail the amount of hazardous waste they produced and to transport such items only if they had no ability to destroy them in a manner that was environmentally sound. The convention permitted commerce with nonparties, but only if another agreement, be it bilateral or regional in nature, guaranteed the disposal of that detritus in a manner at least equivalent to that demanded by Basel. Signatories could not ship wastes to Antarctica. Finally, Basel set up a secretariat that would hold future conferences of the parties.[53]

Who benefited most from these provisions has generated debate. Despite the existence of PIC, write some observers, it was LDCs that gained the most, for they had forced concessions favorable to the South. Others argued that ultimately it was DCs that had the upper hand. For one, Basel said nothing about pesticides, which pleased agrochemical companies, many of them based in the North. Though dangerous chemicals themselves, pesticides were sent to other nations not for disposal but to promote food production. Nor did the convention cover radioactive materials, which were considered outside the document's scope. Additionally, knowing that there were poorer countries willing to import wastes, governments in the North established a "veto coalition," telling those in the South that either they had to accept the proposed PIC regime or forget having a convention at all. Just how much of an advantage the developed nations had, argue critics, was apparent when members of the Organization of African Unity (OAU) suggested amendments to ban the shipment of hazardous materials to countries in the South that did not have treatment facilities equal to those in the North. To the OAU's dismay, developed nations successfully rejected those proposals. Just how displeased African states were became clear when every country on the continent refused to sign or ratify Basel. In fact, when the agreement went into force in 1992 after the requisite consent by twenty nations, virtually no African state was among those to endorse it.[54]

Because of the Basel Convention's limitations, sixty-eight African, Caribbean, and Pacific (ACP) countries, most of them former European colonies, insisted that their former metropoles accept a ban on hazardous exports. The British and French began to worry about impairing their relationship with their one-time dependencies. At first, the EC attempted to convince the ACP nations to accept waste if the industrialized countries sent along as well technology designed to assist in the elimination of that material. When ACP members balked, the EC, as well as thirty other nations in the North—minus, importantly, the United States—adopted a ban on waste exports.[55]

What this new ban failed to cover was pesticides. It was LDCs that became the world's fastest-growing recipients of such poisons. In Africa alone, sales of pesticides grew by 180 percent between 1980 and 1984. Governments that sought to encourage production of export crops, the need to employ ever-larger doses to kill resistant insects, and development projects—oftentimes funded by international financial institutions—encouraged such widespread use. A lack of clarity insofar as the pesticides' application, improperly labeled or unmarked containers, and a failure to wear proper clothing or equipment killed off large scores of fish, animals, and beneficial insects, and contributed to 220,000 human deaths annually. Adopting the precautionary principle, fifty-one African countries in 1991 signed the Bamako Convention, prohibiting the import of hazardous material, including radioactive items and pesticides, from any nation, as well as dangerous substances banned in the country from which they came. Seven years later, enough African states had ratified it to bring it into force. Yet in the name of national self-interest, some African countries known to import hazardous waste, most notably Nigeria, have failed to ratify it.[56]

# To Rio

The reluctance of at least some LDCs to address the hazardous waste trade appeared in negotiations on the ozone layer. The pessimistic findings of British scientists regarding the Montreal agreement, and pressure from the UK chapters of Greenpeace and Friends of the Earth, broke down Thatcher's resistance to doing more to protect the environment. Now, she adopted the view already held in some quarters that one could not separate the planet's environmental well-being from war and security. She then endorsed the appeal made at the time of the Montreal Protocol for an 85 percent reduction in CFCs and asked for a meeting in London, the purpose of which was to get more countries to sign on to the Montreal Protocol and toughen its provisions.[57]

Indicative of just how much ozone depletion had entered international discourse, over 120 countries sent delegates to the London meeting. There, the EC promised to eliminate all CFC manufacturing by the year 2000. Developing countries, however, continued to hesitate for a variety of reasons. Some blamed the developed world for the globe's environmental difficulties. It was the West's "excessive consumption of all materials and . . . large scale industrialization intended to support their styles of life" that was the crux of the problem, stated India's president, Ramaswamy Venkataraman. Moreover, LDCs insisted that the elimination of CFCs jeopardized their ability to improve their standard of living. As the price of abandoning CFCs, they demanded financial help so they could develop or gain access to more environmentally friendly technology. It became clear to Western nations that if they were to protect the ozone layer, they would have to meet LDCs' request for assistance. With that in mind, the attendees in London created an interim fund of US$160–240 million for the developing world. Additionally, the London agreements included provisions for technology transfer.[58]

Whether the meeting of the minds that apparently had taken place at London might extend to climate change was another matter. There was reason for optimism, particularly as the year 1988 came to a close. That year was one of the hottest ever recorded, with the United States experiencing the worst droughts since the Dust Bowl of the 1930s. American and international opinion became more aware of climate change, evidenced by the decision of *Time* magazine to change its "Man of the Year" edition for 1988 to "Planet of the Year: Endangered Earth." That same year, the United States joined with the World Health Organization and other UN agencies in creating the Intergovernmental Panel on Climate Change (IPCC), which established a number of working groups aimed at writing a convention designed to shrink the amount of $CO_2$ in the atmosphere. In June, Toronto, Canada, became the site of a meeting attended by government officials and representatives of environmental and industrial NGOs from nearly four dozen nations. The convention ended with a call for cutting $CO_2$ emissions by 2005 to one-fifth of 1988 levels and a global fund that would receive financial support partly from a tax on the use of fossil fuels. Most importantly, it was here that the first entreaties were made for a convention and protocols to create an international regime to combat climate change.[59]

But such a regime required convincing humans to reduce their use of fossil fuels, which was no easy task. The US government, which had taken a lead in getting rid of CFCs and had helped established the IPCC, resisted going after $CO_2$. Reagan's successor, George H. W. Bush, insisted that the causes of climate change were still unclear. He also was under intense domestic pressure from energy companies, and his own conservative views made him anathema to government regulation of the economy. A recession that began in 1990 further restrained him from taking actions that he felt would add to his country's economic woes.[60]

Developing states too demonstrated recalcitrance, particularly when talk of combating climate change intersected with demands to combat "tropical deforestation"—a phrase that became part of the international lexicon starting in the early 1970s. In 1989, 142,000 square kilometers of the world's rain forest was lost, reducing the total number of square kilometers globally by 1.8 percent. While the percentage itself appeared small, that 142,000 square kilometers was 90 percent higher than a decade earlier. Much of this foliage lay in LDCs, which saw them as a source of revenue derived from the sale of lumber. In other cases, locals in those nations removed the tropical foliage, sometimes through the use of fire, and replaced it with either pastures for grazing animals or trees—such as those that produced coffee beans or fruit—that would provide them income. Or they burned the wood for fuel. One estimate was that four-fifths of the wood cut in developing countries was for providing heat or power. Whenever fire entered the mix, it meant the release of more $CO_2$ into the atmosphere. Disconcerting as well was that rain forests are "carbon sinks." Like all plants, they absorb atmospheric $CO_2$. Rain forests in particular take in and store more $CO_2$ than they emit. Destroying them meant not only the absorption of less $CO_2$ but the emission into the atmosphere of the $CO_2$ they had taken in.[61] As the world's largest rain forest was in the Amazon basin of South America, particular attention was drawn to that part of the world. Coming to grips with the destruction of those forests, however, meant addressing a debt crisis that had taken hold in not just South America but Central America.

Latin America's indebtedness resulted from a combination of sociocultural and economic forces. The region's small, financially well-off elite devoted little of its own capital to development, encouraging governments in that part of the world to borrow even more than they might have otherwise. Much of those funds came from IFIs and foreign countries. Having decided that cattle-ranching offered the best means of maximizing profit, a good portion of that outside money went into that industry. Indeed, by the 1980s, two-thirds of Central America's best agricultural acreage was allocated to ranching, leading not only to less being used to grow crops but the destruction of the local ecology. (Central America, for instance, had 40 percent fewer forests and woodlands in 1983 than it had had in 1950.) Ranching expanded as well in the Amazon basin. The cattle themselves required more grain than other animal protein sources, such as chicken or fish. More land was thus put toward growing feed. With not enough food for their own populations, these countries had to import it, adding to their debt. As the money they owed grew, these states had less to put toward development, if not pay off creditors, forcing them to clear still more acres of forest to make way for economic activities that would raise capital. The consequence of these decisions was a regional debt crisis that began in the early 1980s.[62] It was not until the late 1980s that lenders began to forgive some of those obligations, with the caveat that in return, those countries made changes to their economies so they could pay off what remained.

By the mid-1980s, it appeared Brazil might change its ways insofar as doing more to defend the environment. After being in power for twenty years, its military dictatorship had come to an end, and a democratic government had assumed power. Having borrowed money from IFIs and foreign governments for development projects, its external debt was the largest of any LDC. Instead, international urging to do more to protect flora and fauna evoked a strong nationalist response that emphasized the need for developing Brazil's resources. Brazilians also accused the North of trying to keep their country in a state of subservience, and of hypocrisy by citing Brasilia for destroying nature when the accusers were far more responsible for the globe's environmental problems. Consequently, when creditors offered to reduce Brazil's debt in return for the adoption of more environmentally friendly policies, Brasilia refused. Brazil then led a half-dozen other Latin American nations in 1989 in rejecting any effort to link financial aid to their own environmental initiatives on the grounds that it was a threat to their national sovereignty.[63]

Brasilia's uncompromising stand drew it censure at home and abroad. In early 1989, Brazilian Indian tribes, which formerly had fought one another, united in opposition to a dam project that would have forced 70,000 of them off their lands. NGOs began an effort to cut Brazil off from capital from the multinational lenders, the United States successfully stopped a $500 million World Bank loan meant for Brazil's energy sector, and the IADB turned away from giving Brazil $65 million for road construction. A stung Brazil sought to mollify its critics. In April 1989 it began a program called Our Nature and sought to portray itself as environmentally responsible by starting several initiatives: monitoring and controlling the burning of trees in the Amazon, suspending tax incentives that encouraged ranching and the growing of crops in that same part of Brazil, and a calling for the creation of reserves of rubber trees for tapping. Indeed, between 1989 and 1990, the amount of Amazon rain forest cleared fell by 80 percent. Furthermore, the Brazilian government reached the conclusion that it could take advantage of the international interest in the environment to push even harder for Northern consideration of sustainable development. Accordingly, it offered to host the UN Conference on Environment and Development (UNCED).[64]

# The Rio conference

UNCED's story began in the early 1980s, when scientists started to agree that the number of animal and plant species that had gone extinct had increased significantly. The causes were multifold, and included the destruction of wetlands, changes in climate, population growth, economic development, and deforestation. Still other flora and fauna had been forced to retreat into ever-smaller portions of what once had been wider habitats. Therefore, IUCN called for a convention to establish a global regime to protect the diversity of the planet's animal and plant species. The United States jumped on board and convinced UNEP to form a working group to begin the process of reaching such an agreement. In a sense, this initiative was not new, for the idea of protecting the world's flora and fauna went as far back as the 1900 London Convention. But it and more recent agreements, like CITES, had focused on individual species as opposed to the ecosystems of which they were a part.[65]

In 1988, Tolba convened the first of a series of working groups, each of them attended by an increasing number of representatives from national governments, both LDCs and DCs, and from nongovernmental and intergovernmental organizations, among them the IUCN, the UN's FAO, and the World Wildlife Federation (WWF). There was concurrence among them that existing conventions did not do enough to protect the planet's biodiversity. Getting from there to a more comprehensive agreement required crossing a number of hurdles, many of them involving North-South differences. One had to do with the fact that the most diverse ecosystems are naturally located in or near the tropics. The countries in this region labeled as "mega-diverse" because of the large number of species living in them tend to be LDCs. Among them are India, Indonesia, Malaysia, Madagascar, Zaire, Colombia, Ecuador, Mexico, Brazil, and Peru.[66] Lesser developed nations were certain to argue that they were being unfairly picked on by their more industrially advanced and richer counterparts.

Another touchy subject was that of property rights. Countries in the North argued that a benefit of biodiversity was that a wider variety of plants allowed for the greater likelihood of splicing one species' genes with another, thereby creating new variants that might produce more per acre or be resistant to insects or disease. Or the plants themselves might be useful in creating new medicines. The companies that made these discoveries, which were usually based in the North, patented them, angering LDCs on two levels. First, the firms involved claimed their new plants or pharmaceuticals were "intellectual property" and refused to share their findings with the nations from which the original resources came. Second, by prohibiting LDCs from replicating those discoveries, those same states oftentimes had to purchase the final product from Northern companies and at high prices. What nations in the South wanted was the right to the North's biotechnology and a share of the profits made from product sold. Not until just before UNCED took place did the attendees at Tolba's working groups complete a draft convention that addressed these disagreements.[67]

Held in Rio de Janeiro, UNCED, also called the Earth Summit, had far better attendance than Stockholm, indicating the globe's expanding interest in environmental matters. Whereas only two heads of state came to Stockholm, over one hundred were present at Rio. The 1,400 NGOs and 8,000 journalists from 111 nations also greatly outnumbered those in Sweden twenty years earlier. Additionally, the Earth Summit reflected the growing power of LDCs in environmental decision-making. It was the first environmental conference hosted by a nation in the South. Its title too was noteworthy. LDCs had long argued that economic development was of central importance to them. In their mind, though, UNEP and Tolba had given too much attention to climate change and the decline of biodiversity, subjects that were primarily of interest to DCs. Hence, they succeeded in getting the words "and Development" added to the conference title.[68]

This continued North-South dichotomy indicated that, as in past environmental conferences, DCs and LDCs were likely to clash at Rio. That proved the case. LDCs were irate when industrial states complained about deforestation, pollution, and species loss among countries in the South. Conversely, LDCs again accused their more developed counterparts for generating most of the planet's climate change-causing pollution. They disliked as well the wariness of countries in the North to provide them with technological or financial help so that they could eliminate poverty and do more to protect the environment.[69]

Despite this discord, the delegates at Rio adopted twenty-seven principles, many of them related to sustainable development, but others that addressed the shipment of hazardous waste, the effect of natural disasters and war on the environment, and the roles women, youth, and indigenous people could play in protecting the environment's well-being. The attendees also were able to hammer out two conventions. The first, the Framework Convention on Climate Change (FCCC), received the endorsement of 154 nations. This was largely because it imposed virtually no requirements. "It would not be profitable to draft a treaty that lays out highly specific policies that only a few countries could agree to," commented Argentina's ambassador to the UN, Raoul Estrada. Hence, the FCCC established a "goal" of restricting greenhouse gas emissions to "earlier levels" by the year 2000 without saying when "earlier" was. It set no goals for any year after 2000. Probably the only portion that was enforceable was a stipulation for each party to submit national reports. To environmentalists, the conservatively worded convention was a disappointment, one that did not go far enough to protect the planet from climate change.[70]

The second, the Convention on Biological Diversity (CBD), had 157 signatories, representing over 80 percent of the world's states at the time. A clear example of the precautionary principle in action, it called on each country to inventory its species of flora and fauna, and to develop a strategy to protect that diversity. Though not stated outright, such plans of protection recognized the importance of maintaining not just individual plants or animals, but the ecosystems in which they lived. In this respect, the CBD was unlike previous international conventions. Additionally, while recognizing national sovereignty, it encouraged sustainable use of flora and fauna, and for all parties to share what they learned from the utilization of those resources. In an attempt to encourage every nation—particularly those in the South—to sign on, the convention included provisions for the transfer of technology to protect Earth's biodiversity, including technology protected by "patents and other intellectual property rights."[71]

Only one nation refused to become a party to the CBD. President Bush liked the language of the FCCC and signed on to it, but the biological diversity convention was another matter. The CBD specifically would require him to strengthen the Endangered Species Act—a law passed by Congress in 1973 that Bush contended interfered with domestic economic growth—and its provisions regarding technology transfer would harm American companies, particularly at a time when the United States was in the midst of a recession. Among those encouraging his hardline stance were American pharmaceutical companies, which did not want to have to share their discoveries with others. The United States, therefore, did not join the CBD.[72]

The representatives in Rio reached one other accord. Called Agenda 21, it was a nonbinding agreement on "sustainable development." This idea had been around since the early 1970s, but the term itself was first used extensively in the World Conservation Strategy of 1980. Prepared by the IUCN, the WWF, and UNEP, and backed by the UN General Assembly, Agenda 21 was a conservationist, anthropocentric document that underscored that any program of economic development had to avoid exploiting nature to the point that it could not provide for humans' needs. It covered every issue and international policy related to the environment and development in its nearly three hundred pages. Among its thirty-eight chapters were provisions calling upon developing nations to have local citizens participate in sustainable development initiatives. Others urged decentralization of decision-making so as to give communities a greater say in addressing such matters as desertification, poverty, and agriculture. Agenda 21 also enjoined national governments to do more to permit women a greater part in sustainable development. To oversee Agenda 21's implementation, the delegates at Rio established the Commission on Sustainable Development (CSD), a fifty-three-nation body chosen by the UN's Economic and Social Council. Envisioned as a complement rather than a replacement for UNEP, the CSD offered another means of coordinating decision-making among the UN's agencies[73]

## The resistance to environmental regimes

Despite leaving much unaccomplished, the two decades between Stockholm and Rio had witnessed a continuation of environmentalists' desire to compel humans to go further to protect their planet's well-being. This led to the creation of international regimes aimed at ending shipments of hazardous waste, reducing acid rain, preserving the ozone layer, preventing climate change, and focusing on not just single species of animals or plants, but entire ecosystems. Anthropocentrism, however, was not by any means dead. In both the North and South, resistance to these regimes persisted, particularly when they threatened national sovereignty or economic development.

There were additional complications. One was the provisions of the agreements themselves. The FCCC was weak, the Basel Convention covered neither pesticides nor radioactive waste, and the Bamako Convention's provisions regarding radioactive materials focused solely on their import. Individual articles within the conventions were subject to interpretation. The Basel Convention's call for "environmentally sound management" of waste was one such case. The CBD's Article 9 called for creating "a system of protected areas or areas where special measures need to be taken to conserve biological diversity," but what constituted "protected areas" or "special measures" was not clear.[74]

Funding from IFIs provided another stumbling block in creating international regimes. In 1979, UNEP decided to look more closely into nine of these institutions' lending practices. It found "a general absence (with the partial exception of the World Bank) of systematic attention to environmental impacts of all stages of project conception, design, and execution." NGOs joined the cause, accusing the IFIs of not doing enough to incorporate environmental considerations into their decision-making, and found a U.S. Congress willing to listen. American lawmakers began environmental oversight of the IADB, the Overseas Private Investment Corporation, and the Export-Import Bank. Indeed, the IDB refused a request from Brazil for money for a highway on the grounds that it would encourage deforestation in the Amazon.[75]

NGOs and members of the U.S. Congress also called on the World Bank to heed protection of the environment. Although Capitol Hill could not directly affect the Bank's lending policies, it could indirectly do so by not providing funding for it. Then, in 1986, Barber Conable, who had formerly represented the State of New York in the U.S. Congress, became the World Bank's new head. Cognizant of the demands that his institution do more to underwrite "green" projects rather than those that destroyed the environment, he announced the creation of a new Environment Department within the bank and of a Tropical Forest Action Plan (TFAP) that would offer hundreds of millions of dollars to combat deforestation in tropical areas. Shortly before he resigned his position in 1991, he formed the Global Environment Facility (GEF) to oversee funding to address climate change, water pollution, depletion of the ozone layer, and the loss of biodiversity.[76]

For all their hype, neither TFAP nor the GEF met expectations. The FAO, which was given the job of implementing the Action Plan, directed relatively little funding toward the welfare of forests, nor did it try to encourage policy reforms by the countries targeted. Instead, money oftentimes went to "brown" projects that encouraged further exploitation of flora. Not until the early 1990s did an expansion in the number of "green" projects take place, but even then, more support went to "brown" ones. The GEF has provided billions of dollars toward the projects it oversees. But the Facility views its primary purpose as encouraging investment to the four problems it is charged with solving. Since 1992, it has provided or raised over $100 billion for numerous problems worldwide. Yet $100 billion is only a fraction of what is necessary. The Asian Development Bank in 1994, for example, estimated that India alone would need $135 billion.[77]

The questions of interpretation of international agreements and IFI funding were tied to the greatest challenge to creating international environmental regimes, that of bringing national sovereignty and national interest in accord with those regimes. One example was the unwillingness of developed nations to offer the aid they had promised at UNCED to LDCs, citing economic expediency. Another was the moratorium on whaling. It was to end in 1990, and both Japan and Norway looked forward to once again hunting the cetaceans. To their anger, the IWC decided in 1990 to extend the suspension for another year. In 1994, it went further by banning all whaling south of 40° south latitude, thus establishing a sanctuary for a sizable portion of the planet's whale population. Norway, which had resisted the moratorium, resumed whaling in 1993, despite international objections. Japan, for its part, found a way around it. The 1946 International Convention for the Regulation of Whaling permitted the killing of whales for "scientific purposes," so the Japanese government used that rationale to furnish a large number of whaling permits. In 1987, it instituted the Japanese Whale Research Program under Special Permit in the Antarctic, or JARPA, which it continued even after the creation of the Antarctic sanctuary. In 1994, Tokyo undertook a similar program for the Northwest Pacific, called JARPN. Despite its claims regarding science, much of the whale meat ended up not in laboratories but on the commercial market.[78]

If Japan represented the continued resistance coming from advanced nations, its neighbor, the People's Republic of China (PRC), which had considered itself a representative for LDCs, offered challenges of its own. Following the death in 1976 of its founder, Mao Zedong, the PRC entered an era of economic reform and became more aware of the need to protect the environment. Both were easier said than done. The Chinese Communist Party (CCP) refused to permit the level of political freedom witnessed in the Soviet bloc, fearful that to do so would mean its downfall. Such fear became apparent in the party's harsh crackdown on pro-democracy activists in Beijing's Tiananmen Square in 1989. Scientists with concerns about the Three Gorges Dam—a massive hydroelectric project that began in 1994—had to express their caution with the utmost care, lest they find themselves out of a job. That corruption infused the CCP did not help matters. Finally, the PRC's infrastructure, which the CCP sought to modernize, was deficient. A lack of sewage plants meant that even in the mid-1980s, 90 percent of the country's effluents went untreated. With a large population and relatively little acreage for growing crops, it relied heavily on fertilizers and pesticides. Its energy sector rested largely on coal, so much so that during the first half of the 1980s, China witnessed the most rapid increase of $CO_2$ emissions of any nation. The number of so-called cancer villages and people suffering from pollution-induced illnesses rose.[79] Thus, despite all of the steps taken forward by the early 1990s, it was clear that creating international regimes in the face of individual countries' interests, differences between North and South, and the IFIs' perceived mandates, was going to be a long, drawn-out process.

# CHAPTER SIX

# The Anthropocene epoch?

The UN Conference on the Environment and Development (UNCED) ended with guarded optimism. "The Miracle was that it happened at all and that, in the end, some agreement however tentative and laced with compromise— was reached between the representatives of such a diverse group of over 170 countries," commented Frank McDonald of the *Irish Times*. "Yet the vast bulk of them started their journeys home yesterday having committed themselves, at least in theory, to setting out on the path of 'sustainable development.'" Paul Lewis, writing in the *New York Times*, adopted a similar tone. "The Earth Summit, which wound up with predictable fanfare today, has given the world its first real glimpse of the kind of global diplomacy that is becoming possible now that the cold war is over," he wrote. "But the conference has also shown how difficult negotiating worldwide solutions to worldwide problems is likely to be."[1]

The dichotomy between identifying problems and finding solutions for them indeed proved hard to overcome over the next two decades. New international environmental agreements, among them the Convention to Combat Desertification, the Rotterdam Convention on Pesticides, and the Stockholm Convention on Persistent on Organic Pollutants, were steps forward. So were the 2002 World Summit on Sustainable Development (WSSD) held in Johannesburg, South Africa, and, more significantly, the United Nations Climate Change Conference that took place in Paris in 2015. Differences, though, lingered over how to stop desertification and overexploitation of forests, address genetically modified organisms, protect marine life, regulate the shipments of hazardous waste, and come to grips with climate change. In many cases, these differences continued to fall along a North-South axis, with lesser developed countries (LDCs) giving priority to economic growth. But DCs, especially the United States, and, at times, IFIs, dug in their heels as well in the name of national or economic security. Nature's power, especially the 2011 tsunami that damaged the nuclear power plant in Fukushima, Japan, raised anew questions about nuclear power and drew worldwide attention to the trash dumped by humans in the ocean. By the time of Paris, some scientists and academics suggested that the planet was well into a new historical epoch, the Anthropocene, and warned that unless humans adopted more serious efforts to protect the globe's ecosystem of which they were a part, Earth's future looked dim.

## Addressing the Rio Agenda

As excited as the delegates who left UNCED were with having agreed to the Framework Convention on Climate Change, the Convention on Biological Diversity, and Agenda 21, there was a realization that the agenda remained incomplete. Protection of forests was one example. DCs sought some form of international regulations but met resistance from developing states, who argued that DCs were infringing of their national sovereignty. Frustrated with the lack of progress, the World Wildlife Fund (WWF) in 1993 created the Forest Stewardship Council (FSC). Its purpose is to bring together environmental groups, forest owners, and timber companies in finding common measures to regulate forest use. It established a voluntary process by which those who own or exploit forests can receive an FSC certificate by permitting an inspector to determine if the owner or industry is following FSC standards of responsible practice. To the WWF, this cooperative means of protecting forests was more likely to achieve success than the past tactic of embargoing timber.[2]

The possibility of an environmental NGO establishing a method of certifying forest products did not sit well with the timber industry in Canada, Australia, and New Zealand. At the Intergovernmental Panel on Forests (IPF), a body established by the UN to meet Agenda 21's call to combat deforestation, these three nations called the FSC's certification system a form of "disguised protectionism" that endangered free trade and proposed their own certification program. Further, they wanted both national governments and international organizations to regulate schemes like that tabled by the FSC. The European Union (EU) and a number of NGOs regarded the stance adopted by Canada, New Zealand, and Australia as too stringent. Searching for a middle ground, the IPF in 1997 adopted language that called for states to "ensure, as necessary, that [certification] schemes are not used as a form of disguised protectionism." That counterstance failed to stop the growing influence of the FSC, which by the start of 1999 had certified fifteen million hectares of timber in over two dozen countries.[3]

As before, though, IFIs and the governments of developing countries did not necessarily comply with these efforts to encourage protection of forests. During 1997 and 1998, the World Bank and International Monetary Fund both provided loans to Indonesia, with each of them insisting on reforms designed to protect that country's forests. That annoyed both Indonesia's government and its lumber industry. Plywood was and remains one of Indonesia's top exports, and the companies involved had little incentive to engage in programs that threatened to cut into their profits. Accordingly, Jakarta failed to meet pledges to do more to protect its forests. Even then, though, the World Bank provided $400 million in loans to Indonesia in 1999, thus giving away an opportunity to use financial leverage to promote greater environmental protections.[4]

Protections for forests and the North-South divide became tied to another matter left unresolved at Rio, desertification. Despite millions of dollars in assistance, including a $750 million loan from the UN's International Fund for Agricultural Development in 1985, desertification had worsened as the 1990s got underway. Lesser developed nations had wanted to see progress on writing a desertification convention at Rio, but the only industrialized state to join them was France, which had a history of connections to Africa. Other DCs and the World Bank balked, blaming desertification on policies adopted by African governments rather than on the lack of an international agreement to combat it. A sudden shift in position by the United States changed the atmosphere at UNCED. Desirous for African help to resolve other outstanding issues then on the agenda at Rio, including forests, the US government declared itself supportive of a desertification convention. Additional industrialized nations followed suit, leading the plea for an international desertification agreement to become part of Agenda 21.[5]

Negotiations to produce a convention began in 1993. The Organization of African Unity, which assumed a central role in the negotiations, insisted that the foreign debts owed by African nations and the price of international commodities weakened their ability to put money toward combating desertification. Moreover, LDCs, including China and some members of the Group of 77, contended that developed nations should establish a fund to help fight desertification. Countries in the North resisted. They favored addressing international economic matters in a different forum and rejected the thought of being financially responsible in assisting LDCs to combat a problem that they believed those lesser developed nations had created. DCs eventually agreed to "give due attention" to questions of debts and trade. As for financing, the United States succeeded in breaking that impasse by proposing a "global mechanism" that would be placed "within an existing institution" and that would be overseen by the convention's parties.[6]

Having found language acceptable to all sides, the Convention to Combat Desertification was opened for signature in the fall of 1994 and went into force two years later. It was unique in that it originally had been proposed by developing nations and became reality in the face of opposition among DCs. Its language gives primacy to Africa. However, desertification was not just an African problem, and so each region received its own annex. The convention addressed the social, economic, physical, and biological effects of desertification, as well as action programs to combat it. Since being opened for signature, every member of the UN has ratified the convention. Even so, desertification continued to present a serious challenge, particularly in Africa, where as late as the year 2000, some 300 million people faced the threat of water shortages.[7]

Unlike forests and desertification, the delegates at Rio had tackled biodiversity and signed the Convention on Biological Diversity (CBD). In 1993, the CBD went into force, thanks in part to the decision of the recently elected president of the United States, Bill Clinton, to reverse US policy and endorse it. But the CBD had some important shortcomings. In addition to the vagueness of some of its articles, parties to the convention had resisted mandates on particularly contentious matters, such as forests and marine life. Thus, the CBD's parties turned to less controversial subjects, among them biosafety. At issue here was making sure that any genetically modified organisms (GMOs) created by modern technology could be safely shipped, used, and disposed.[8]

The idea of a biosafety protocol first arose in the 1980s, when it appeared the technology to create GMOs was likely to lead to their commercial sale. LDCs were the strongest advocates of such a protocol, anxious that modified organisms could prove unsafe. The preparatory meetings began in Denmark in 1996, and at first the delegates split along a North-South axis. Gradually, though, rifts appeared among the developed and developing countries. Ethiopia favored a more comprehensive protocol than Latin American nations, including Uruguay, Argentina, and Chile, which believed GMOs could prove highly profitable. The United States, Australia, and Canada joined those Latin American states. But it was the nations that leaned in favor of a more strongly worded protocol that had the upper hand in the negotiations. They had the endorsement of the EU. More amenable to the precautionary principle than the United States, the nations of the EU already had in place restrictions on the sale and use of GMOs. It was in the tropics where most of the raw materials on which the biotech companies relied, and the majority of the states with tropical climates were LDCs. Still, it was not until they met at Cartagena, Colombia, in 2000 that the attendees reached agreement on a Protocol on Biosafety. It took another three years for it to go into effect. Relying on the precautionary principle, it seeks to balance the economic advantage gained from international sale of GMOs with a country's well-being. Specifically, it allows a nation to ban the import of GMOs if it believes those goods might endanger public health or efforts to protect biodiversity.[9] Today, it has 170 parties.

## NAFTA

At the time of his election, one of Bill Clinton's greatest concerns was not the environment but fending off the recession that had taken hold of the

United States in 1990. To him, the route to renewed economic health was to accept the trend toward globalization taking place worldwide. That word, "globalization," had first been coined in 1983 by the editor of the *Harvard Business Review*, Theodore Levitt.[10] It referred to the way in which modern information technology, particularly computers, had revolutionized international trade by creating an integrated global market. It was not necessarily a new concept. By the early 1900s, technological advances, among them the telephone, telegraph, railroad, oil-powered ships, and the Suez and Panama Canals, had tied the world more closely together commercially. Corporations in major industrial nations, with the assistance of the banking sector, were selling their products worldwide, establishing branches in other countries, and augmenting production through horizontal or vertical integration (merging with similar companies to command more of the market or acquiring companies to give the mother firm more control over the manufacturing process of a good).

By the end of the 1900s, that financial, technological, and commercial interconnectedness had become even tighter. There were more than 60,000 parent corporations and nearly 700,000 foreign affiliates. Numerous companies had offices and production facilities in countries around the world. To President Clinton, these facts were proof of capitalism's triumph. Now, with the collapse of communism in the Soviet Union and Eastern Europe, capitalism had the opportunity to spread even further and faster than before. As part of that process, it became important to reduce or eliminate barriers to investment and trade. Companies, the people who worked in them, and the industrialized countries in which they were based would benefit as access to new markets enhanced profit margins. But LDCs would do well also, argued free trade advocates, for the lack of commercial barriers would encourage investment in LDCs, make it easier for those nations in the South to export products, provide them with access to advanced technology, create jobs, and promote economic growth. Convinced that free trade would pull the United States out of its recession, foster a better world, and win him political points at home, Clinton made one of his first acts that of seeking ratification of the North American Free Trade Agreement (NAFTA).[11]

NAFTA's history began in 1987 when President Ronald Reagan and Canadian prime minister Brian Mulroney signed a pact to eliminate tariffs between their countries. Reagan then sought to have Mexico sign on as well, but it was not until after the election of Carlos Salinas de Gortari in 1988 that Mexico exhibited an interest. Like Mulroney and Reagan, Salinas believed a more liberal trade policy would reap economic benefits for his country and a political windfall for himself. The same was the case for George H. W. Bush, Reagan's successor who had to contend with the recession that began on his watch. The negotiations commenced in 1991, and created an unlikely alliance in the United States between organized labor and environmentalists. Labor unions cautioned that Mexico's slack labor standards and meager wages would force business owners in both the United States and Canada to have to do the same to compete. For American environmentalists, as well as their Canadian counterparts, NAFTA increased the likelihood of causing harm to flora and fauna as people moved to take advantage of the job opportunities opened by the agreement, natural resources came under greater pressure, and industry transferred operations to those countries—most likely Mexico—where environmental laws were nonexistent or poorly enforced, and environmental NGOs were weak. Knowing that the U.S. Senate and Canadian Parliament would have to ratify NAFTA gave environmental NGOs in those two countries significant leverage in making sure that their agenda was included in NAFTA's provisions.[12]

An apparently unrelated international dispute served the environmentalists' cause. Since the 1950s, US tuna fishermen working out of California in the Eastern Tropical Pacific Fishery had complained about the use of purse-seine nets—boat-drawn nets as long as a mile—to encircle and catch tuna. The nets worked as intended insofar as tuna, but they also captured and killed or injured large numbers of dolphins. The harm caused to dolphins played a part in the passage of the 1972 Marine Mammal Protection Act (MMPA), one provision of which required reducing dolphin kills to "insignificant levels approaching zero." When environmentalists realized that no information was being kept to ensure dolphins' safety, they succeeded in getting a court-ordered embargo pending evidence that efforts were being taken to protect dolphins. The order primarily affected Mexico and Venezuela, which had been expanding their presence in tuna fishing. An unhappy Bush administration imposed the embargo.[13]

As the United States was (and is) the globe's largest commercial market, the imposition of such sanctions stood to seriously impact whichever nation it targeted. Unwilling to stand pat, Mexico in 1991 filed a complaint with the General Agreement on Tariffs and Trade (GATT). Established shortly after the Second World War, GATT's purpose was to liberalize worldwide commerce through the elimination of trade barriers. Washington fought back, justifying its action not only on the MMPA but on GATT's Article XX, which permitted restrictions on trade to safeguard human health, to conserve animal or plant species, or to prevent depletion of "exhaustible natural resources." The United States declared it had met that criteria by protecting the lives of dolphins and, in so doing, conserving an exhaustible resource. Now joined by Venezuela, Mexico insisted that dolphins were not an endangered species. Furthermore, to buckle under to Washington would harm their countries' economic well-being and deny their people an essential source of protein.[14]

The GATT panel sided with the plaintiffs. For one, it stated, the United States had based its case on the product itself, not on how it was obtained. Additionally, it declared that Article XX could not permit an exception because that provision did not apply beyond US jurisdiction. Simply put, GATT took the position that restricting commerce for environmental reasons risked establishing a precedent that could imperil global trade.

In 1992, Mexico, Venezuela, and the United States reached an accord to impose a five-year moratorium on seine-net fishing in return for permitting imports of tuna from those nations. Furthermore, Mexico and Venezuela accepted a reimposition of the embargo if they violated the agreement. That last provision pleased environmentalists, who otherwise would have resisted the pact.[15]

The protection of dolphins played an important part in the inclusion of environmental provisions in NAFTA. Using their influence in Canada and the United States, environmental NGOs insisted that if GATT was going to be indifferent to Mexico's treatment of dolphins, then it was up to the individuals assigned by Ottawa and Washington to the NAFTA negotiations to make sure that that agreement contained environmental provisions. In that effort, they succeeded. When ratified by the three parties in 1993, NAFTA itself eliminated trade barriers between them. But alongside NAFTA was a supplementary pact, called the North American Agreement on Environmental Cooperation (NAAEC). The NAAEC seeks to promote collaboration among the parties by establishing a review process to enforce measures to protect the environment, with the intention of creating over time a unified environmental policy. NAFTA's signatories established the North American Commission on Environmental Cooperation to enforce the NAAEC and to settle disputes among them via arbitration. Should any party fail to abide by the commission's findings, the NAAEC provides a foundation for the imposition of trade sanctions to force compliance.[16]

NAFTA and the NAAEC have their weaknesses. It is one thing to try to bring harmony among three nations' environmental policies and another to achieve that goal. Citing both national security and sovereignty, NAFTA's signatories have continued to adopt their own environmental initiatives, and each enforces within its borders the environmental standards it has established. NAFTA and the NAAEC are, therefore, similar to numerous other environmental agreements where the desire to create a single regime to protect flora, fauna, and humans have had to contend with each party's individual priorities.[17]

# Marine life

The legal challenge to US restrictions on tuna fishing was just one example of international disagreements regarding who should oversee protections for marine life and how far such protections should extend. The suspension of commercial whaling remained in force, despite attempts by Ireland in 1997 and 1999 to end it. Ireland had suggested permitting catches up to 1 percent of a whale species' population if there was scientific evidence that the population was large enough to permit kills. It also sought to prohibit whaling for scientific purposes. Environmental NGOs and the majority of the IWC's members rejected the Irish approaches, fearful that they would open the door to a resumption of commercial whaling.[18]

It was Japan, though, that proved most defiant. Its provision of financial assistance to other countries bore dividends in 2000, when six Caribbean countries that received Japanese aid joined Tokyo in defeating a plan to establish a whale sanctuary in the South Pacific. More importantly, Japan continued to use the Convention for the Regulation of Whaling (CRW) to justify kills for "scientific purposes." On this score, Tokyo in 2002 and 2005, respectively, initiated JARPN II and JARPA II. Between 1988 and 2007, 10,857 whales fell victim to Japanese whalers, of which nearly 92 percent were killed on "scientific" grounds. This compared to approximately 2,100 whales killed for that same reason between 1948 and 1987.[19]

In 2010, Australia challenged Japan's use of the "scientific" loophole by bringing JARPA II before the UN's International Court of Justice (ICJ). In March 2014, the ICJ found JARPA II was in violation of the CRW and ordered Tokyo to halt further whaling off Antarctica. The ICJ, however, has no enforcement mechanism. In 2015, after abiding by the International Court's decision for a year, Japan announced its intention to resume Antarctic whaling, despite international criticism.[20]

## Hazardous waste

If UNCED had given short shrift to desertification and forests, the delegates had called in Principle 14 and in Agenda 21 for doing more to combat the hazardous waste trade. By the early 1990s, some 100,000 chemicals were being used, generating a growing amount of detritus requiring disposal. With some DCs charging as much as $2,500 per ton to eliminate the waste, exporters searched for less expensive places willing to accept their refuse, and were able to work out at times agreements with African nations for as little as $2.50 a ton. Further confounding those who wanted more regulations over the waste trade was the United States. Not only had that country refused to endorse the Basel Convention—and remains an outlier to the present—but political conservatives, whose influence grew in the United States during the 1990s and into the 2000s, argued that attempts to restrict trade only served to push untoward commercial activities underground. To them, the most effective means of putting a stop to shipments of hazardous waste was to rely on the free market. Once companies realized it was unprofitable to send their detritus elsewhere, stated conservatives, those firms would no longer do so. Finally, and notwithstanding evidence to the otherwise, opponents of Basel claimed that very little of the waste treated in developing nations came from the industrialized world. According to this argument, then, the international community had to stop focusing on the North and take a harder look at LDCs.[21]

Confusing matters even more was the question of the recycling of waste, a subject for which neither the Basel nor the Bamako conventions established separate rules. This loophole permitted industrialized states to argue that the materials on their way to LDCs were not destined for destruction but for reuse. Greenpeace found that whereas just over one-third of all waste was destined for recycling between 1980 and 1988, by 1989, it was just over three-quarters, and in 1993, it had reached nearly 90 percent.[22] As in the case of dumping, a significant amount of items meant for recycling went to countries unable to handle them properly.

There were at least three recycling schemes used by handlers to send their waste abroad. One was reprocessing. The second was "waste-to-energy," by which substances that might otherwise be dumped instead ended up incinerators, where it provided power. The last, which became increasingly common thanks to the increasing number of personal electronics (particularly cell phones, laptops, and media players), was to donate older models to Third World nations, where they could be used for spare parts, turned into scrap, or, once they broke down, thrown out. Recycling did save money for countries concerned about the cost of making those same products from scratch: recycled steel, for instance, needs 60 percent less energy to produce than that made from raw ore. Yet the process increased the amount of pollution in LDCs. According to Greenpeace, Indian recycling companies accepted over 100,000 metric tons of waste from 1998 to 1999, including zinc ash, used batteries, and lubricating oils. In South Africa, a plant owned by the British company Thor Chemicals reprocessed mercury, which left many of the workers with mercury poisoning and a river used for human purposes contaminated. In mid-2003, Thor ended up having to pay twenty-four million South African Rand (or about $1.75 million in current US dollars) to clean up the contamination.[23]

Restricting commerce in hazardous waste continued to draw attention to pesticides. According to some researchers, by the early 1990s, about 80 percent of all pesticide-related deaths occurred in the developing world. Since the 1950s international rules covering the management of pesticides fell under the auspices of the UN's Food and Agriculture Organization, while UNEP did the same for chemicals since its inception in the 1970s. In the 1980s, both agencies adopted the procedure of prior informed consent (PIC) to cover the importation of hazardous materials. In 1996, UNEP and the FAO instituted what became two years of negotiations that would place chemicals and pesticides under a single regulatory umbrella. The Netherlands asked to host the signing ceremony, which took place in the city of Rotterdam.[24]

The Rotterdam Convention on the Prior Informed Consent Procedure for Certain Hazardous Chemicals and Pesticides in International Trade applied PIC to the dozens of chemicals listed in its annexes. Which pesticides appeared on those lists reflected the bargaining that had taken place among the delegates. Much of it had been not between the countries of the North and South but among the DCs themselves. For instance, a group led by the United States wanted to keep the scope of the convention limited to a certain number of chemicals, while the EU favored a broader mandate. It was the former point of view that won out, with the focus placed on those chemicals considered "severely hazardous." Significant as well was that whereas the Basel Convention prohibited the export of chemicals in certain cases, Rotterdam only required the sharing of information, leaving it up to the nations involved to decide how to proceed. Moreover, the convention lacked any requirements for developed nations to provide financial assistance to developing countries. This has been attributed to time constraints as well as the fact that the convention's primary concern was the exchange of information as opposed to wider obligations.[25] Not until 2004, when it had the requisite number of ratifications, did the Rotterdam Convention go into effect.

What Rotterdam did not address were so-called persistent organic pollutants (POPs), defined as chemicals, including some pesticides, that enter the environment, can be transported by the air or living organisms far from where used, accumulate in the food chain, and place humans and the environment in potential danger. Here again, Rio entered the picture, as Agenda 21 called for doing more to tackle such substances. UNEP accordingly called for negotiations to create an international convention, focusing primarily on the so-called dirty dozen: twelve POPs regarded as particularly dangerous, including the insecticides dieldrin, aldrin, and DDT. By restricting the targeted chemicals to twelve allowed the negotiations to gather momentum, with the hope that if a convention resulted, other dangerous substances might later be added. Further pushing the dialogue along was the fact that many nations had already imposed severe regulations on the chemicals in question.[26]

These discussions culminated in 2001 with the signing by 127 nations of the Stockholm Convention on Persistent Organic Pollutants. Relying also on the precautionary principle, the agreement called for restricting or eliminating production of the twelve substances it covers and encouraged development or use of substitutes. Importantly, though, it provided no timelines for doing either. Moreover, it separated polychlorinated biphenyls (PCBs) and DDT from the others. Recognizing that PCBs were (and are) widely used in the manufacture of transformers and electrical equipment, Stockholm called for phasing them out. Determining that DDT was effective in combating mosquito-spread malaria and that alternatives were less effective, the Stockholm pact permitted the production or use of that chemical, but only for "disease-vector control in accordance" with guidelines established by the WHO. The convention provided a procedure for adding new POPs to the existing list. Finally, it established a financial mechanism by which DCs would provide assistance to LDCs. In 2004, the convention went into effect. Yet there remain a few holdouts, among them the United States, which has taken the position that ratifying Stockholm

PHOTO 8 Fogging DDT spray to kill mosquitoes in Thailand, 2016. *Credit: Dreamstime.*

would necessitate defining hazardous waste more broadly than currently accepted by domestic regulations.[27]

# The ozone layer and climate change

By that time, pesticides had entered into the long-standing debate over climate change. Their application, particularly on large farms, required the use of fossil-fuel-burning equipment. Moreover, one of the substances applied on those farms was methyl bromide, a fumigant employed widely around the world to kill insects and rats. In 1992, it was confirmed to be an ozone depleter and added to the list of chemicals covered by the Montreal Protocol.[28]

Elected that same year, Bill Clinton and, even more so, the new vice president, Al Gore, brought with them an agenda calling for greater environmental protection. Clinton expressed his preparedness to move quickly to eliminate the use of methyl bromide. He was less enthusiastic about eliminating hydrochlorofluorocarbons (HCFCs). A substitute for ozone-damaging CFCs, HCFCs were less harmful to the ozone layer but expected to see more use as CFCs were phased out. At a meeting in Copenhagen in 1992, ninety countries agreed to ban all CFCs four years earlier than originally planned and to eliminate HCFCs by 2030. However, when the European Community in 1993 suggested phasing out HCFCs by 2015, Clinton balked. Many US companies had invested in HCFCs, and the Clinton administration wanted to give them more time to recoup any financial losses as they switched to substitutes. If anything, said Washington, getting rid of methyl bromide was more likely to protect the ozone layer than quickly doing away with HCFCs.[29]

Clinton was more amenable to doing what George H. W. Bush had rejected: adopting specific targets designed to reduce carbon emissions. That was the central concern of the more than 6,000 official delegates, hundreds of reporters, and thousands of NGO representatives who attended a summit in Kyoto, Japan, in 1997. The delegates agreed that some three dozen DCs, among them the United States, would curb their carbon emissions by just over 5 percent of 1990 levels between 2008 and 2012. How to achieve that goal was a matter of debate. The United States, which produced 36 percent of the world's $CO_2$, wanted "flexible mechanisms," such as the right to trade emissions credits. Likewise, it favored a "clean development mechanism" in which DCs could compensate for their emissions by working to curb those in less developed nations. Additionally, because rapid industrialization was taking place in countries such as India and China, and because developing nations tended to use fossil fuels less efficiently for transportation or power generation, the United States asked that Kyoto require LDCs to curb their carbon emissions as well. India, China, and other countries of the South attacked such a suggestion, blaming most global warming on the industrialized world. Australia, which had recently elected a conservative government, also fought back, asserting that in light of its growing population and dependence on fossil fuels, it needed more lax targets.[30]

Not wanting to see the talks fail, the Clinton administration sent Gore to Kyoto, where he worked out a compromise. Developed nations accepted what was on average a 5.2 percent reduction in 1990-level emissions by 2012, though the targets themselves varied from one country to another. As an example, members of the EU, which had wanted a 15 percent cut, adopted one of 8 percent, while the United States promised to do the same by 7 percent. Russia and the Ukraine were not required to reduce their greenhouse emissions. Insisting that it faced a unique situation among advanced countries given its size, and reliance on fossil fuels and exports, Australia won an 8 percent *increase* in its 1990 emissions by 2012, which it said amounted to a decrease in what otherwise would have been far higher emissions. Meanwhile, LDCs successfully fended off efforts to include them in the Kyoto agreement, even rejecting a provision that would have permitted them voluntarily to adopt emissions targets. As a further incentive to encourage ratification, the protocol permitted the trading of emissions credits, meaning that a nation like the United States could purchase credits from parties like Russia that did not have to cut emissions. Clinton, however, decided not to submit the protocol to the U.S. Senate for ratification after senators unanimously declared they would not endorse an agreement that failed to include developing nations.[31]

# Johannesburg

Three years after Kyoto, American voters selected George W. Bush as their new president. Long having ties to energy companies, including serving as chairman of the oil company Spectrum 7, Bush vowed to cut back on environmental regulations that he said stifled business and to adopt a more unilateralist foreign policy than had his predecessors. His antienvironmental agenda became evident when he announced shortly after his inauguration America's withdrawal from the agreements reached in Japan. His decision infuriated US allies that had signed Kyoto and triggered protests throughout Europe.[32]

The anger felt toward the Bush administration's demotion of the environment was evident during the 2002 WSSD held in Johannesburg, South Africa. Because its purpose was to review the progress achieved on the UNCED agenda, it lacked the anticipation that had surrounded its predecessor. Affecting the meeting's atmosphere as well was the aftermath of the September 2001 terrorist attacks on the World Trade Center and Pentagon buildings. Stock markets plummeted worldwide and oil prices rose, creating a downturn in the global economy and fear of a worldwide recession. Declaring a "war on terror," the Bush administration, supported by the North Atlantic Treaty Organization, sent military forces to Afghanistan in October 2001 and overthrew that country's Taliban-led government, which had provided a safe haven to al-Qaeda. Early the next year, President Bush announced the existence of an "Axis of Evil," made up of Iraq, Iran, and North Korea, further ratcheting up worldwide tensions. Protecting the environment remained low on the White House's list of priorities. Knowing his disinterest in the environment likely would engender a cold reception if he attended the WSSD, Bush sent as his representative Secretary of State Colin Powell. Hecklers denounced Powell during his speech before the delegates, shouting "Shame on Bush."[33]

Ultimately, little new came out of the WSSD. The United Nations in 2000 had adopted eight Millennium Development Goals (MDGs). Each MDG had targets, designed to promote sustainable international development. Goal 7, "To ensure environmental sustainability," included such targets as achieving a "significant reduction" in biodiversity loss by 2010, and reducing by half by 2015 the number of people lacking "sustainable access to safe drinking water and basic sanitation." The parties at Johannesburg reiterated these goals, and to "restore fisheries to maximum sustainable yield" by 2015. The United States promised $36 million to protect the rain forest in Congo, and it joined the WWF, Brazil, and other countries in offering $81 million to increase the amount of land protected in Brazil. Canada and Russia declared they would ratify Kyoto, giving the accords enough endorsements to go into effect. For the most part, though, hard targets were not adopted. The United States, joined by Australia, Japan, Canada, and Saudi Arabia, objected to deadlines by when they would convert from using fossil fuels to renewable energy sources. Johannesburg lacked the country-specific targets on greenhouse gas emissions adopted at Kyoto. And developing countries joined with the United States in opposing language that would have required them "to significantly reduc[e] the threat that dangerous chemicals pose to health and the environment." Still, UNEP executive director Klaus Toepfer tried to put a positive spin on the WSSD, stating that it was "more workmanlike" than Rio, "reflecting perhaps a feeling among many nations that they no longer want to promise the earth and fail, that they would rather step forward than run too fast."[34]

## The challenges persist

Despite such positive assessments of the WSSD, old problems persisted, if not grew worse, and new ones appeared. Many of them related to the impact of globalization and the emphasis in LDCs on economic growth. The Mexico City conference on population and development was followed with a meeting in Cairo in 1994, where the delegates adopted a twenty-year action plan to encourage greater education for women; reduce the rate of immorality among pregnant women, infants, and children; and give families greater access to contraception and family planning services. Conferences to mark the fifth and ninth anniversaries of the Cairo gathering took place, in 1999 and 2003, respectively. In 2014, the UN General Assembly held a special session during which it called on all members to abide by the commitments they had made at Cairo. But the lack of international summits since 2003 on overpopulation suggests that the subject lacks the political consequence of other global matters.[35]

Feeding a world population that had reached six billion as of 1999 and almost seven billion a decade later intensified the search for higher-yield crops and better ways of eliminating the weeds and pests that menaced foodstuffs. Thanks to research conducted at the US agricultural company Monsanto in the mid-1990s, increasing yields appeared a certainty. In 1974, Monsanto had developed Roundup, a highly effective glyphosate herbicide that was soon sold worldwide. The problem with Roundup was that it was nonselective. Hence, if applied incorrectly, it killed not just weeds but the crops farmers wanted to protect. In 1996, however, Monsanto unveiled the first of its so-called Roundup ready crops: soybean seeds that were immune to Roundup. Accordingly, it was possible for a farmer to grow foodstuffs and use a glyphosate compound simultaneously, with the added benefit of producing a higher yield.[36]

In Argentina, a country once known for its beef industry, farmers saw a lucrative opportunity and started buying Monsanto's seeds. By 2013, soy farming had expanded to 47 million acres (300 percent). Genetically modified corn, cotton, and wheat also became widely used. But there were serious problems with these crops. The seeds they produced were sterile, forcing farmers to buy the latest plant-ready seeds from the manufacturer. Weeds became resistant to Roundup. So did insects that agriculturalists had tried to eliminate using existing pesticides. Farmers in Argentina, therefore, had to increase how many chemicals they used, reaching as much as 4.3 pounds per acre, or double that of their counterparts in the United States. Furthermore, Argentina's provinces had no consistent rules regarding where chemicals could be sprayed. Thus, as in Africa, pesticides were used by people lacking proper protection and near populated areas. Doctors began to record a higher rate of birth defects following the approval of genetically modified crops. Yet rarely were those who broke the law punished.[37]

The encouragement of economic growth also contributed to the destruction of forest. Government officials converted mangrove forests in Southeast Asia and South America to aquaculture. The fish and shrimp population declined, as some species relied on mangroves to reproduce. In Cambodia, the government in the 1990s began to offer land concessions to spur its economy. Socfin, a company based in Luxembourg that encourages the development of rubber and oil palm plantations, took advantage of the offer and signed a joint venture with Phnom Penh. Socfin in 2008 began to bulldoze the fields and forests on which Cambodia's Bunong people lived to clear the land for rubber plantations that would provide for China's growing automobile industry. The Bunong argued that they were neither warned nor offered compensation for the land as required by Cambodian law. When presented with remuneration, many felt they had no choice but to accept it, even though they considered it too little to make up for all they had lost.[38]

The desire to generate income continued as well to make nations in the South willing to accept hazardous waste. Much of it was electronic waste (or e-waste), such as computers, mobile phones, and televisions, with up to 80 percent of American e-waste being sent to LDCs as the second decade of the 2000s got underway. By the early 2010s, China was importing millions of pounds of waste. Tens of thousands of Chinese worked in waste recycling, with at times entire villages focused on individual products. A large proportion of that trash was unrecyclable, while other items ended up in poorly designed smelters, where they polluted the air, soil, and water. UNEP executive director Achim Steiner in 2015 warned of a "tsunami of e-waste rolling out over the world" that posed a threat to flora, fauna, and humans.[39]

Even when the trends looked promising, the desire to encourage growth discouraged environmentalists. The Convention on Long-Range Transboundary Air Pollution gained new members as a result of the breakup of the Soviet Union and the desire of the former Soviet states to win favor among members of the EU. Consequently, in Europe and North America, sulfur dioxide emissions fell by more than three-quarters and nitrogen oxide by about 30 percent in the twenty-five years after the convention was opened for signing.[40]

Freed of the shackles of the Kremlin, though, those same former Soviet states regarded it as essential to give priority to economic growth and political stability. The Aral Sea revealed the aftereffects. The former Soviet republics surrounding that body of water signed in 1992 an agreement on "Cooperation in the Management, Utilization, and Protection of Water Resources of Interstate Sources." In it, each party promised not to use Aral Sea's water to the detriment of the others, and to determine how much water could be used each year to keep it from drying up. Yet the demand for irrigation had reduced the size of that body of water by 90 percent by 2007.[41]

Outside of the former Soviet bloc, Lake Chad, once sixth on the list of the planet's biggest lakes, suffered a fate similar to the Aral Sea. By 2013, it too had shrunk in size by 90 percent, depriving about thirty million Africans of water. More than one-half of Nigerians lacked clean water, placing it third, behind China and India, in the number of people without such access. Low incomes in Nigeria meant that some families had to devote half their income to water purchases.[42]

What happened to Lake Chad became particularly important given its link to the question of security. A number of reasons were offered as to why the lake began disappearing, though they all appear to intersect. Nigerians' need for wood led that country by 2005 to have among the world's highest rate of deforestation. Fewer trees permitted more silt to enter the lake, and contributed to desertification and a dryer climate. Climate change and drought only made a bad situation worse. With the lake drying up, farmers and herders residing nearby moved elsewhere, where they competed with locals for land. Still others traveled to the cities, adding to the size

**PHOTO 9** The ship graveyard of the Aral Sea. *Credit: Dreamstime.*

of slums in them and taxing even further the ability to provide for their inhabitants. Some analysts believed that the sense of hopelessness allowed terrorist groups such as Boko Haram, founded in 2002 in Nigeria, to recruit new members. Unlike the Aral Sea, however, hope for Lake Chad began to appear by the 2010s. To encourage reforestation of the land near Lake Chad, several African countries in the 1980s initiated Operation Sahel. Between 2008 and 2012, over 550,000 trees were planted, covering nearly 41,000 acres, and satellite imagery pointed to an increase in the lake's size.[43]

Desertification did not challenge only people living in Africa. By 2015, approximately 600,000 square kilometers of Brazilian land had desertified. In Mexico, desert annually was eating up 250,000 square kilometers of what had once been farmland. As in Africa, those who relied on those acres for their survival had no choice but to move to the cities. According to one researcher, the combination of lack of water and increase in both the overall and urban population will leave at least eighty million people in Latin America lacking sufficient water supplies by the year 2055.[44]

One method increasingly used to address water scarcity was desalinization. Salty seawater is dangerous to humans, animals, and plants, and therefore, must have the salt removed to be used. By the early 2010s, there were over 16,000 desalinization plants worldwide, with more under construction. They produced 6.7 billion cubic meters of desalinized water per day by 2011, an increase of 276 percent since 2001. There was a price to be paid, though, as the desalinization process required an enormous amount of energy and generated "nearly twice the emissions as treating and reusing the same amount of fresh water."[45]

## The climate conundrum continues

That methods of providing for humans' welfare, including desalinization, emitted greenhouse gases helps explain why no topic continued to draw as much attention as the 2000s got underway as climate change. By 2003, 105 nations had ratified Kyoto, but they included less than half of the world's developed states. It was not until 2005, when Canada and Russia acceded to it, that the protocol finally entered into force. Still, there remained outliers, most notably the United States. Scientists and government officials continued to place the subject before world opinion, not only to continue the momentum created by Kyoto but to convince Washington to join the ratifying parties. In 2006, the British government released a study that tied climate change to global security: if global warming reached as high as many scientists thought possible, then by the year 2100, global domestic product would fall by 5 percent, if not more. Military officials began to worry about the implications of a refugee crisis driven by people forced to leave countries or regions left uninhabitable by climate change. Those in and out of the scientific community who questioned or denied the existence of climate change, whose numbers had been in decline, argued that the world went through warm and cool cycles or used satellite data to show a cooling of temperatures at middle levels of the atmosphere. But their evidence could not offset the enormous amount of data that demonstrated a warming of global temperatures.[46]

Hollywood sought to demonstrate how dangerous the greenhouse effect could be. In 2004, it released *The Day after Tomorrow*, which depicted a paleoclimatologist who sought to locate his son after climate change caused the planet to descend into a new ice age. Two years later, *An Inconvenient Truth* appeared in theaters, documenting Gore's efforts to educate the world's citizenry on the dangers posed by global warming. The former US vice president's warnings drew wide airplay and the attention of the Nobel Prize Committee, which gave him and the IPCC one of its awards in 2007.

The year 2007, as it turned out, brought the link between the environment on the one hand, and war and security on the other, to the forefront of the debate over climate change. The warnings issued by individuals such as Fairfield Osborn, Richard Falk, and Margaret and Harold Sprout received little traction until after the end of the Cold War. By the early 2000s, environmental security had become part of official policy in Russia, Hungary, and Finland. Then, in 2007, British foreign minister Margaret Beckett, who was serving as the president of the UN Security Council, got the Council for the first time to discuss what was an environmental subject, that of climate change. She warned that global warming's impact could "reach to the very heart of the security agenda."[47]

The Arctic Ocean reflected the extent to which climate change had entered the dialogue regarding national and international security. Political, military, and business interests had long sought out in the Northwest Passage, a sea route that would link the Atlantic and Pacific Oceans through the Arctic Ocean. Yet because it was covered by ice, the Arctic was impossible to traverse without proper equipment, such as icebreaking ships. That changed "in September 2007 when for the first time in recorded history," the Northwest Passage became ice-free. Not only did this offer a northern route for interocean shipping comparable to the Panama Canal, but it was known by then that the Arctic Ocean seabed had large stores of minerals. Corporations and militaries sought to claim, use, and protect their interests in the region. Russia exhibited a greater desire to use the Arctic for submarine operations, Canadian prime minister Stephen Harper asserted his country's sovereign interest in the Arctic, China placed a research station on the Norwegian island of Svalbard, and Norway moved the headquarters of its armed forces from near Stavanger in the country's southwest to near Bodo in its north. These moves were worrisome enough to lead the U.S. Navy, Marines, and Coast Guard in 2007 to issue a joint report warning that such "developments . . . are potential sources of competition and conflict for access and natural resources."[48]

The national and international pressure began to force the United States to yield. In 2005, the US government phased out the use of methyl bromide (though it provided an exemption for "critical uses"). In 2007, President George W. Bush admitted that his country had to "confront the serious challenge of global climate change." At a conference held later that year in Indonesia, the delegation of Papua New Guinea spoke directly to the United States, telling the American representatives that "if for some reason you are not willing to lead, leave it to the rest of us. Please, get out of the way." In an unexpected move, the Americans promised to endorse global opinion. Following a moment of surprise, the entire convention hall "erupted in applause."[49]

Exciting to the world community as well was the 2008 election of Barack Obama as Bush's successor to the presidency. More liberal in his political and social views than Bush, he promised a foreign policy that was more multilateral in orientation than his predecessor and gave greater attention to environmental protection. His first trip abroad was to Canada in May 2009, during which he and Canadian prime minister Stephen Harper announced cooperation to encourage "the development of clean energy technologies." He made a similar declaration following a visit two months later with Mexican president Felipe Calderón.[50] At home, he enacted fuel efficiency standards for vehicles and provided more funding for clean energy technology.

Tempering the excitement, however, was a worldwide recession that had begun in the United States in 2008 when a bubble in the real estate market burst. Imbalances in international commerce made the so-called Great Recession worse. Resolving this economic downturn became a top priority in numerous countries. In turn, it remained impossible to reach binding targets aimed at curbing greenhouse gas emissions. Instead, numerous countries downgraded their commitments to reducing carbon dioxide ($CO_2$) emissions and other environmental achievements. The decline in enthusiasm became apparent at the 2009 UN climate summit in Copenhagen, where the signatories promised by 2020 to prevent world temperatures from rising more than 2°C than they had been at the time of the First Industrial Revolution. Yet nothing required signatories to reduce their emissions. Indeed, the World Bank cautioned that the planet was on a path to see temperatures rise nearly 4°C by the year 2100.[51]

In 2014, several climate change reports appeared, including one from the US government's National Climate Assessment, and another from the IPCC. They emphasized that "man-made climate change is a real and ongoing threat." In a study published in March 2015 in *The Proceedings of the National Academy of Sciences*, researchers argued that a drought in Syria that lasted from 2006 to 2009 was likely the result of climate change. That drought, wrote the authors, was one of the reasons for the Syrian civil war that began in 2011. Three months later, Pope Francis issued an encyclical to emphasize the danger posed by climate change, calling it "a global problem with grave implications: environmental, social, economic, political and for the distribution of goods. It represents one of the principal challenges facing humanity in our day."[52]

# Paris

Five months after the encyclical, 196 nations sent representatives to Paris to attend the most significant climate change summit since Kyoto, the United Nations Climate Change Conference. With the nonbinding agreement reached at Copenhagen to expire in 2020, the goal of Paris was to get the world community to adopt mandatory targets to prevent temperatures from increasing more than 2°C than was the case in preindustrial times.

China's position at the summit was of particular significance. It had long sided with LDCs in encouraging economic development over environmental protection. Between 1980 and 2000, its gross domestic product had grown 300 percent. Much of that growth, however, rested on the use of fossil fuels, especially coal. In 2012, China used as much coal as all of planet's other countries combined. The emissions from those power plants threw ever more $CO_2$ into the atmosphere, to the point that since 2005 China's emissions have exceeded those of the United States. In 2014, its per capita $CO_2$ emissions surpassed those of the EU. So much pollution drew China international criticism and pressure to abide by a climate change agreement. Domestically, it created highly dangerous conditions for the Chinese people, if not for the government in Beijing itself. The WHO had declared more than twenty-five micrograms per cubic meter (ug/m³) of fine particles of air pollutants a danger to human health. The United States adopted a looser standard, placing it at 250 micrograms per cubic meter. Yet in January 2013, Beijing, China, reached 526 micrograms per cubic meter, with the smog created being so thick that airlines had to cancel flights. A year later, Beijing's was 671 micrograms per cubic meter. The number of so-called cancer villages, where cases of cancer had increased dramatically over a decade, was as many as four hundred as of 2013, or three hundred more than were recorded five years earlier. With their health at risk, Chinese began to protest against coal-fired power plants. In December 2011, for instance, 30,000 people in the city of Hainan demonstrated against plans to expand a coal-powered facility, going so far as to block a highway and to withstand days of police who attacked them with batons and tear gas. Chen Jiping, a former official of the Chinese Communist Party, warned that pollution had become the single greatest cause of social unrest in the PRC. Realizing the environmental and human consequences of their efforts to grow their nation's economy quickly, China's leaders by late 2015 began to take environmental protection more seriously, and postponed or canceled energy projects that used dirty forms of fuel.[53]

What came out of Paris was more ambitious than the agreement reached in Kyoto. The attendees vowed to keep global temperatures from rising more than 2°C versus preindustrial times. However, even 2°C could melt enough ice and cause the seas to rise high enough to inundate low-lying lands, including island nations, so the delegates expressed their desire to restrict the temperature increase to 1.5°C. Whereas Kyoto required only

DCs to announce publicly by 2020 their measures to reduce emissions Paris imposed that mandate on LDCs as well. Every five years afterward, each party would issue a national report—called an Intended Nationally Determined Contribution, or INDC—to take stock of how well it was doing to reach the goals set forth at Paris. In a concession to LDCs like India that wanted to focus on economic development before emissions reductions, the signatories promised to "reach global peaking of greenhouse gas emissions as soon as possible, recognizing that peaking will take longer for developing country parties, and to undertake rapid reductions thereafter." Additionally, DCs offered to provide $100 billion each year by 2020 to LDCs to help them adopt more environmentally friendly policies.[54] In 2016, with the 55th state ratification, the agreement went into effect.

How possible it was to achieve these goals was (and is) unclear. Brazil, South Africa, India, and China explained in their INDCs how much they plan to reduce their emissions—India, for one, called for reducing it by 33–35 percent of 2005 levels by 2030—but none of them have yet stated what their peak emissions will be. To avoid a review by a potentially hostile U.S. Senate, the $100 billion fund was placed within the "decision" portion of the Paris agreement, not the "action" section. Moreover, it was only a fraction of the total estimated by LDCs; India alone believed it would need US$2.5 trillion to achieve its INDC by 2030. The lack of financial support from public sources has encouraged the parties to Paris to look at private ones. Finally, it was uncertain whether holding to a temperature increase of less than 1.5°C was possible. In fact, the plans submitted by the attending countries were likely to permit an increase of more than 3°C.[55]

Ultimately, what the attendees agreed to at Paris left them and observers with mixed emotions. Pessimists, including representatives of small island and some African states, were anxious that an inability to impose stringent controls on climate change would lead to a worsening of drought, desertification, or inundation by rising waters. Others believed that the INDCs would grow more stringent over time, thereby allowing the international community to reach the 2°C goal set at Paris. A third group took a middle ground. South Africa's minister of Water and Environmental Affairs, Edna Molewa, commented that the Paris accord was "not perfect, but . . . it represents a solid foundation from which we can launch our enhanced action with renewed determination . . . the Agreement is balanced and the best we can do at this historic moment."[56]

## Nuclear power and plastics

Aside from the signing of the Paris climate agreement, the year 2015 was the deadline for achieving the targets set by the MDGs. The UN acknowledged progress toward them was uneven. It thus adopted a resolution, *Transforming*

*Our World: The 2030 Agenda for Sustainable Development*, which presented to the global community seventeen sustainable development goals (SDGs) to supersede the MDGs. They included ending poverty and hunger, encouraging more healthy lifestyles, providing everyone with cheap and clean energy, combating climate change, and sustainably using the planet's oceans.

Nuclear energy offered one potential means of providing climate-friendly power to the world community. However, it had shortcomings. One was safe storage of the radioactive waste they produced. Another was accidents. In 1979, a partial meltdown of a reactor at the Three Mile Island nuclear plant in the U.S. state of Pennsylvania released radioactivity in the atmosphere and created a backlash against atomic power in the United States. The Chernobyl accident in 1986 caused far greater harm to the environment. Still, a significant number of countries, among them Japan, South Korea, France, and Belgium, relied heavily on the atom for power.

In 2011, a massive earthquake measuring 9.0 or 9.1 on the Richter scale occurred off the coast of Japan, shaking buildings throughout much of that country and creating tsunami waves as high as 39.6 meters (130 feet). One of those waves, measuring about fifteen meters (fifty feet), swamped the nuclear power plant at Fukushima and damaged the cooling systems. Three of the four reactors melted down, releasing dangerous levels of radiation into the atmosphere and the surrounding waters. The local and global reaction was quick and intense. Japanese public opinion, which had endorsed nuclear plants as a safe means of providing the country with the power it needed, began to turn to renewable sources, such as solar and wind power. Germany declared it planned to phase out its nuclear power plants and also turn to renewables. France, which relied on the atom for 80 percent of its power, announced its preparedness to reduce that number. Climatologists, energy experts, and the UN's International Atomic Energy Agency insisted that the atom remained one of the surest and safest ways to provide electricity without releasing the greenhouse gases the Paris agreement sought to cut.[57] A significant number of countries signaled that they would continue to pursue nuclear energy or stand behind ongoing atomic programs, and by the fall of 2017 even Tokyo had begun to reconsider reducing its dependence on nuclear power. Still, the antinuclear sentiment expressed following the Fukushima accident has appeared outside of Japan and Europe.[58]

The tsunamis also drew worldwide attention to the amount of trash deposited in the seas. The water picked up enough debris to send an "island" of waste seventy miles long across the ocean. Starting in 2012, that detritus began to arrive on the U.S. West Coast. But there was also waste already in the oceans in so-called trash vortexes. The largest, the "Great Pacific Garbage Patch," is actually two vortexes, one located east of Japan and the other between Hawaii and California. How big it is remains in dispute, with some sources stating it is 700,000 square kilometers and others declaring it is in fact twenty times that size. About 80 percent of the waste in those patches comes from materials deposited from land-based sources. The overwhelming majority of the materials were (and are) made up of plastics, which are buoyant, easily driven by ocean and wind currents, and can survive for as long as a half-century. Arguably, the delegates at Paris championed a reduction in waste by encouraging recycling and discouraging landfills and waste incineration, both of which release greenhouse gases into the air.[59] But the subject was not addressed directly in the final agreement.

## In the Anthropocene?

In the year 2000, atmospheric chemist Paul Crutzen and biologist Eugene Stoermer wrote that the historical era called the Holocene, which had begun around 11,000 years earlier as the last ice age came to an end, had since the late 1700s been replaced by a new epoch called the Anthropocene. "We choose this date," they commented, "because, during the past two centuries, the global effects of human activities have become clearly noticeable. This is the period when data retrieved from glacial ice cores show the beginning of a growth in the atmospheric concentrations of several 'greenhouse gases,' in particular $CO_2$ and $CH_4$. Such a starting date also coincides with James Watt's invention of the steam engine in 1784." Fourteen years later, a series of studies published in the highly respected academic journal *Science* seconded them. The planet itself had gone through five mass extinctions, the last taking place sixty-five million years ago and bringing an end to the dinosaurs. Now, stated the scientists in *Science*, the planet was in a sixth "'mass extinction' of life." In just the past thirty-five years, the human population had doubled. During that same period, the number of invertebrate animals had declined by 45 percent, resulting in what they called an "anthropocene defaunation."[60]

The Crutzen-Stoermer thesis is not universally accepted. Many geologists argue that there is not enough evidence in the Earth's strata to begin talking about replacing the Holocene with the Anthropocene.[61] And for scientists and academics to agree that the planet has entered a new epoch is far different from getting government officials to develop solutions for the myriad of issues involved. Finding that meeting of the minds has posed, and will continue to present, the greatest challenge for international environmental policymaking.

# Accomplishments and challenges

In 2009, the movie *Avatar* appeared in theaters around the world. Set in the year 2154, it depicts an Earth depleted of its resources. Forced to search for raw materials elsewhere, humans, some of them beneficent scientists and others from the unscrupulous Resources Development Administration (RDA), discover an extrasolar moon named Pandora, which is inhabited by ten-foot-tall humanoids called the Na'vi. Unable to breathe Pandora's atmosphere, the scientists create Na'vi-humanoid hybrids called Avatars to study the indigenes, and the plants and animals with which they lived in harmony. But one of the Avatars, operated by a former marine named Jake Sully, is given a more malevolent job: to learn about a holy Na'vi meeting place, which stood atop a deposit of a valuable mineral called unobtanium. At first, Sully dutifully follows his orders, but over time he comes to identify with the Na'vi and turns against the RDA. With the help of other humans, the Na'vi, and Pandora's animals, Sully defeats the RDA and its private security force. Afterward, the Na'vi expel all but a few humans from Pandora.

*Avatar* went on to receive three Academy Awards and become one of the highest-grossing movies ever, grossing over $2.5 billion worldwide. Its environmental overtones, namely the horrific destruction humans had caused to their own planet and were prepared to inflict elsewhere, was clear. However, it was one of only a number of big-screen films released in the first two decades of the twenty-first century that reflected the international community's growing attention to the environment. *The Day After Tomorrow* had appeared in cinemas in 2004, followed by *An Inconvenient Truth* two years afterward. In 2007, Warner Pictures released *The 11th Hour*. Produced and narrated by actor Leonardo DiCaprio, it offers insights from dozens of scientists, activists, and political leaders, who warn of the devastation humans were inflicting on their planet. The following year, the Disney production *WALL-E* appeared, portraying a planet Earth that had been abandoned, with no sign of human habitation save for the piles of waste left behind. In 2012, Illumination Entertainment adapted Dr. Seuss's 1971 book, *The Lorax*, to the big screen, where it offered a strong criticism of the deforestation taking place around the world in the name of profit. In 2017, the sequel to *An Inconvenient Truth*, appropriately titled *An Inconvenient Sequel*, ran in theaters, detailing former vice president Al Gore's efforts to combat climate change and encourage the development of renewable energy sources.

The intersection between popular culture and the environment, however, was no longer just a phenomenon among DCs. Possibly the best example was the 2016 Summer Olympics, held in Rio de Janeiro, Brazil. No doubt aware of the international condemnation Brazil had received for not doing more to protect its rain forests, the opening day ceremony had as a centerpiece Brazil's leadership in encouraging environmentally friendly sustainable development. In fact, the organizers wrote, "It is not enough to stop harming the planet, it is time to start healing it." Marathon runner Vanderlei Cordeiro de Lima lit an environmentally friendly Olympic cauldron. Later appeared scientific maps produced by NASA that warned of the crisis facing the planet's ecosystems, particularly that posed by climate change. The ceremony then offered a message of hope, as the more than 10,000 competing athletes marched into the main stadium, each carrying a seed and a small amount of soil to plant an "Athlete's Forest" at one site of the Games. Following that, towers covered in mirrors opened up to create five rings of vegetation, giving viewers an idea of the rich, lush forest that would eventually emerge from those seeds.[1]

Yet for all of the recognition of humans' impact on Earth, old challenges persisted. In 2015, China's leadership permitted release of *Under the Dome*, a documentary produced by a Chinese journalist about that nation's severe pollution. It aired for four days on China's internet company, Tencent, before the Chinese Communist Party censored it. Holding to his highly nationalistic, America First platform, US president Donald Trump, in addition to withdrawing from the Paris climate agreement, sought to cut funding for the EPA; named as the EPA's head, Scott Pruitt, an Oklahoma politician who had sued that same agency on the grounds that it imposed too many regulations on industry; and announced that he would reverse President Barack Obama's clean energy initiatives and give more support to increasing the production of fossil fuels. In August 2017, Brazil's president, Michael Temer, issued a decree permitting commercial mining in a nature reserve in the Amazon larger than the country of Denmark. A Brazilian court suspended the order, drawing a rebuke from Temer, who argued that he was trying to "boost the country's economy."[2]

These examples point to the continued influence of anthropocentrism in international efforts to protect the environment. Despite the evidence of the human impact on the climate, biodiversity, and ecosystems, humans have repeatedly viewed the environment through the extent to which they can exploit or change it for humankind's benefit. Subsumed within that broader theme are subthemes. One is the difficulty of creating international regimes when those regimes are believed to endanger an individual country's well-being. Another, reflected in Brazil's preparedness to open up more of the Amazon to development despite international pressure not to do so, is the continued emphasis of economic development among the LDCs of the "South." Giving the economy precedence over the environment has been a cause of disputes among the DCs of the "North," but it has generated even greater disharmony between LDCs and DCs.

Yet there is also a final subtheme, that of wars caused by humans' geopolitical and economic impulses. In her 2012 book, *Wartime*, the historian Mary Dudziak argued that war is no longer something unusual with a clear beginning and conclusion, but a constant fact, particularly (though not solely) for Americans. The Second World War paved the way for the Cold War. Then came the "war on terror," which appears to have no end. Wars, though, do not have to be international in scope to have an environmental impact. They can be civil, such as those in Rwanda and Zaire in the 1990s. The civil strife in Zaire, for example, was the cause for the slaughtering of numerous animals in Virunga National Park. The possibility of a nuclear exchange between the United States and North Korea reignited discussion over what effect radioactive fallout would have on humans and, more broadly, the planet's ecosystems.[3] Hence, while much has been accomplished from the turn of the twentieth century through the Paris climate accords, and progress continues insofar as efforts to protect the environment, many of the issues that have divided the international community endure and run the risk of becoming worse if not addressed.

## Accomplishments

From the turn of the twentieth century into the twenty-first, international efforts to protect the environment made significant headway. The Convention for the Preservation of Wild Animals, Birds and Fish in Africa, which had only a few signatories and no one willing to ratify it, reflected a desire to protect the planet's fauna, even if it was less to champion the animals themselves than to make sure that they were not overexploited. Other agreements that were designed to protect flora and fauna but that, at their core, were anthropocentric in nature, included the Convention for the Regulation of Whaling, the Convention Relative to the Preservation of Flora and Fauna in Their Natural State, the International Convention for the Prevention of Pollution of the Sea by Oil, and the Convention on Wetlands of International Importance.

Those endeavors to offer protection for the planet's ecosystems intensified in the period following the 1972 Stockholm Convention. Indeed, of the approximately 140 multilateral environmental agreements reached between 1920 and 2009, more than half were signed since 1973.[4] Still, anthropocentrism made its influence felt, whether it be efforts to reduce or eliminate acid rain, stop the trade in hazardous waste and pesticides, protect animal species, close the hole in the ozone layer, or address climate change.

It would be wrong to give the credit for these agreements, despite their weaknesses or humans-first orientation, solely to national political leaders.

Hunters, scientists, authors, and NGOs could and did have substantial influence within and beyond their home countries. Hunters' warnings about the extirpation of animals stimulated efforts to protect fauna in Africa and in North America. Scientists expressed their misgivings regarding humans' impact on the environment with some, such as Rachel Carson, having an international impact. Authors like Farley Mowat played a part in creating the "Save the Whales!" movement. By offering their expertise and putting pressure on governments to do more for the planet's well-being, NGOs could and did encourage international environmental meetings and the signing of numerous multination agreements, among them the Convention for the Preservation of Wild Animals, Birds and Fish in Africa, the Convention Relative to the Preservation of Flora and Fauna in Their Natural State, the Convention on the Conservation of Nature and Natural Resources, the whaling moratorium, the MAR conference, the Convention on Wetlands of International Importance, the Rio conference, and Agenda 21. Even international financial institutions (IFIs) began to take greater interest in the environment, as demonstrated by the World Bank's creation of the Tropical Forest Action Plan and the Global Environment Facility. More often than not, though, IFIs have tended to give the nod to development projects, even if they caused harm to the environment.

Efforts have continued to improve the globe's environmental well-being. Greenpeace had long called for banning microbeads, small, round pieces of plastic first introduced in the 1970s and used as an exfoliant in consumer products. In 2015, the United States outlawed their use on the grounds that they were increasing the amount of plastic in the oceans. Great Britain followed suit in January 2018. Measures to control acid rain have led to a significant decline in its occurrence.[5]

Meanwhile, a number of countries have taken additional measures to enforce CITES. In 2016, the United States prohibited the sale of nearly all ivory products, China announced its intention to end its domestic trade in ivory in 2017, and in April of that year, Kenya's government burned over one hundred tons of elephant tusks. In fact, 2016 marked the fifth straight year that the poaching of elephants declined. That same year marked the greatest seizure of illegal ivory since 1999, an indication of, on the one hand, the determination of the international community to enforce CITES and, on the other hand, that poaching remained a serious challenge to that effort. With regard to flora, the International Tropical Timber Organization, an intergovernmental body formed in 1985 to sustainably manage the world's tropical forests, has joined CITES to enforce the latter. Meanwhile, the Forest Stewardship Council has maintained its activities. By the end of 2017, it had certified over 196 million hectares of forest in eighty-three nations.[6]

The international community's bid to safeguard ozone layer and combat climate change achieved some success as well. In mid-2016, researchers reported by that the hole over the ozone layer, which had reached its peak in the year 2000, had contracted by over 1.5 million square miles. China, one of the world's largest emitters of carbon dioxide ($CO_2$), announced in early 2017 the cancellation of over one hundred coal-powered plants, and its intention to invest $360 billion into renewables by the year 2020. Some nations have started to look at abandoning the use of fossil-fueled vehicles. As of July 2017, Great Britain and France had announced they would cease selling fossil-fueled automobiles by 2040. Norway set a similar goal for 2025, India declared its desire to have only electric vehicles sold within its borders by 2030, and China, Austria, Germany, Denmark, Portugal, South Korea, and Spain set targets of their own for the sale of electric cars. Volvo in 2017 declared that by 2019, it would produce only hybrid vehicles that used both gas and electricity, and electric-only models.[7]

## Challenges at sea

Despite such progress, there remain challenges to international initiatives to protect the environment. On the high seas, steps taken over the past century to reduce the amount of pollution have made headway but have not eliminated the problem. Oil tankers entering the Persian Gulf illegally wash their tanks, polluting the gulf, which is itself not a large body of water. How much longer the moratorium on whaling will remain in place is unclear. Some whales have come off the endangered species list, including gray whales in 1994 and, in 2016, the majority of humpbacks. Their growing populations may offer an incentive to members of the IWC to lift permit hunting those species once again. Meanwhile, Japan has continued to resist limitations on whaling. After having announced their decision in 2015 to resume "scientific whaling," Japanese whalers in March 2016 returned from a nearly four-month "scientific" expedition to the Antarctic, during which they killed 333 minke whales, the majority of which were pregnant.[8]

Bringing pressure to bear on sea life as well are oceanic disputes. A recent and particularly volatile example concerns China's determination to exert its control over the South China Sea. That body of water is not only an important transportation route but is believed to have large deposits of oil and natural gas. Beijing has claimed islands in the South China Sea as its own, constructed new ones, and placed military facilities on some of them. It has, in turn, drawn the ire of the United States, Vietnam, the Philippines, Malaysia, and other nations, which charge China with endangering regional shipping or asserting control over islands that belong to others. In 2016, the Philippines won one of these land claims in a suit brought by it against China before the Permanent Court of Arbitration at The Hague, Netherlands. The tribunal, though, went a step further, contending that artificial islands constructed by China had caused "permanent irreparable harm to the coral reef ecosystem."[9] Beijing, however, has shown no preparedness to give up its existing claims or to stop building new islands.

**PHOTO 10** Adult and young minke whale brought aboard a Japanese whaling ship, 2008. *Credit: Australian Customs and Border Protection Service.*

## Challenges on land: Poaching, poison, and radiation

Despite the passage of CITES and agreements regarding protecting avian life, protections for mammals remain at risk. One reason is a growing human population. Here, there is reason for some hope. A 2016 report found that despite a 23 percent increase in the human population between 1993 and 2009, and global economic growth of over 150 percent during that same period, the impact of humans on land increased by only 9 percent. This suggests that more people are living in cities and that resources are being used more sustainably. In turn, there is cause for optimism when it comes to protecting biodiversity. These findings, though, are not across the board. In some cases, such as Western Europe, the East Coast of the United States, China, India, and portions of Brazil, the pressure on the environment was the greatest. Those areas with the least incursions were generally inhospitable: the Sahara and Gobi deserts, and the forests of the Congo and the Amazon. Yet even in these regions, humans' presence has grown.[10]

All the while, warnings continue to appear that humans are destroying animal and insect life on the planet. Despite new protections, the elephant population has continued to decline, with about one hundred of them dying each day at the hands of poachers. Some poachers have started employing poison to kill elephants, as well as lions—the bones of which have been used in Africa and Asia for medicinal purposes. Scavengers also fall victim to the poison as they feed off the carcasses. A decision by the government of South Africa in June 2017 to permit an online auction of rhino horn, despite an international ban of such sales, drew fire from critics who said it will serve to encourage poaching. They point out that most rhinos live in South Africa, where over 1,000 of them were killed in 2016.[11]

Agricultural development has entailed the use of pesticides, which present perils of their own. As of 2017, the Stockholm Convention on Persistent Organic Pollutants had 180 parties. Significantly, the United States and Italy are the only industrialized nations that have failed to accept its provisions. Yet even for those countries that have signed on, disposing of shipping containers remains problematic, particularly in the developing world. Insecticides, moreover, can and do unintentional harm nontargets. A noticeable decline in the bee population was linked by the mid-2010s to the use of neonicotinoids, a pesticide that attacked bees' nervous system and harmed their ability to fly and direct hives to plants. As pollination is vitally important to 70 percent of the world's one hundred most important species of crops, the loss of bees would mean the destruction of foods on which humans rely. Although the EU has banned the use of neonicotinoids, they remain popular in the United States.[12]

Deadly as well is the radioactivity that has persisted since the Cold War. That conflict created such widespread environmental damage in the former Soviet Union that much of it may never recover. Copper-nickel smelters in the towns of Monchegorsk and Nikel-Zapolyarnyi in northwestern Russia left behind what appears to be permanent damage to pine trees there. Other towns, among them Lipetsk and Chelyabinsk, have higher cancer rates than those of others. Similarly, the recent collapse of a tunnel containing nuclear waste at the Hanford nuclear site in Washington State, and the leakage of radioactive materials from underground storage tanks at that same location, pointed to the failure of US officials during the Cold War to give greater attention to the long-term disposal of atomic detritus. At the Savannah River nuclear reservation in South Carolina, where, starting in the 1950s, the US government refined atomic materials for use in weapons, an effort is underway to clean up contaminated groundwater. At that site too is radioactive waste in outdated tanks.[13]

## Demographic challenges

Feeding a growing human population while protecting the globe's biodiversity remains another daunting task. Around 1800, there were one billion people living on Earth. It took 120 years for that number to double. By 1986, it had reached five billion. It took only another thirteen years to reach six billion, and twelve to reach seven billion. Since the 1970s, 99 percent of that growth has taken place in LDCs. This is largely due more to advancements in health care and greater knowledge about public health than economic development. Furthermore, it is those nations with the highest growth rate that tend to have the youngest populations, meaning more people who are at an age to reproduce.[14]

How to feed that population is not clear. The growing emphasis on biofuels—petrol created from plants such as corn, sugarcane, or palm plants—runs the risk of farmers selling their crops to companies that produce the fuel and, in turn, curtailing the amount of food available for consumers. In that case, food prices would rise and millions of additional people could find themselves living in poverty. That, in turn, could jeopardize achievement of the UN's sustainable development goals. A potential solution, aside from restrictions on the acreage that could be devoted to biofuel, is genetically modified organisms (GMOs). They have permitted for the growing of more crops per acre, and in weather conditions that in the past would have been impossible. But there are two risks. One, noted previously and expressed by the EU, is that they might be unsafe. The second is that by relying on single species of plants, especially grains, rather than a greater diversity of them, makes food supplies susceptible to disruptions,[15] such as disease.

A growing population additionally means more pollution. Trash ends up not just at sea, on roadsides, or in domestic landfills, but is shipped elsewhere, oftentimes in the name of recycling. China in 2016 imported forty-five million tons of waste, worth over US$18 billion. In 2017 it announced it would stop taking in two dozen types of foreign detritus, declaring it was doing so in the name of environmental protection. A likely effect of this decision, though, will be to shift the trade to other nations in the region, such as Malaysia and Vietnam.[16]

Then there is air pollution. The United Kingdom, United States, Spain, and Poland still have not signed the Helsinki Protocol on sulfur emissions. Acid rain, though less common than in the past, continues to affect water quality. Following the Fukushima nuclear disaster, German chancellor Angela Merkel announced she would phase out the use of atomic power plants in her country but said nothing about coal. Despite its reduction in coal capacity, China has not stopped building coal-powered plants. Even by 2020, the amount of power generated by coal in that country would be three times as great as that produced by American coal plants (assuming no additional coal plants were built under the current US administration). Indeed, some countries are having difficulty curbing pollution. In China and India, three million people died in 2015 from contaminated air. In those two states, the demand for facial masks has increased, as has a preparedness to purchase cans and bottles filled with nothing more than fresh air from places like Canada's Rocky Mountains.[17]

# The atmospheric challenge: Climate change

Biofuels are advertised as environmentally friendly, and Brazil and the United States have become the world leaders in using plants as an energy source for vehicles. But aside from the possibility of diverting foodstuffs elsewhere, the process of producing biofuels may contribute to climate change. Palm oil, for instance, necessitates destroying palm trees in rain forests that are themselves carbon sinks. According to one study, acquiring a ton of palm oil releases thirty-three tons of $CO_2$ into the atmosphere. The process of clearing the land or converting it to biofuel-producing crops requires the use of equipment that releases greenhouse gases. The same is true for the power needed for the factory machinery that turns the plants into fuel.[18]

It is the desire to curb greenhouse gas emissions that has pushed countries and companies to look into hybrid or electric-only vehicles, but there is a dark side to that effort, particularly insofar as electric-powered transportation. The electricity for those automobiles has to come from sources of energy, which may include fossil-fuel power plants. A coal-powered facility, which produces greenhouse-causing $CO_2$, would have to increase its output to meet higher demand as more people drove electric cars.[19] The key will be to find means of producing that electricity with sources that do not produce greenhouse gases.

"Remember when this water hazard was just a puddle? Global warming is ruining my game."

PHOTO 11 *Credit: IN THE BLEACHERS © 2016 Steve Moore. Reprinted with permission of ANDREWS MCMEEL SYNDICATION. All rights reserved.*

Locating those cleaner sources of energy has become ever more pressing. The years 2014, 2015, and 2016 each set a record for the hottest Earth had ever seen. In September 2016, for the first time, the amount of $CO_2$ in the atmosphere reached more than 400 parts per million. Even if humans were to stop immediately using all carbon-emitting devices, numerous scientists have argued that $CO_2$ would remain in the atmosphere for decades, making it even harder to combat climate change. Confusing matters further is recent evidence that found methane emissions from livestock were higher than originally believed. Methane constituted approximately 16 percent of all greenhouse gas emissions in 2015, but it is estimated to be twenty-eight times as potent as $CO_2$ in contributing to climate change. The amount of methane produced by cattle was 11 percent greater than estimated by the UN's Intergovernmental Panel for Climate Change, thereby adding to the challenge of reaching the goals set at Paris.[20]

Whether the environment is or could be a cause of war remains a matter of debate within the scholarly community. Supporters point not only to such examples as Boko Haram or the Northwest Passage, but also to a 1980 conflict in Africa along the Senegal River fought between black Mauritanians and Arabic Mauers, the fight against the leftist Shining Path in Peru that lasted through the 1980s, and El Salvador's civil war of 1980–92. Critics argue that poverty is more often a cause of war than the environment, or that resource scarcity has a greater chance of encouraging diplomatic cooperation than armed confrontation.[21] It is important not to dismiss those who argue environmental security has been overplayed as a cause of military clashes. Still, it is equally crucial not to disregard the potential for the environment to be a cause of armed conflict.

There are other perils posed by climate change. Rising sea levels caused by the melting of ice in the North and South Poles may inundate low-lying cities and countries. Dhaka, Bangladesh, with over fourteen million inhabitants, could end up under water, as could Tokyo and Singapore. Much of the US state of Florida is less than fifty feet above sea level. The small island nations of Kiribati, Nauru, Tuvalu, the Seychelles, and the Marshall Islands could find themselves overwhelmed. Warmer sea temperatures also have the effect of bleaching coral reefs, which not only draw dollars from ecotourists but provide a haven for fish that provide both sustenance and livelihoods in many countries. The loss of land or livelihoods has raised the specter of numerous "environmental refugees" escaping drought, desertification, food shortages, or floods. How many such refugees there might be remains in contention. A 1995 estimate placed the number at twenty-five million, while a more recent study by the United Nations suggests it could reach twice that number. Using arguments similar to those who challenge the concept of the environment as a cause of war, critics have stated these numbers are inflated or ignore other factors. Even taking into account the position adopted by detractors, there is clear evidence of a potential crisis. In 2012, the president of the Maldives, Mohamed Nasheed, declared that his country had set up an account to purchase land in other nations and was looking at Australia, Sri Lanka, and India as a new home for his 350,000 people. Tuvalu also approached Australia about taking in its 12,000 residents.[22] An influx of refugees fleeing environmental disaster could put intense economic pressure on the recipient countries.

Achieving any progress on climate change, as is the case with any international environmental regime, will continue to face the same long-expressed challenges posed by national interest, differences between the North and South, and disagreements within those same blocs. For example, a 2013 report by the Organization for Economic Cooperation and Development declared, "The poorest country in 2011 was poorer than the poorest country in 1980. And much of humankind continues to live on less than USD$1 a day. . . . In many countries, inequalities have deepened." Many LDCs place this gap at the feet of DCs, charging the latter with providing inadequate financial assistance.[23] Nations in the North argue that they provide enormous sums of aid to their counterparts in the South, that LDCs need to do a better job of using the money provided them more effectively, and that by focusing on development, the nations of the South are making it more difficult to solve global environmental problems.

Yet there remain divisions within the North. Countries in the EU tend to believe that environmental protection is as important as other global subjects, including trade and social issues. Furthermore, they contend that a healthy environment is necessary for the well-being of a society. Consequently, there is widespread agreement in the EU that people must do more to curb pollution, reduce consumption, and accept lifestyle changes. Many Americans, however, are inclined to look at the environment through the lens of free trade, corporate interests, and individual as opposed to societal well-being. Despite Russia's ratification of Kyoto, Russian president Vladimir Putin has made numerous statements suggesting that he does not see climate change a serious issue. Indeed, he once commented that "an increase of two or three degrees wouldn't be so bad for a northern country like Russia. We could spend less on fur coats, and the grain harvest would go up."[24]

One must be cautious in making generalities, for divisions can exist within countries themselves. The United States is an obvious case. The overwhelming majority of climate scientists believe humans are the cause of climate change, but critics point to the small number of dissenters to question the majority's assessment. This has allowed politicians who doubt or deny the validity of human-induced climate change to make it a political issue. In the United States, this divergence became apparent following the Kyoto Protocol, with Republicans increasingly doubtful that climate change was manmade, and Democrats ever more certain. Consequently, by 2016, Americans, who live in one of the world's greatest emitters of $CO_2$, were more split over humans' responsibility for the climate than they were twenty years earlier.[25]

At present, China, the United States, and the EU are the top emitters of greenhouse gases, accounting for more than 50 percent of the world's emissions. Add to that list India, Russia, Japan, Brazil, Indonesia, Canada, and Mexico, and one can account for three-quarters of the globe's climate-changing discharges. Meanwhile, 3.5 percent of emissions come from the bottom one hundred nations.[26] Finding a way to get these nations, as well as the dozens of others on the planet, to balance common cause with national priorities, has been and will continue to be one of the greatest challenges facing the international community.

# NOTES

## Preface

1  "Statement by President Trump on the Paris Climate Accord," June 1, 2017, accessed October 14, 2017. https://www.whitehouse.gov/the-press-office/2017/06/01/statement-president-trump-paris-climate-accord; World Economic Forum, "Which Countries Emit the Most Greenhouse Gas?" July 21, 2015, accessed October 14, 2017. https://www.weforum.org/agenda/2015/07/countries-emitting-most-greenhouse-gas/; and Tom DiChristopher, "Trump is Still Pulling Out of Paris Agreement, Despite Chatter of Reversal, Experts Say," *CNBC*, September 19, 2017, accessed October 14, 2017. https://www.cnbc.com/2017/09/19/trump-is-not-reversing-on-paris-agreement-heres-why.html.

## Chapter 1

1  John M. MacKenzie, *The Empire of Nature: Hunting, Conservation and British Imperialism* (New York: Manchester University Press, 1988), 87, 89–90, 92, 116.

2  MacKenzie, *Empire of Nature*, 207–08; Michael Bowman, Peter Davies, and Catherine Redgwell, *Lyster's International Wildlife Law*, 2nd ed. (New York: Cambridge University Press, 2010), 262.

3  Peter Brimblecombe, "History of Air Pollution," in *Composition, Chemistry, and Climate of the Atmosphere*, ed. Hanwant B. Singh (New York: Reinhold, 1995), 3; John McCormick, *Reclaiming Paradise: The Global Environmental Movement* (Bloomington: Indiana University Press, 1989), 127; Mostafa K. Tolba, with Iwona Rummel-Bulska, *Global Environmental Diplomacy: Negotiating Environmental Agreements for the World, 1973-1992* (Cambridge, MA: MIT Press, 1998), 11; C. Donald Aherns, *Essentials of Meteorology: An Invitation to the Atmosphere*, 7th ed. (Stamford, CT: Cengage, 2015), 432.

4  Clarence J. Glacken, *Traces on the Rhodian Shore: Nature and Culture in Western Thought from Ancient Times to the End of the Eighteenth Century* (Berkeley: University of California Press, 1967), 336–39; Ramachandra Guha, *Environmentalism: A World History* (New York: Longman, 2000), 33.

5  Alfred W. Crosby, *Ecological Imperialism: The Biological Expansion of Europe, 900-1900* (New York: Cambridge University Press, 1986), 74–78, 94–97.

6   Richard Grove, *Green Imperialism: Colonial Expansion, Tropical Island Edens, and the Origins of Environmentalism, 1600-1860* (New York: Cambridge University Press, 1995), 64–65, 67, 150, 175; Stephen G. Bunker, *Underdeveloping the Amazon: Extraction, Unequal Exchange, and the Failure of the Modern State* (Urbana: University of Illinois Press, 1985), 61–64.

7   Nathan Nunn and Nancy Quinn, "The Columbian Exchange: A History of Disease, Food, and Ideas," *Journal of Economic Perspectives* 24 (2010): 165; Crosby, *Ecological Imperialism*, 205–08, 231–33.

8   Myles Osborne and Susan Kingsley Kent, *Africans and Britons in the Age of Empires, 1660-1980* (New York: Routledge, 2015), 8.

9   John A. Garraty and Peter Gay, eds., *The Columbia History of the World* (New York: Harper and Row, 1981), 848, 851.

10   Osborne and Kent, *Africans and Britons in the Age of Empires*, 8.

11   Benjamin Kline, *First Along the River: A Brief History of the Environmental Movement*, 2nd ed. (Lanham, MD: Acada Books, 2000), 38–43.

12   Grove, *Green Imperialism*, 157, 159–60, 165, 195–96, 347, 357.

13   Ibid., 199; Paul Hawken, *Blessed Unrest: How the Largest Movement in the World Came into Being and Why No One Saw It Coming* (New York: Viking, 2007), 44.

14   Guha, *Environmentalism*, 33–34.

15   Gregory Allen Barton, *Empire Forestry and the Origins of Environmentalism* (New York: Cambridge University Press, 2002), 137–40; Kline, *First Along the River*, 2nd ed., 56.

16   Guha, *Environmentalism*, 10–12, 16–17; Kline, *First Along the River*, 2nd ed., 33, 48; J. Baird Calicott, *Beyond the Land Ethic: More Essays in Environmental Philosophy* (Albany: State University of New York Press, 1999), 197.

17   For a detailed study of this dispute, see Robert W. Righter, *The Battle over Hetch Hetchy: America's Most Controversial Dam and the Birth of Modern Environmentalism* (New York: Oxford University Press, 2005), esp. chaps. 3–6.

18   Peter Dauvergne, *Historical Dictionary of Environmentalism* (Lanham, MD: Scarecrow, 2009), xxii.

19   Mark Cioc, *The Game of Conservation: International Treaties to Protect the World's Migratory Animals* (Athens: Ohio University Press, 2009), 21.

20   Harri Olavi Siiskonen, "The Concept of Climate Improvement: Colonialism and Environment in German South West Africa," *Environment and History* 21 (2015): 288–89, 296, 298; Thomas Hietala, *Manifest Design: American Exceptionalism and Empire*, rev. ed. (Ithaca, NY: Cornell University Press, 2005), 133–34, 194.

21   On this score, see Mark David Spence, *Dispossessing the Wilderness: Indian Removal and the Making of the National Parks* (New York: Oxford University Press, 1999), chaps. 4–5.

22   Frederick B. Pike, *The United States and Latin America: Myths and Stereotypes of Civilization and Nature* (Austin: University of Texas Press, 1992), 125;

Thomas R. Dunlap, *Nature and the English Diaspora: Environment and History in the United States, Canada, Australia, and New Zealand* (New York: Cambridge University Press, 1999), 49.

23  Dunlap, *Nature and the English Diaspora*, 60.

24  MacKenzie, *Empire of Nature*, 44, 152–53; Mario Prost and Yoriko Otomo, "British Influences on International Environmental Law: The Case of Wildlife Conservation," in *British Influences on International Law, 1915-2015*, eds. Robert McCorquodale and Jean-Pierre Gauci (Leiden, Netherlands: Brill Nijholt, 2016), 195.

25  Cioc, *Game of Conservation*, 30–31; Dunlap, *Nature and the English Diaspora*, 61–62.

26  Bernhard Gissibl, *The Nature of German Imperialism: Conservation and the Politics of Wildlife in Colonial East Africa* (New York: Berghahn, 2016), 38; MacKenzie, *Empire of Nature*, 163, 206.

27  Cioc, *Game of Conservation*, 21–23, 29; MacKenzie, *Empire of Nature*, 89–90.

28  MacKenzie, *Empire of Nature*, 201, 202–03, 229; Cioc, *Game of Conservation*, 29; Karen Brown, "Cultural Constructions of the Wild: The Rhetoric and Practice of Wildlife Conservation in the Cape Colony at the Turn of the Twentieth Century," *South African Historical Journal* 47 (2002): 89–90.

29  Gissibl, *Nature of German Imperialism*, 44–45, 72; Brown, "Cultural Constructions of the Wild," 78, 79; Russell J. Dalton, "The Environmental Movement in Western Europe," in *Environmental Politics in the International Arena: Movements, Parties, Organizations, and Policy*, ed. Sheldon Kamieniecki (Albany: State University of New York Press, 1993), 44; Cioc, *Game of Conservation*, 31.

30  Cioc, *Game of Conservation*, 33; Gissibl, *Nature of German Imperialism*, 211–12, 236; Committee on Ungulate Management in Yellowstone National Park, Board of Environmental Studies and Toxicology, Division on Earth and Life Studies, National Research Council, *Ecological Dynamics on Yellowstone's Northern Range* (Washington, DC: National Academy Press, 2002), 92.

31  Cioc, *Game of Conservation*, 32; Gissibl, *Nature of German Imperialism*, 38, 85–87; MacKenzie, *Empire of Nature*, 205.

32  Cioc, *Game of Conservation*, 33.

33  Ibid., 34; Sherman Strong Hayden, *The International Protection of Wild Life: An Examination of Treaties and Other Agreements for the Preservation of Birds and Mammals* (New York: Columbia University Press, 1942), 36–37.

34  Gissibl, *Nature of German Imperialism*, 246, 250; Cioc, *Game of Conservation*, 34.

35  Cioc, *Game of Conservation*, 35–39.

36  Ibid., 39–40; MacKenzie, *Empire of Nature*, 211–13; Gregory H. Maddox, *Sub-Saharan Africa: An Environmental History* (Santa Barbara, CA: ABC-CLIO, 2006),144, 145; Gissibl, *Nature of German Imperialism*, 201.

37  MacKenzie, *Empire of Nature*, 227, 230–31; Cioc, *Game of Conservation*, 47.

38  MacKenzie, *Empire of Nature*, 234–37.

39  Cioc, *Game of Preservation*, 62.

40  Vaclav Smil, *Harvesting the Biosphere: What We Have Taken from Nature* (Cambridge, MA: MIT Press, 2013), 92.

41  Hayden, *International Protection of Wild Life*, 70.

42  Otto Herman, *The International Convention for the Protection of Birds Concluded in 1902 and Hungary* (Budapest: Victor Horyánszky, 1907), 21–22.

43  Hayden, *International Protection of Wild Life*, 92, 95–96; Michael J. Bowman, "The 1902 Convention for the Protection of Birds in Historical and Juridical Perspective," *Ardeola* 61 (2014): 175–76.

44  Charlotte Epstein, *The Power of Words in International Relations: Birth of Anti-Whaling Discourse* (Cambridge, MA: MIT Press, 2008), 56–57.

45  Kurkpatrick Dorsey, *Whales and Nations: Environmental Diplomacy on the High Seas* (Seattle: University of Washington Press, 2013), 4–5.

46  Ibid., 6–7; Epstein, *Power of Words*, 32, 46.

47  Epstein, *Power of Words*, 28–29, 32–34, 36, 37; J. N. Tønnessen and A.O. Johnsen, *The History of Modern Whaling*, trans. R. I. Christophersen (Berkeley: University of California Press, 1982), 370.

48  Callum Roberts, *The Unnatural History of the Sea* (Washington, DC: Island Press, 2007), 100, 102, 103–04, 105–07.

49  Roberts, *Unnatural History of the Sea*, 110; Richard Ellis, *The Empty Ocean: Plundering the World's Marine Life* (Washington, DC: Island Press, 2003), 201.

50  Kurkpatrick Dorsey, *The Dawn of Conservation Diplomacy: U.S.-Canadian Wildlife Treaties in the Progressive Era* (Seattle: University of Washington Press, 2009), 113–15.

51  Charles S. Campbell, Jr., "The Anglo-American Crisis in the Bering Sea, 1890-1891," *Mississippi Valley Historical Review* 48 (1961): 393–414.

52  Charles S. Campbell, "The Bering Sea Settlements of 1892," *Pacific Historical Review* 32 (1963): 347–67.

53  Dorsey, *Dawn of Conservation Diplomacy*, 121; Thomas A. Bailey, "The North Pacific Sealing Convention of 1911," *Pacific Historical Review* 4 (1935): 1–6.

54  Bailey, "North Pacific Sealing Convention," 6–9.

55  Ibid., 9–13; Roberts, *Unnatural History of the Sea*, 112.

56  Grove, *Green Imperialism*, 20; J. R. McNeill, "Woods and Warfare in World History," *Environmental History* 9 (2004): 398; Ted Widmer, "The Civil War's Environmental Impact," in *The New York Times Disunion: A History of the Civil War*, ed. Ted Widmer (New York: Oxford University Press, 2016), 327; MacKenzie, *Empire of Nature*, 229.

57  Kathryn Shively Meier, *Nature's Civil War: Common Soldiers and the Environment in 1862 Virginia* (Chapel Hill: University of North Carolina Press, 2013), 50.

58  Dorothee Brantz, "Environments of Death: Trench Warfare on the Western Front, 1914-18," in *War and the Environment: Military Destruction in*

*the Modern Age,* ed. Charles E. Closmann (College Station: Texas A&M University Press, 2009), 78, 79–80.

59   Ibid., 80; Hazel Hutchinson, *The War that Used Up Words: American Writers and the First World War* (New Haven, CT: Yale University Press, 2015), 1; "The Real 'No-Go Zone' of France: A Forbidden No Man's Land Poisoned by War," May 26, 2015, accessed May 30, 2015. http://www.messynessychic. com/2015/05/26/the-real-no-go-zone-of-france-a-forbidden-no-mans-land-poisoned-by-war/.

60   McNeill, "Woods and Warfare," 399; Richard P. Tucker, "The British Empire and India's Forest Resources: The Timberlands of Assam and Kumaon, 1914-1950," in *World Deforestation in the Twentieth Century*, eds. John F. Richards and Richard P. Tucker (Durham, NC: Duke University Press, 1988), 95; Peter Hough, *Environmental Security: An Introduction* (New York: Routledge, 2014), 59; Robert Wilson, "Birds on the Home Front: Wildlife Conservation in the Western United States during World War II," in ed. Closmann, 132–33; J. R. McNeill, *Something New Under the Sun: An Environmental History of the Twentieth-Century World* (New York: Norton, 2000), 346.

61   Robert Boardman, *International Organization and the Conservation of Nature* (London: Macmillan, 1981), 28–29; Gissibl, *Nature of German Imperialism,* 251.

62   Dorsey, *Whales and Nations,* 33; Epstein, *Power of Words,* 43–44.

63   MacKenzie, *Empire of Nature,* 230, 231.

64   Dorsey, *Dawn of Conservation,* 170–71, 180–88, 200, 206–08.

65   Cioc, *Game of Conservation,* 72–74.

66   Ibid., 74–77, 81–83, 101; Dunlap, *Nature and the English Diaspora,* 222; Graeme Wynn, *Canada and Arctic North America: An Environmental History* (Santa Barbara, CA: ABC-CLIO, 2007), 412; Hayden, *International Protection of Wild Life,* 77.

67   Barton, *Empire Forestry,* 144–45, 158, 160; Dorsey, *Whales and Nations,* 33–34.

68   Gabriela Kütting and Sandra Rose, "The Environment as a Global Issue," in *Palgrave Advances in Environmental Politics,* eds. Michele M. Betsill, Kathryn Hochstetle, and Dimitris Stevis (New York: Palgrave Macmillan, 2006), 178; Anna-Katharina Wöbse, "Oil on Troubled Waters? Environmental Diplomacy in the League of Nations," *Diplomatic History* 32 (2008): 520–21.

69   Wöbse, "Oil on Troubled Waters?" 521–22.

70   Ibid., 522–24.

# Chapter 2

1   Frederick W. Haberman, ed., *Peace,* vol. 1 (Amsterdam: Elsevier Publishing, 1972), 329.

2   Wöbse, "Oil on Troubled Waters?" 524–25.

3   Dorsey, *Whales and Nations*, 34, 39–40, 291–92; Epstein, *Power of Words in International Relations*, 76–77. A blue whale unit (BWU) assumed that each blue whale produced 110 barrels of oil and established a ratio based on that number. In 1932, it took two fin whales, five sei whales, or three humpbacks to produce a single BWU. In 1944, that ratio was changed to one blue equaling two fins or two-and-a-half humpbacks. See Dorsey, *Whales and Nations*, 52, 104.

4   Dorsey, *Whales and Nations*, 40–42, Epstein, *Power of Words*, 75–76.

5   Dorsey, *Whales and Nations*, 6, 42–44.

6   Ibid., 44–45, 47–48, 59; Epstein, *Power of Words*, 46.

7   Dorsey, *Whales and Nations*, 49–50.

8   Ibid., 52, 57, 59, 60–61; Epstein, *Power of Words*, 47–48.

9   Dorsey, *Whales and Nations*, 66–68, 72; Epstein, *Power of Words*, 79.

10   Dorsey, *Whales and Nations*, 72, 74–75, 76, 81; Anthony A. D'Amato, *International Law Studies* (The Hague, Netherlands: Kluwer Law International, 1997), 79.

11   Erik J. Dahl, "Naval Innovation: From Coal to Oil," *Joint Force Quarterly* 27 (2000–01): 51, 54–55; Wöbse, "Oil on Troubled Waters?" 526.

12   Wöbse, "Oil on Troubled Waters?" 525–26.

13   Ibid., 526–27.

14   Ibid., 528–29.

15   Ibid., 530–35; Ronald Mitchell, "International Oil Pollution of the Oceans," in *Institutions for the Earth: Sources of Effective International Environmental Protection*, eds. Peter M. Haas, Robert O. Keohane, and Marc A. Lev (Cambridge, MA: MIT Press, 1993), 197–98.

16   Tuomas Kuokkanen, *International Law and the Environment: Variations on a Theme* (The Hague, Netherlands: Kluwer Law International, 2002), 122–24, 124n84; Bowman, "The 1902 Convention for the Protection of Birds in Historical and Juridical Perspective," 184.

17   Roger D. Smith, *Japan's International Fisheries Policy: Law, Diplomacy, and Policy Governing Resource Security* (New York: Routledge, 2015), 4; Micah S. Muscolino, *Fishing Wars and Environmental Change in Late Imperial and Modern China* (Cambridge, MA: Harvard University Asia Center, 2009), 99–105.

18   Muscolino, *Fishing Wars and Environmental Change*, 106–09.

19   Ibid., 122–23.

20   Naomichi Ishige, *The History and Culture of Japanese Food* (New York: Routledge, 2001), 131; Edward Miles, et al., *The Management of Marine Regions: The North Pacific: An Analysis of Issues Relating to Fisheries, Marine Transportation, Marine Scientific Research, and Multiple Use Conditions and Conflicts* (Berkeley: University of California Press, 1982), 90; Dietrich Sahrhage and Johannes Lundbeck, *A History of Fishing* (Berlin: Springer-Verlag, 1992), 183; Ramachandra Guha, *Environmentalism: An International History* (New York: Longman, 2000), 128–29; Miles, et al., *Management of Marine Regions*, 90.

21 Miles, et al., *Management of Marine Regions*, 90–91; Douglas R. Weiner, *A Little Corner of Freedom: Nature Protection from Stalin to Gorbachev* (Berkeley: University of California Press, 1999), 38–44; Guha, *Environmentalism*, 129.

22 Harry N. Scheiber, *Inter-Allied Conflicts and Ocean Law, 1945-53: The Occupation Command's Revival of Japanese Whaling and Marine Fisheries* (Taipei: Institute of European and American Studies, Academica Sinica, 2001), 14–16.

23 Miles, et al., *Management of Marine Regions*, 91.

24 Cioc, *Game of Conservation*, 41–43; MacKenzie, *Empire of Nature*, 220–21.

25 Cioc, *Game of Conservation*, 47–48.

26 Ibid., 48–50.

27 Ibid., 50–52; MacKenzie, *Empire of Nature*, 217; Convention Relative to the Preservation of Flora and Fauna in Their Natural State, accessed March 17, 2017. http://iea.uoregon.edu/treaty-text/1933-PreservationFaunaFloraNatu ralStateENtxt; Lynton Keith Caldwell, *International Environmental Policy: Emergence and Dimensions*, 2nd ed. (Durham, NC: Duke University Press, 1990), 34.

28 Cioc, *Game of Conservation*, 52; MacKenzie, *Empire of Nature*, 218–20.

29 MacKenzie, *Empire of Nature*, 264, 306.

30 Ibid., 262, 286–87, 289; Cioc, *Game of Conservation*, 53.

31 Cioc, *Game of Conservation*, 86, 87, 89.

32 Ibid., 89–93.

33 Ibid., 94–95.

34 Ibid., 95–97.

35 John D. Wirth, *Smelter Smoke in North America: The Politics of Transborder Pollution* (Lawrence: University Press of Kansas, 2000), 2, 12, 14–16, 21; "Treaty Between the United States and Great Britain Relating to Boundary Waters, and Questions Arising between the United States and Canada," 1909, accessed March 14, 2017. http://ijc.org/en_/BWT.

36 Wirth, *Smelter Smoke in North America*, 3–4, 10, 22–29, 37–42.

37 Ibid., 3, 43.

38 Ibid., 4.

39 Robert J. T. Joy, "Malaria and American Troops in the South and Southwest Pacific in World War II," *Medical History* 43 (1999): 193, 198; Frank McLynn, *The Burma Campaign: Disaster into Triumph, 1942-45* (New Haven, CT: Yale University Press, 2011), 92.

40 Marcus Hall, "World War II and the Axis of Disease: Battling Malaria in Twentieth-Century Italy," in *War and the Environment: Military Destruction in the Modern Age*, ed. Charles E. Closmann (College Station: Texas A&M University Press, 2009), 113, 115–16.

41 Wilson, "Birds on the Home Front" and J. R. McNeill and David S. Painter, "The Global Environmental Footprint of the U.S. Military, 1789-2003," in

ibid., 26, 134; E. B. Sledge, *With the Old Breed: At Peleliu and Okinawa* (New York: Ballantine, 2007), 146.

42  McNeill and Painter, "Global Environmental Footprint," 18; Seth Garfield, *In Search of the Amazon: Brazil, the United States, and the Nature of a Region* (Durham, NC: Duke University Press, 2013), 49, 53, 65–68; Thaddeus Sunseri, "World War II and the Transformation of the Tanzanian Forests," in *Africa and World War II*, eds. Judith A. Byfield, et al. (New York: Cambridge University Press, 2015), 253–54.

43  Paul Josephson, "War on Nature as Part of the Cold War: The Strategic and Ideological Roots of Environmental Degradation in the Soviet Union," in *Environmental Histories of the Cold War*, eds. J. R. McNeill and Corinna R. Unger (New York: Cambridge University Press, 2010), 28–29, 31–32, 34, 37–38.

44  Dorsey, *Whales and Nations*, 92, 101–04; Epstein, *Power of Words in International Relations*, 79–80; Alessandro Bonanno and Douglas Constance, *Caught in the Net: The Global Tuna Industry, Environmentalism, and the State* (Lawrence: University Press of Kansas, 1996), 121; McNeill and Painter, "Global Environmental Footprint," 26–27.

45  Judith A. Bennett, *Natives and Exotics: World War II and the Environment in the South Pacific* (Honolulu: University of Hawai'i Press, 2009), 202; Joshua Horwitz, *War of the Whales: A True Story* (New York: Simon and Schuster, 2014), 198; Wöbse, "Oil on Troubled Waters?," 535.

46  Cecil C. Konijnendijk, *The Forest and the City: The Cultural Landscape of Urban Woodland* (New York: Springer, 2008), 73; Richard Albright, *Cleanup of Chemical and Explosive Munitions: Locating, Identifying Contaminants, and Planning for Environmental Remediation of Land and Sea Military Ranges and Ordnance Dumpsites*, 2nd ed. (Amsterdam: Elsevier, 2012), 32; Nils Petter Gleditsch, "Conversion and the Environment," in *Green Security or Militarized Environment*, ed. Jyrki Käkönen (Aldershot, UK: Dartmouth, 1994), 138; "The Ticking Time Bomb at the Bottom of the Baltic Sea" *The Economist*, November 21, 2013, accessed January 28, 2017. http://www.economist.com/blogs/easternapproaches/2013/11/baltic-sea; Sheldon H. Harris, *Factories of Death: Biological Warfare, 1932-1945, and the American Cover-up*, rev. ed. (New York: Routledge, 2002), 329; "China Says 2,500 Wartime Japanese Chemical Weapons Destroyed," Associated Press, January 17, 2017, accessed March 17, 2017. http://bigstory.ap.org/article/1ec6b853e84 f4e4db9048e78a94f28dc.

47  Edmund Russell, *War and Nature: Fighting Humans and Insects with Chemicals from World War I to Silent Spring* (New York: Cambridge University Press, 2001), 75–76, 80–81, 86.

48  Russell, *War and Nature*, 124–25, 127, 129; McNeill and Painter, "Global Environmental Footprint," 19.

49  John McCormick, *Reclaiming Paradise: The Global Environmental Movement* (Bloomington: Indiana University Press, 1989), 28.

50  McCormick, *Reclaiming Paradise*, 33–36; Dalton, "The Environmental Movement in Western Europe," 49.

51  MacKenzie, *Reclaiming Paradise*, 34.

# Chapter 3


1 J. Samuel Walker, *Prompt and Utter Destruction: Truman and the Use of the Atomic Bombs against Japan* (Chapel Hill: University of North Carolina Press, 1997), 38; Martin J. Sherwin, *A World Destroyed: Hiroshima and Its Legacies*, 3rd ed. (Stanford, CA: Stanford University Press, 2003), 223; Jon Hunner, *J. Robert Oppenheimer, the Cold War, and the Atomic West* (Norman: University of Oklahoma Press, 2009), 111.

2 Nayef R. F. Al-Rodhan, *Meta-Geopolitics of Outer Space: An Analysis of Space Power, Security and Governance* (Houndsmills, UK: Palgrave Macmillan, 2012), 193.

3 Quoted in Marc Trachtenberg, *A Constructed Peace: The Making of the European Settlement, 1945-1963* (Princeton, NJ: Princeton University Press, 1999), 52.

4 Dorsey, *Whales and Nations*, 129.

5 Jeffrey R. Bernstein, "Japanese Capitalism," in *Creating Modern Capitalism: How Entrepreneurs, Companies, and Countries Triumphed in Three Industrial Revolutions*, ed. Thomas K. McGraw (Cambridge, MA: Harvard University Press, 1997), 465; Bonanno and Constance, *Caught in the Net*, 121; Smith, *Japan's International Fisheries Policy*, 31–33; Carmel Finley, *All the Fish in the Sea: Maximum Sustainable Yield and the Failure of Fisheries Management* (Chicago: University of Chicago Press, 2011), 72; Sahrhage and Lundbeck, *A History of Fishing*, 209.

6 Smith, *Japan's International Fisheries Policy*, 33–35, 48; Harry N. Scheiber, *Inter-Allied Conflicts and Ocean Law*, 86–87.

7 Dorsey, *Whales and Nations*, 129, 134–37; Smith, *Japan's International Fisheries Policy*, 31–35; Scheiber, *Inter-Allied Conflicts and Ocean Law*, 121–23.

8 Dorsey, *Whales and Nations*, 130, 138–39, 152; Sahrhage and Lundbeck, *History of Fishing*, 150.

9 Dorsey, *Whales and Nations*, 110, 117–18, 122.

10 Ibid.,121.

11 E. C. M. Parsons, with Amy Bauer, et al., *An Introduction to Marine Mammal Biology and Conservation* (Burlington, MA: Jones and Barlett, 2013), 218; Dorsey, *Whales and Nations*, 165–69.

12 Dorsey, *Whales and Nations*, 156–60, 170–76.

13 Daniela Liggett, "An Erosion of Confidence?: The Antarctic Treaty System in the Twenty-First Century," in *Diplomacy on Ice: Energy and the Environment in the Arctic and Antarctic*, eds. Rebecca Pincus and Saleem H. Ali (New Haven, CT: Yale University Press, 2015), 62; Charlotte Epstein, *The Power of Words in International Relations: Birth of Anti-Whaling Discourse* (Cambridge, MA: MIT Press, 2008), 59–61.

14 Liggett, "Erosion of Confidence?" 62–63; James E. Heg, "Conference on the Conservation on Antarctic Seals," *Antarctic Journal* 7 (1972): 45.

15 Heg, "Conference on the Conservation on Antarctic Seals," 45.

16   William M. McClenehan, Jr. and William H. Becker, *Eisenhower and the Cold War Economy* (Baltimore: Johns Hopkins University Press, 2011), 177; James Bamberg, *British Petroleum and Global Oil, 1950-1975: The Challenge of Nationalism* (New York: Cambridge University Press, 2000), 76; Ronald Mitchell, "Intentional Oil Pollution of the Oceans," in *Institutions for the Earth: Sources of Effective International Environmental Protection*, eds. Peter M. Haas, Robert O. Keohane, and Marc A. Levy (Cambridge, MA: MIT Press, 1993), 199.

17   Wöbse, "Oil on Troubled Waters?" 535; Mitchell, "Intentional Oil Pollution," 199–200.

18   Mitchell, "International Oil Pollution," 200–04, 232.

19   Greg Bankoff, "A Curtain of Silence: Asia's Fauna in the Cold War," in *Environmental Histories of the Cold War*, eds. J. R. McNeill and Corinna R. Unger (New York: Cambridge University Press, 2010), 212; Lisa M. Brady, "Life in the DMZ: Turning a Diplomatic Failure into an Environmental Success," *Diplomatic History* 32 (September 2008): 585, 586, 587, 595, 596.

20   Jacob Darwin Hamblin, *Arming Mother Nature: The Birth of Catastrophic Environmentalism* (New York: Oxford University Press, 2013).

21   Joseph J. Corn and Brian Horrigan, *Yesterday's Tomorrows: Past Visions of the American Future* (Baltimore: Johns Hopkins University Press, 1984), 45; Andrew F. Wood, *New York's 1939-1940 World's Fair* (Charleston, SC: Arcadia, 2004), 55, 121; Elizabeth Ram, "The Electric Kitchen," accessed May 2, 2017. http://exhibitions.nypl.org/biblion/worldsfair/enter-world-tomorrow-futurama-and-beyond/essay/essay-ram-electric-kitchen.

22   Andrew J. Dunar, *America in the Fifties* (Syracuse, NY: Syracuse University Press, 2006), 234; Jamie Bronstein and Andrew Harris, *Empire, State, and Society: Britain since 1830* (Malden, MA: Wiley, 2012), 267; Lori Maguire, "Introduction," in *The Cold War and Entertainment Television*, ed. Lori Maguire (Newcastle Upon Tyne, UK: Cambridge Scholars, 2016), 10.

23   Kristine C. Harper and Ronald E. Doel, "Environmental Diplomacy in the Cold War: Weather Control, the United States, and India, 1966-1967," in *Environmental Histories of the Cold War*, eds. J. R. McNeill and Corinna R. Unger (New York: Cambridge University Press, 2010), 115–37; Hamblin, *Arming Mother Nature*, 27, 30–35, 42–47, 63, 70–71.

24   Christian C. Young, *The Environment and Science: Social Impact and Interaction* (Santa Barbara, CA: ABC-CLIO, 2005), 84, 87–89; Dunlap, *Nature and the English Diaspora*, 142, 145–46, 151–52; Hamblin, *Arming Mother Nature*, 72–73.

25   Russell, *War and Nature*, 165, 189–90.

26   Ibid., 171–74, 179, 197.

27   Ibid., 135–36, 159, 170.

28   Marcos Cueto, "Metaphors of Malaria Eradication in Cold War Mexico," in *Plagues and Epidemics: Infected Spaces Past and Present*, eds. D. Ann Herring and Alan C. Swedlund (Oxford, UK: Berg, 2010), 290; Frank M. Snowden, *The Conquest of Malaria: Italy, 1900-1962* (New Haven, CT: Yale University

Press, 2006), 204; Rockefeller Foundation Home Page, accessed September 15, 2017. https://www.rockefellerfoundation.org/; Marcus Hall, "World War II and the Axis of Disease: Battling Malaria in Twentieth-Century Italy," in *War and the Environment: Military Destruction in the Modern Age*, ed. Charles E. Closmann (College Station: Texas A&M University Press, 2009), 121–22.

29  G. Mathys, "Society Supported Disease Management Activities," in *Plant Disease: An Advanced Treatise*, vol. I, *How Disease is Managed*, eds. James G. Horsfall and Ellis B. Cowling (New York: Academic, 1977), 365; H. S. Chaube and V. S. Pundhir, *Crop Diseases and Their Management* (New Delhi: PHI Learning, 2009), 214; Caldwell, *International Environmental Policy*, 2nd ed., 220–21.

30  Victor S. Kaufman, *Confronting Communism: U.S. and British Policies toward China* (Columbia: University of Missouri Press, 2001), 8–9.

31  John Lewis Gaddis, *Russia, the Soviet Union, and the United States: An Interpretive History* (New York: Wiley, 1978), 222; Dick Wilson, *Zhou Enlai: A Biography* (New York: Viking, 1984), 211–12; Han Suyin, *Eldest Son: Zhou Enlai and the Making of Modern China, 1898-1976* (New York: Hill and Wang, 1994), 270.

32  Stanley Karnow, *Mao and China: A Legacy of Turmoil*, 2nd ed. (New York: Penguin, 1990), 85.

33  Judith Shapiro, *Mao's War against Nature: Politic and the Environment in Revolutionary China* (New York: Cambridge University Press, 2001), 21–22, 30–32, 51–52.

34  Shapiro, *Mao's War against Nature*, 61, 62–23, 80–81, 82–83; Penny Kane, *Famine in China, 1959-1961: Demographic and Social Implications* (New York: St. Martin's, 1988), 47–48, 89; Karnow, *Mao and China*, 91–92.

35  Karen Brown, *Plutopia: Nuclear Families, Atomic Cities, and the Great Soviet and American Plutonium Disasters* (New York: Oxford University Press 2013), 3.

36  Brown, *Plutopia*, 4; Thomas B. Cochran, Robert Standish Norris, and Kristen L. Suokko, "Radioactive Contamination at Chelyabinsk-65, Russia," *Annual Review of Energy and the Environment* 18 (1993): 507–08, 511, 513–15, 518–23; Samira Goetschel, "'The Graveyard of the Earth': Inside City 40, Russia's Deadly Nuclear Secret," *The Guardian*, July 20, 2016, accessed February 9, 2017. https://www.theguardian.com/cities/2016/jul/20/graveyard-earth-inside-city-40-ozersk-russia-deadly-secret-nuclear.

37  Annette Cary, "Final Hanford Downwinder Lawsuit Settled after 24 Years," *Seattle Times*, October 8, 2015, accessed April 16, 2017. http://www.seattletimes.com/seattle-news/environment/final-hanford-downwinder-lawsuit-settled-after-24-years/.

38  Jacob Darwin Hamblin, *Poison in the Well: Radioactive Waste in the Oceans at the Dawn of the Nuclear Age* (New Brunswick, NJ: Rutgers University Press, 2008), 28, 126–30, 167–72, 183–86.

39  Hamblin, *Poison in the Well*, 193–94.

40  Mark D. Merlin and Richard M. Gonzalez, "Environmental Impacts of Nuclear Testing in Remote Oceania, 1946-1996," in *Environmental Histories of the Cold War*, eds. J. R. McNeill and Corinna R. Unger (New York: Cambridge University Press, 2010), 170; Scott Kaufman, *Project Plowshare: The Peaceful Use of Nuclear Explosives in Cold War America* (Ithaca, NY: Cornell University Press, 2013), 9.

41  Merlin and Gonzalez, "Environmental Impacts," 175, 178.

42  Ibid., 184–85; "This Dome in the Pacific Houses Tons of Radioactive Waste—and It's Leaking," *The Guardian*, July 3, 2015, accessed February 12, 2017. https://www.theguardian.com/world/2015/jul/03/runit-dome-pacific-radioactive-waste.

43  J. Christopher Jolly, "Linus Pauling and the Scientific Debate over Fallout Hazards," *Endeavour* 26 (2002): 149; Michael Egan, *Barry Commoner and the Science of Survival: The Remaking of American Environmentalism* (Cambridge, MA: MIT Press, 2007), 51–52.

44  Robert A. Divine, *Blowing on the Wind: The Nuclear Test Ban Debate, 1954-1960* (New York: Oxford University Press, 1978), 3–4, 5, 7–8; David Tal, *The American Nuclear Disarmament Dilemma, 1945-1963* (Syracuse: Syracuse University Press, 2008), 64–65.

45  Divine, *Blowing on the Wind*, 41, 78–81, 123.

46  Ibid., 200–01; Jolly, "Linus Pauling," 150–51.

47  George H. Gallup, *The Gallup Poll: Public Opinion, 1935-1971*, vol. 2 (New York: Random House, 1972), 1229, 1488; Richard Terry Sylves, *The Nuclear Oracles: A Political History of the General Advisory Committee of the Atomic Energy Commission, 1947-1977* (Ames: Iowa State University Press, 1987), 59, 60; Kaufman, *Project Plowshare*, 20.

48  Divine, *Blowing on the Wind*, 206–07, 209–11.

49  Record of Meeting, August 18, 1958, *Foreign Relations of the United States, 1958-1960*, 3:644–46; Thanos P. Dokos, *Negotiations for a CTBT, 1958-1994: Analysis and Evaluation of American Policy* (Lanham, MD: University Press of America, 1995), 7–8; *Public Papers of the Presidents of the United States, Dwight D. Eisenhower*, 1958, 636; Stephen E. Ambrose, *Eisenhower*, vol. 2: *The President* (New York: Simon and Schuster, 1984), 480.

50  Dokos, *Negotiations for a CTBT*, 7, 13–14.

51  Ibid., 43; Glenn T. Seaborg, *Kennedy, Khrushchev, and the Test Ban* (Berkeley: University of California Press, 1981), 209–11; Benjamin P. Greene, *Eisenhower, Science Advice, and the Nuclear Test-Ban Debate, 1945-1963* (Stanford, CA: Stanford University Press, 2007), 239–40.

52  Simon Dalby, *Security and Environmental Change* (Cambridge, UK: Polity, 2009), 37; Kaufman, *Project Plowshare*, 91, 92–93.

53  Paul Kennedy, *The Parliament of Man: The Past, Present, and Future of the United Nations* (New York: Random House, 2006), 156–57.

54  Thomas Davies, *NGOs: A New History of Transnational Civil Society* (New York: Oxford University Press, 2014), 144.

# Chapter 4

1 Yuri Smertin, *Kwame Nkrumah* (New York: International Publishers, 1987), 58.

2 Dunlap, *Nature and the English Diaspora*, 276.

3 J. Edmund de Steiguer, *The Origins of Modern Environmental Thought* (Tucson: University of Arizona Press, 2006), 33; Tony Brenton, *The Greening of Machiavelli: The Evolution of International Environmental Politics* (London: Royal Institute of International Affairs, Energy and Environmental Programme, 1994), 18; Mark Hamilton Lytle, *The Gentle Subversive: Rachel Carson,* Silent *Spring, and the Rise of the Environmental Movement* (New York: Oxford University Press, 2007), 165, 176, 186; David Kinkela, *DDT and the American Century: Global Health, Environmental Politics, and the Pesticide that Changed the World* (Chapel Hill: University of North Carolina Press, 2011), 124.

4 Ramachandra Guha, *Environmentalism: An International History* (New York: Longman, 2000), 72; Bill Freedman, *Environmental Ecology: The Ecological Effects of Pollution, Disturbance, and Others Stresses*, 2nd ed. (San Diego: Academic Press, 1995), 168; Brenton, *Greening of Machiavelli*, 22; Thomas R. Wellock, *Preserving the Nation: The Conservation and Environmental Movements, 1870-2000* (Wheeling, IL: Harlan Davidson, 2007), 172–73.

5 Brenton, *Greening of Machiavelli*, 21, 23.

6 Ibid., 22–23; McCormick, *Reclaiming Paradise*, 64.

7 Hough, *Environmental Security*, 40; David Adamson, *Defending the World: The Politics and Diplomacy of the Environment* (London: I.B. Tauris, 1990), 31–32; de Steiguer, *Origins of Modern Environmental Thought*, 166, 167, 171.

8 Barbara Jancar-Webster, "Eastern Europe and the Former Soviet Union," in *Environmental Politics in the International Arena: Movements, Parties, Organizations, and Policy*, ed. Sheldon Kamieniecki (Albany: State University of New York Press, 1993), 208; McCormick, *Reclaiming Paradise*, 132; Brett D. Schaefer, "Green Creep: The Increasing Influence of Environmentalism in U.S. Foreign Policy," in *The Greening of U.S. Foreign Policy*, eds. Terry L. Anderson and Henry I. Miller (Stanford, CA: Hoover Institution Press; Bozeman, MT: Political Economy Research Center, 2000), 44–45.

9 Dalton, "Environmental Movement in Western Europe," 53–54, 61; Davies, *NGOs*, 145.

10 Burt K. Carnahan, "The Canadian Arctic Waters Pollution Prevention Act: An Analysis," *Louisiana Law Review* 31 (1971): 632; Dalton, "Environmental Movement in Western Europe," 53; R. J. Owell and L. M. Wharton, "Development of the Canadian Clean Air Act," *Journal of the Air Pollution Control Association* 32 (1982): 62–65; A. Radha Krishnan and Malcolm Tull, "Resource Use and Environmental Management in Japan, 1890-1990," *Australian Economic History Review* 34 (1994): 14–17; Peter Haas, *Saving the Mediterranean: The Politics of International Environmental Cooperation* (New York: Columbia University Press, 1990), 14.

11   Marc Cioc, "Europe's River: The Rhine as Prelude to International
     Cooperation and the Common Market," in *Nation-States and the Global
     Environment: New Approaches to International Environmental History*, eds.
     Erika Marie Bsumek, David Kinkela, and Mark Atwood Lawrence (New York:
     Oxford University Press, 2013), 27; Caldwell, *International Environmental
     Policy*, 2nd ed., 98, 131; "The Berne Convention," accessed June 22, 2017.
     https://www.iksr.org/fileadmin/user_upload/Dokumente_en/convention_on_
     tthe_protection_of_the_rhine.pdf; Daniel Bodansky, *The Art and Craft of
     International Environmental Law* (Cambridge, MA: Harvard University Press,
     2010), 26–27; Robert L. Paarlberg, "Managaing Pesticide Use in Developing
     Countries," in *Institutions for the Earth: Sources of Effective International
     Environmental Protection*, eds. Peter M. Haas, Robert O. Keohane, and Marc
     A. Levy (Cambridge, MA: MIT Press, 1993), 314.

12   Memorandum for the Record, March 21, 1967, *Foreign Relations of the
     United States, 1964-1968*, 5: 275; Stanley Karnow, *Vietnam: A History* (New
     York: Penguin, 1997), 272–73.

13   David Zierler, *The Invention of Ecocide: Agent Orange, Vietnam, and the
     Scientists Who Changed the Way We Think about the Environment* (Athens:
     University of Georgia Press, 2010), 84–85; Edwin A. Martini, *Agent Orange:
     History, Science, and the Politics of Uncertainty* (Amherst: University of
     Massachusetts Press, 2012), 2, 64–70.

14   Zierler, *Invention of Ecocide*, 93–94, 95–96.

15   Ibid., 97–99, 100, 107–08, 109–10.

16   Ibid., 119–20.

17   Ibid., 122–23, 124–25.

18   J. Brooks Flippen, "Richard Nixon, Russell Train, and the Birth of Modern
     American Environmental Diplomacy," *Diplomatic History* 32 (2008): 613–15,
     617, 624.

19   Flippen, "Richard Nixon, Russell Train, and the Birth of Modern American
     Environmental Diplomacy," 626–27; Hough, *Environmental Security*, 27.

20   Zierler, *Invention of Ecocide*, 3, 15, 122, 138, 144–46, 152, 155–56, 157.

21   Dorsey, *Whales and Nations*, 189, 194. For more on the Soviet Union's
     violations of the ICRW and its effect on whale populations, see Yulia V.
     Ivashchenko, Phillip J. Clapham, and Robert L. Brownell, Jr., "Soviet Illegal
     Whaling: The Devil and the Details," *Marine Fisheries Review* 73 (2011):
     1–19.

22   Dorsey, *Whales and Nations*, 209, 213–18.

23   Ibid., 218, 220–21, 225–26.

24   Paul R. Josephson, "When Stalin Learned to Fish: Natural Resources,
     Technology, and Industry under Socialism," in *City, Country, Empire:
     Landscapes in Environmental History*, eds. Jeffry M. Diefendorf and Kurk
     Dorsey (Pittsburgh: University of Pittsburgh Press, 2005), 174–81; Erika
     Weinthal, "The Promises and Pitfalls of Environmental Peacemaking in the
     Aral Sea Basin," in *Environmental Peacemaking*, eds. Ken Conca and Geoffrey
     D. Dabelko (Washington, DC: Woodrow Wilson Center Press/Baltimore: Johns
     Hopkins University Press, 2002), 86.

25 Josephson, "When Stalin Learned to Fish," 181–83, 187.

26 Nicolai Lagoni, *The Liability of Classification Societies* (New York: Springer, 2007), 273–74; Elli Louka, *International Environmental Law: Fairness, Effectiveness, and World Order* (New York: Cambridge University Press, 2006), 159.

27 Carnahan, "Canadian Arctic Waters Pollution Prevention Act," 636–43; Willy Østreng, et al., *Shipping in Arctic Waters: A Comparison of the Northeast, Northwest and Trans Polar Passes* (Heidelberg, Germany: Springer, 2013), 26–27.

28 Thomas Rodney Christofferson and Michael Scott Christofferson, *France during World War II* (New York: Fordham University Press, 2006), 18; William L. Hosch, ed., *World War II: People, Politics, and Power* (New York: Britannica Educational, 2010), 185; Richard Goff, et al., *The Twentieth Century: A Brief Global History*, 6th ed. (Boston: McGraw-Hill, 2002), 262; David Kennedy and Elizabeth Cohen, *The American Pageant: A History of the American People*, 15th ed. (Boston: Wadsworth, 2014), 789; Mark Pilisuk, with Jennifer Achord Roundtree, *Who Benefits from Global Violence and War: Uncovering a Destructive System* (Westport, CT: Praeger, 2008), 136.

29 Willard W. Cochrane, *The Development of American Agriculture: A Historical Analysis* (Minneapolis: University of Minnesota Press, 1993), 127; Jonathan Harwood, *Europe's Green Revolution and Others Since: The Rise and Fall of Peasant-Friendly Plant Breeding* (New York: Routledge, 2012), 116–18.

30 Caldwell, *International Environmental Policy*, 2nd ed., 48; Anthony H. F. Li, "Hopes of Limiting Global Warming? China and the Paris Agreement on Climate Change," *China Perspectives* no. 1 (2016): 51; Lester Ross, "Environmental Policy in Post-Mao China," *Environment* 29 (1987): 34.

31 William M. Adams, *Against Extinction: The Story of Conservation* (Sterling, VA: Earthscan, 2004), 169–70; McCormick, *Reclaiming Paradise*, 43.

32 Adams, *Against Extinction*, 53.

33 Ibid., 170; IUCN International Law Programme, *An Introduction to the African Convention on the Conservation of Nature and Natural Resources*, 2nd ed. (Gland, Switzerland: IUCN, 2006), 4–6; Frans Viljoen, *International Human Rights Law in Africa*, 2nd ed. (New York: Oxford University Press, 2012), 269.

34 Erik Carp, *Directory of Wetlands of International Importance in the Western Palearctic* (Nairobi: UNEP/Gland, Switzerland: World Wildlife Fund, 1980), 1–3.

35 John Temple Lang, "Biological Conservation and Biological Diversity," in *International Environmental Negotiation*, ed. Gunnar Sjöstedt (Newbury Park, CA: Sage, 1993), 171–72; Caldwell, *International Environmental Policy*, 2nd ed., 225.

36 Lang, "Biological Conservation and Biological Diversity," 172; "The Ramsar Sites," accessed September 9, 2017. https://www.ramsar.org/sites-countries/the-ramsar-sites; McCormick, *Reclaiming Paradise*, 177.

37 Marc A. Levy, "European Acid Rain: The Power of Tote-Board Diplomacy," in *Institutions for the Earth: Sources of Effective International Environmental*

*Protection*, eds. Peter M. Haas, Robert O. Keohane, and Marc A. Levy (Cambridge, MA: MIT Press, 1993), 78–79; Gareth Porter, Janet Welsh Brown, and Pamela S. Chasek, *Global Environmental Politics*, 3rd ed. (Boulder, CO: Westview, 2000), 83.


38   Caldwell, *International Environmental Policy*, 2nd ed., 49–50, 52.

39   Brenton, *Greening of Machiavelli*, 42–44; Peter S. Thacher, "The Mediterranean: A New Approach to Marine Pollution," in *International Environmental Negotiation*, ed. Gunnar Sjöstedt (Newbury Park, CA: Sage, 1993), 119.

40   McCormick, *Reclaiming Paradise*, 98–100, 103; SEQ CHAPTER \h \r 1Error! Main Document Only.Epstein, *The Power of Words in International Relations*, 105.

41   McCormick, *Reclaiming Paradise*, 104–05; Stephen J. Macekura, *Of Limits and Growth: The Rise of Global Sustainable Development in the Twentieth Century* (New York: Cambridge University Press, 2015), 92.

42   Jennifer A. Elliott, *An Introduction to Sustainable Development*, 3rd ed. (New York: Routledge, 2006), 32–33; Macekura, *Of Limits and Growth*, 117; Tolba and Rummel-Bulska, *Global Environmental Diplomacy*, 2; Brenton, *Greening of Machiavelli*, 37–38.

43   Adamson, *Defending the World*, 33; "Declaration of the United Nations Conference on the Human Environment," June 1972, accessed June 10, 2017. http://www.un-documents.net/unchedec.htm.

44   Douglas A. Schuler, "The NAFTA and the Environment: Trade, Diplomacy, and Limited Protection," *The International Trade Journal* 10 (1996): 357; Tolba and Rummel-Bulska, *Global Environmental Diplomacy*, 15.

45   Kate O'Neill, *The Environment and International Relations* (New York: Cambridge University Press, 2009), 27–28; McCormick, *Reclaiming Paradise*, 101–02, 139; 150; Adamson, *Defending the World*, 133.

46   Dalton, "Environmental Movement in Western Europe," 52–53; David Vogel, "Environmental Policy in the European Community," in *Environmental Politics in the International Arena: Movements, Parties, Organizations, and Policy*, ed. Sheldon Kamieniecki (Albany: State University of New York Press, 1993), 182; Marc Cioc, *The Rhine: An Eco-Biography, 1815-2000* (Seattle: University of Washington Press, 2002), 179; Tolba and Rummel-Bulska, *Global Environmental Diplomacy*, 18; Caldwell, *International Environmental Policy*, 2nd ed., 99.

47   Levy, "European Acid Rain," 81; Johan Sliggers and Willem Kakebeeke, *Clearing the Air: 25 Years of the Convention on Long-Range Transboundary Air Pollution* (Geneva: Economic Commission for Europe, 2004), 9.

48   Levy, "European Acid Rain," 81–82.

49   Roderick W. Shaw, "Acid-Rain Negotiations in North America and Europe: A Study in Contrast," in *International Environmental Negotiation*, ed. Gunnar Sjöstedt (Newbury Park, CA: Sage, 1993), 94–95, 97–98; McCormick, *Reclaiming Paradise*, 183, 186; Sliggers and Kakebeeke, *Clearing the Air*, 11; Haas, *Saving the Mediterranean*, 239–40; Levy, "European Acid Rain," 82.

50  Shaw, "Acid-Rain Negotiations," 92–93, 100–01; Levy, "European Acid Rain," 83.

51  Hamblin, *Poison in the Well*, 220, 230–34, 242–52.

52  Haas, *Saving the Mediterranean*, 11.

53  Ibid., 27–30, 83–84, 86–88.

54  Ibid., 72–74, 79; Tolba and Rummel-Bulska, *Global Environmental Diplomacy*, 40.

55  Haas, *Saving the Mediterranean*, 97, 101–03, 107–08, 110; UNEP, *United Nations Environment Programme Mediterranean Action Plan*, January 16, 2015, accessed November 14, 2017. https://wedocs.unep.org/rest/bitstreams/7804/retrieve.

56  Brenton, *Greening of Machiavelli*, 101; Richard Caldwell, "Inter-Treaty Cooperation, Biodiversity Conservation and the Trade in Endangered Species," *RECIEL* 22 (2013): 266.

57  Ed Couzens, "CITES at Forty: Never Too Late to Make Lifestyle Changes," *RECIEL* 22 (2013): 317–18; Prost and Otomo, "British Influences on International Environmental Law," 207–08; Porter, Brown, and Chasek, *Global Environmental Politics*, 3rd ed., 100.

58  Dorsey, *Whales and Nations*, 222–23, 225.

59  Ibid., 229, 260–62; Epstein, *Power of Words in International Relations*, 108. For a detailed description of the confrontation between Greenpeace and the Soviet whalers, see Frank S. Zelko, *Make It a Green Peace!: The Rise of Cultural Environmentalism* (New York: Oxford University Press, 2013), 219–23.

60  Cioc, *The Game of Conservation*, 98–99; Boardman, *International Organization and the Conservation of Nature*, 95; Convention on the Conservation of Migratory Species of Wild Animals, accessed June 16, 2017. http://www.cms.int/en/convention-text.

61  Macekura, *Of Limits and Growth*, 93.

62  Hough, *Environmental Security*, 22; Ken Conca, "The Case for Environmental Peacemaking," in *Environmental Peacemaking*, eds. Ken Conca and Geoffrey D. Dabelko (Washington DC: Woodrow Wilson Center Press/Baltimore: Johns Hopkins University Press, 2002), 1.

# Chapter 5

1  Caldwell, *International Environmental Policy*, 87, 89.

2  Michele M. Betsill, "Transnational Actors in International Environmental Politics," in *Palgrave Advances in International Environmental Politics*, eds. Michele M. Betsill, Kathryn Hochstetler, and Dimitris Stevis (New York: Palgrave Macmillan, 2006), 178; Peter Haas, *Saving the Mediterranean: The Politics of International Environmental Cooperation* (New York: Columbia University Press, 1990), 15.

3  Jessica Tuchman Mathews, "Introduction and Overview," in *Preserving the Global Environment: The Challenge of Shared Leadership*, ed. Jessica Tuchman Mathews (New York: Norton, 1991), 20–24.

4  Cioc, *Game of Conservation*, 99–100; Parties and Range States of Convention on the Conservation of Migratory Species of Wild Animals, accessed June 16, 2017. http://www.cms.int/en/parties-range-states; Kirsti-Liisa Sjoblom and Gordon Linsley, "Sea Disposal of Radioactive Wastes: The London Convention of 1972," *IAEA Bulletin* 36 (1994): 12.

5  Jessica Duncan, *Global Food Security Governance: Civil Society Engagement in the Reformed Committee on World Food Security* (New York: Routledge, 2015), 50; Cynthia Rosenzweig and Daniel Hillel, *Climate Variability and the Global Harvest: Impacts of El Niño and Other Oscillations on Agro-Ecosystems* (New York: Oxford University Press, 2008), 94–95.

6  Robert L. Paalberg, "Managing Pesticide Use in Developing Countries," in *Institutions for the Earth: Sources of Effective International Environmental Problems*, eds. Peter M. Haas, Robert O. Keohane, and Marc A. Levy (Cambridge, MA: MIT Press, 1993), 315; Council of Europe Parliamentary Assembly, Resolution 583, January 22, 1975, accessed July 7, 2017. http://www.assembly.coe.int/nw/xml/XRef/Xref-XML2HTML-en.asp?fileid=15996&lang=en.

7  John McNeill, "Deforestation in the Araucaria Zone of Southern Brazil, 1900-1983," in *World Deforestation in the Twentieth Century*, eds. John F. Richards and Richard P. Tucker (Durham, NC: Duke University Press, 1988), 17; Mostafa K. Tolba, "A Commitment to Life," in *Environment and Diplomacy in the Americas*, ed. Heraldo Muñoz (Boulder, CO: Lynne Rienner, 1992), 26; Ramachandra Guha, *Environmentalism: A World History* (New York: Longman, 2000), 116–17; Javier A. Barrientos, Jr., "Mexico's Energy Policy: 1976-1982," in *Energy Options and Conservation: Proceedings of the Fourth International Conference*, eds. Ragaei El Mallakh and Dorothea El Mallakh (Boulder, CO: International Research Center for Energy and Economic Development, 1978), 278; "Constitution of the Union of Soviet Socialist Republics," 1977, accessed June 15, 2017. http://www.departments.bucknell.edu/russian/const/77cons01.html; Paul R. Josephson, "When Stalin Learned to Fish: Natural Resources, Technology, and Industry under Socialism," in *City, Country, Empire: Landscapes in Environmental History*, eds. Jeffry M. Diefendorf and Kurk Dorsey (Pittsburgh: University of Pittsburgh Press, 2005), 191–92.

8  Porter, Brown, and Chasek, *Global Environmental Politics*, 3rd ed., 53.

9  Terry L. Anderson, "Bucking the Tide of Globalism: Developing Property Rights from the Ground Up," in *The Greening of U.S. Foreign Policy*, eds. Terry L. Anderson and Henry I. Miller (Stanford, CA: Hoover Institution Press; Bozeman, MT: Political Economy Research Center, 2000), 256–57; Lisa Friedman, "Coal-Fired Power in India May Cause More than 100,000 Premature Deaths Annually," *Scientific American*, March 11, 2013, accessed September 19, 2017. https://www.scientificamerican.com/article/coal-fired-power-in-india-may-cause-more-than-100000-premature-deaths-annually/.

10  Kwasi Nsiah-Gyabaah, "Human Security and the Environment in Sub-Saharan Africa: The Challenge of the New Millennium," in *Human Security*

*and the Environment: International Implications*, eds. Edward A. Page and Michael Redclift (Cheltenham, UK: Edward Elgar, 2002), 230–31; O'Neill, *Environment and International Relations*, 158.

11  United Nations, "Declaration of the United Nations Conference on the Human Environment," June 1972, accessed June 30, 2017. http://www.un-documents. net/unchedec.htm; Guha, *Environmentalism*, 112; Louis Emmerij, Richard Jolly, and Thomas G. Weiss, *Ahead of the Curve?: UN Ideas and Global Challenges* (Bloomington: Indiana University Press, 2001), 95–96; Hough, *Environmental Security*, 41.

12  Diana K. Davis, *The Arid Lands: History, Power, Knowledge* (Cambridge, MA: MIT Press, 2016), 2; Hough, *Environmental Security*, 106, 108, 110; Porter, Brown, and Chasek, *Global Environmental Politics*, 3rd ed., 130, 132.

13  Brian Fagan, *Floods, Famines, and Emperors; El Niño and the Fate of Civilizations* (New York: Basic Books, 1999), 216–19; Tolba and Rummel-Bulska, *Global Environmental Diplomacy*, 49.

14  Porter, Brown, and Chasek *Global Environmental Politics*, 3rd ed., 132; Brenton, *Greening of Machiavelli*, 121.

15  Byron W. Daynes and Glen Sussman, *White House Politics and the Environment: Franklin D. Roosevelt to George W. Bush* (College Station: Texas A&M Press, 2010), 87.

16  Daynes and Sussman, *White House Politics and the Environment*, 176, 184.

17  Rüdiger K. W. Wurzel, *Environmental Policy-Making in Britain, Germany, and the European Union: The Europeanisation of Air and Water Pollution Control* (New York: Manchester University Press, 2002), 127.

18  Otis L. Graham, Jr., *Presidents and the American Environment* (Lawrence: University Press of Kansas, 2015), 295; Dunlap, *Nature and the English Diaspora*, 304; McCormick, *Reclaiming Paradise* 137, 141–42; Caldwell, *International Environmental Policy*, 2nd ed., 141–43.

19  Smith, *Japan's International Fisheries Policy*, 86; Porter, Brown, and Chasek, *Global Environmental Politics*, 3rd ed., 95; Dorsey, *Whales and Nations*, 254–55; Epstein, *The Power of Words in International Relations*, 158–60.

20  Dorsey, *Whales and Nations*, 265, 267, 274; Caldwell, *International Environmental Policy*, 2nd ed., 288.

21  Smith, *Japan's International Fisheries Policy*, 32, 67–68, 69–72; Scheiber, *Inter-Allied Conflicts and Ocean Law*, 11.

22  Sarhhage and Lundbeck, *A History of Fishing*, 68, 74, 75, 76–77.

23  Porter, Brown, and Chasek, *Global Environmental Politics*, 3rd ed., 84.

24  Levy, "European Acid Rain," 94; B. W. Clapp, *An Environmental History of Britain* (New York: Longman, 1994), 57; Daynes and Sussman, *White House Politics and the Environment*, 166, 185; Randolph P. Angle, "The Canada-US Air Quality Agreement and Its Impact on Air Quality Management in Canada," in *Air Quality Management: Canadian Perspectives on a Global Issue*, eds. Eric Taylor and Ann McMillan (New York: Springer, 2014), 326.

25  Paul N. Edwards, "Representing the Global Atmosphere," in *Changing the Atmosphere: Expert Knowledge and Environmental Governance*, eds. Clark

A. Miller and Paul N. Edwards (Cambridge, MA: MIT Press, 2001), 39, 40; Christopher Herrick, with Patricia B. McRae, *Issues in American Foreign Policy* (New York: Longman, 2003), 283; Fagan, *Floods, Famine, and Emperors*, 19–20.

26  Spencer Weart, *The Discovery of Global Warming*, rev. and expanded ed. (Cambridge, MA: Harvard University Press, 2008), 19, 34–35, 37, 41.

27  Weart, *The Discovery of Global Warming*, 42, 67–68, 76–77; Sonja Boehmer-Christiansen, "The International Research Enterprise and Global Environmental Change: Climate-change Policy as a Research Process," in *The Environment and International Relations*, eds. John Vogler and Mark F. Imber (London: Routledge, 1996), 179.

28  Weart, *Discovery of Global Warming*, rev. and expanded ed., 122–23; Edward A. Parson, "Protecting the Ozone Layer," in *Institutions for the Earth: Sources of Effective International Environmental Protection*, eds. Peter M. Haas, Robert O. Keohane, and Marc A. Levy (Cambridge, MA: MIT Press, 1993), 28; Richard Elliot Benedick, *Ozone Diplomacy: New Directions in Safeguarding the Planet*, enlarged ed. (Cambridge, MA: Harvard University Press, 1998), 10–11.

29  Porter, Brown, and Chasek, *Global Environmental Politics*, 3rd ed., 88; Tolba and Rummel-Bulska, *Global Environmental Diplomacy*, 57; Parson, "Protecting the Ozone Layer," 36–37.

30  Adamson, *Defending the World*, 109; Paul Vitello, "Joseph Farman, 82, Who Discovered the Hole in the Ozone Layer, Dies," *New York Times*, May 19, 2013.

31  Tolba and Rummel-Bulska, *Global Environmental Diplomacy*, 57–59; Weart, *Discovery of Global Warming*, rev. and expanded, ed., 123–24.

32  Benedick, *Ozone Diplomacy*, 42–43; Tolba and Rummel-Bulska, *Global Environmental Diplomacy*, 59.

33  Srini Sitaraman, "Evolution of the Ozone Regime: Local, National, and International Influences," in *The Environment, International Relations, and U.S. Foreign Policy*, ed. Paul G. Harris (Washington DC: Georgetown University Press, 2001), 124.

34  Greenpeace, *The Chernobyl Catastrophe: Consequences on Human Health* (Amsterdam: Greenpeace, 2006), 9; Anne Nadakavukaren, *Our Global Environment: A Health Perspective*, 7th ed. (Long Grove, IL: Waveland, 2011), 262.

35  Dalton, "Environmental Movement in Western Europe," 58; Caldwell, *International Environmental Policy*, 2nd ed., 188; Convention on Early Notification of a Nuclear Accident, accessed September 22, 2017, https://www.iaea.org/publications/documents/treaties/convention-early-notification-nuclear-accident; Convention on Assistance in the Case of a Nuclear Accident or Radiological Emergency, accessed September 22, 2017, https://www.iaea.org/publications/documents/treaties/convention-assistance-case-nuclear-accident-or-radiological-emergency.

36  Vogel, "Environmental Policy in the European Community," 186–87, 188; Dalton, "Environmental Movement in Western Europe," 58; Brenton, *Greening of Machiavelli*, 112–13.

37 Jancar-Webster, "Eastern Europe and the Former Soviet Union," 200–01, 207–08; Adamson, *Defending the World*, 202–03.

38 On this score, see Weiner, *A Little Corner of Freedom*.

39 Jancar-Webster, "Eastern Europe and the Former Soviet Union," 208.

40 Ibid., 204–05, 211–14; Brenton, *Greening of Machiavelli*, 66.

41 Jurgen Brauer, *War and Nature: The Environmental Consequences of War in a Globalized World* (Lanham, MD: AltaMira, 2009), 81–82, 108–09; Mohammad Sadiq and John C. McCain, *The Gulf War Aftermath: An Environmental Tragedy* (Boston: Kluwer Academic, 1993), 80; Hough, *Environmental Security*, 63.

42 Benedick, *Ozone Diplomacy*, 15, 18; Tolba and Rummel-Bulska, *Global Environmental Diplomacy*, 62.

43 Benedick, *Ozone Diplomacy*, 26, 30–31, 33; Tolba and Rummel-Bulska, *Global Environmental Diplomacy*, 63, 64–65; Parson, "Protecting the Ozone Layer," 41.

44 Tolba and Rummel-Bulska, *Global Environmental Diplomacy*, 66, 71; Porter, Brown, and Chasek, *Global Environmental Politics*, 3rd ed., 89; Daynes and Sussman, *White House Politics and the Environment*, 185; Benedick, *Ozone Diplomacy*, 35, 39.

45 John J. Cohrssen, "U.S. International Interests, Sustainable Development, and the Precautionary Principle," in *The Greening of U.S. Foreign Policy*, eds. Terry L. Anderson and Henry I. Miller (Stanford, CA: Hoover Institution Press; Bozeman, MT: Political Economy Research Center, 2000), 133; Vogel, "Environmental Policy in the European Community," 188; Porter, Brown, and Chasek, *Global Environmental Politics*, 3rd ed., 90; Benedick, *Ozone Diplomacy*, 93.

46 Barbara J. Bramble and Gareth Porter, "Non-Governmental Organizations and the Making of US International Environmental Policy," in *The International Politics of the Environment*, eds. Andrew Hurrell and Benedict Kingsbury (Oxford, UK: Clarendon, 1992), 337–38; Benedick, *Ozone Diplomacy*, 113–14.

47 Jennifer Clapp, *Toxic Exports: The Transfer of Hazardous Wastes from Rich to Poor Countries* (Ithaca, NY: Cornell University Press, 2001), 35; Bruno Dente, Paolo Fareri, and Josee Ligteringen, *The Waste and the Backyard: The Creation of Waste Facilities: Success Stories in Six European Countries* (Dordrecht, Netherlands: Kluwer Academic, 1998), 165.

48 Clapp, *Toxic Exports*, 24, 27.

49 Ibid., 23.

50 Ibid.

51 Ibid., 23, 32, 36; Brenton, *Greening of Machiavelli*, 131.

52 Stanley Johnson, *UNEP: The First 40 Years: A Narrative* (Nairobi, Kenya: United nations Environment Programme, 2012), 98, 103; 50; Clapp, *Toxic Exports*, 39–44; Johnson, *UNEP*, 103.

53 Clapp, *Toxic Exports*, 44–46.

54 Ibid., 46–47, 56; Porter, Brown, and Chasek, *Global Environmental Politics*, 3rd ed., 105.

55 Porter, Brown, and Chasek, *Global Environmental Politics*, 3rd ed., 106; Clapp, *Toxic Wastes*, 48–49.

56 Margo Brett Baender, "Pesticides and Precaution: The Bamako Convention as a Model for An International Convention on Pesticides Regulation," *New York University Journal of International Law and Politics* 24 (1991): 557–67, 571; Elizabeth R. DeSombre, *Global Environmental Institutions*, 2nd ed. (New York: Routledge, 2017), 154.

57 Benedick, *Ozone Diplomacy*, 114.

58 Ibid., 123–24; Naomi Klein, *This Changes Everything: Capitalism vs. the Climate* (New York: Simon and Schuster, 2014), 75; Porter, Brown, and Chasek, *Global Environmental Politics*, 3rd ed., 90; Tolba and Rummel-Bulska, *Global Environmental Diplomacy*, 80–81; Parson, "Protecting the Ozone Layer," 50.

59 Philip Shabecoff, "Global Warmth in '88 is Found to Set a Record," *New York Times*, accessed August 5, 2017, http://www.nytimes.com/1989/02/04/us/global-warmth-in-88-is-found-to-set-a-record.html; Klein, *This Changes Everything*, 74; Weart, *Discovery of Global Warming*, rev. and expanded ed. 150–51; Porter, Brown, and Chasek, *Global Environmental Politics*, 3rd ed., 116; Brenton, *Greening of Machiaevelli*, 166.

60 Daynes and Sussman, *White House Politics and the Environment*, 160; Brenton, *Greening of Machiavelli*, 170–71.

61 Garfield, *In Search of the Amazon*, 216; United Nations Population Fund, *Population, Resources, and the Environment: The Critical Challenges* (New York: United Nations Population Fund, 1991), 43; Adamson, *Defending the World*, 93–94.

62 Philip J. O'Brien, "Debt and Sustainable Development in Latin America," and Michael Redclift and David Goodman, "The Machinery of Hunger: The Crisis of Latin American Food Systems," in *Environment and Development in Latin America: The Politics of Sustainability*, eds. David Goodman and Michael Redclift (New York: Manchester University Press, 1991), 26–27, 57–58, 61–63, 65; Kenton R. Miller, Walter V. Reid, and Charles V. Barber, "Deforestation and Species Loss: Responding to the Crisis," in *Preserving the Global Environment: The Challenge of Shared Leadership*, ed. Jessica Tuchman Mathews (New York: Norton, 1991), 81; O'Neill, *Environment and International Relations*, 158; J. B. Veiga, et al., "Cattle Ranching in the Amazon Rain Forest," paper presented at the 12th World Forestry Congress, Québec City, Canada, accessed July 5 2017. http://www.fao.org/docrep/ARTICLE/WFC/XII/0568-B1.HTM.

63 Andrew Hurrell, "Brazil and the International Politics of Amazonian Deforestation," in *International Politics of the Environment*, eds. Andrew Hurrell and Benedict Kingsbury (Oxford UK: Clarendon, 1992), 404–07; Michael Redclift and David Goodman, "Introduction," in *Environment and Development in Latin America: The Politics of Sustainability*, eds. David Goodman and Michael Redclift (New York: Manchester University Press, 1991), 16.

64 Bron Taylor, et al., "Grass-Roots Resistance: The Emergence of Popular Environmental Movements in Less Affluent Countries," in *Environmental Politics in the International Arena: Movements, Parties, Organizations, and Policy*, ed. Sheldon Kamieniecki (Albany: State University of New York Press, 1993), 81–82; Eduardo J. Viola, "The Environmental Movement in Brazil: Institutionalization, Sustainable Development, and Crisis of Governance since 1987," in *Latin American Environmental Policy in International Perspective*, eds. Gordon J. MacDonald, Daniel L. Nielson, and Marc A. Stern (Boulder, CO: Westview, 1997), 96; Hurrell, "Brazil and the International Politics of Amazonian Deforestation," 417, 418–19; Bruce A. Byers, "Armed Forces and the Conservation of Biological Diversity," in *Green Security or Militarized Environment*, ed. Jyrki Käkönen (Aldershot, UK: Dartmouth, 1994), 118.

65 Porter, Brown, and Chasek, *Global Environmental Politics*, 3rd ed., 124; Brenton, *Greening of Machiavelli*, 197–98.

66 Tolba and Rummel-Bulska, *Global Environmental Diplomacy*, 136–40, 144–46, 148, 152–58; Brenton, *Greening of Machiavelli*, 201.

67 Porter, Brown, and Chasek, *Global Environmental Politics*, 3rd ed., 124–25; Brenton, *Greening of Machiavelli*, 202; Tolba and Rummel-Bulska, *Global Environmental Diplomacy*, 136–58.

68 Ken Conca, "Rethinking the Ecology-Sovereignty Debate," in *Green Planet Blues: Environmental Politics from Stockholm to Johannesburg*, 3rd ed., eds. Ken Conca and Geoffrey D. Dabelko (Boulder, CO: Westview, 2004), 74; Kennedy, *The Parliament of Man*, 162; Porter, Brown, and Chasek, *Global Environmental Politics*, 3rd ed., 47.

69 Kennedy, *Parliament of Man*, 162–63.

70 Porter, Brown, and Chasek, *Global Environmental Politics*, 3rd ed., 118; Tolba and Rummel-Bulska, *Global Environmental Diplomacy*, 95–96.

71 Tolba and Rummel-Bulska, *Global Environmental Diplomacy*, 159; Cohrssen, "U.S. International Interests," 133; Convention on Biological Diversity, accessed June 28, 2017. https://www.cbd.int/convention/text/.

72 Daynes and Sussman, *White House Politics and the Environment*, 167–68; Porter, Brown, and Chasek, *Global Environmental Politics*, 3rd ed., 127.

73 Hans Bruyninckx, "Sustainable Development: The Institutionalization of a Contested Policy Concept," in *Palgrave Advances in Environmental Politics*, eds. Michele M. Betsill, Kathryn Hochstetler, and Dimitris Stevis (New York: Palgrave Macmillan, 2006), 266–67; Peter S. Thacher, "The Role of the United Nations," in *International Politics of the Environment*, eds. Andrew Hurrell and Benedict Kingsbury (Oxford UK: Clarendon, 1992), 189; Porter, Brown, and Chasek, *Global Environmental Politics*, 3rd ed., 26–27; Emmerij, Jolly, and Weiss, *Ahead of the Curve?*, 94.

74 Porter, Brown, and Chasek, *Global Environmental Politics*, 3rd ed., 127–28.

75 Thacher, "Role of the United Nations," 190; Schaefer, "Green Creep," 58–59; Haas, *Saving the Mediterranean*, 14.

76 Daniel L. Nielson and Marc A. Stern, "Endowing the Environment: Multilateral Development Banks and Environmental Lending in Latin America," in *Latin American Environmental Policy in International*

*Perspective*, eds. Gordon J. MacDonald, Daniel L. Nielson, and Marc A. Stern (Boulder, CO: Westview, 1997), 142–43; Porter, Brown, and Chasek, *Global Environmental Politics*, 3rd ed., 163; Caldwell, *International Environmental Policy*, 2nd ed., 81.

77  Nielson and Stern, "Endowing the Environment," 143–44; Norman Myers, "The Anatomy of Environmental Action: The Case of Tropical Deforestation," in *International Politics of the Environment*, eds. Andrew Hurrell and Benedict Kingsbury (Oxford, UK: Clarendon, 1992), 441–42; Porter, Brown, and Chasek, *Global Environmental Politics*, 3rd ed., 50, 163, 166; Global Environment Facility, "About Us," Forest Stewardship Council, accessed October 18, 2017.

78  Paul G. Harris, "International Development Assistance and Burden Sharing," in *Green Giants?: Environmental Policies of the United States and the European Union*, eds. Norman J. Vig and Michael G. Faure (Cambridge, MA: MIT Press, 2004), 256; Porter, Brown, and Chasek, *Global Environmental Politics*, 3rd ed., 96–97; Peter H. Sand, "Japan's 'Research Whaling' in the Antarctic Southern Ocean and the North Pacific Ocean in the Face of the Endangered Species Convention (CITES)," *RECIEL* 17 (2008): 56.

79  Adamson, *Defending the World*, 10, 208–9; Ross, "Environmental Policy in Post-Mao China," 37–38; Bao Maohong, "The Evolution of Environmental Problems and Environmental Policy in China," in *Environmental Histories of the Cold War*, eds. J. R. McNeill and Corinna R. Unger (New York: Cambridge University Press, 2010), 337.

# Chapter 6

1  Frank McDonald, "Despite Limited Progress, Rio Marks a Modest Step Forward," *Irish Times*, June 15, 1992, 6; Paul Lewis, "Battle in Rio: The Day After," *New York Times*, June 15, 1992.

2  Mason C. Carter, Robert C. Kellison, and R. Scott Wallinger, *Forestry in the U.S. South: A History* (Baton Rouge: Louisiana State University Press, 2015), 305; Sébastian Duyck, "Polar Environmental Governance and Nonstate Actors," in *Diplomacy on Ice: Energy and the Environment in the Arctic and Antarctic*, eds. Rebecca Pincus and Salem H. Ali (New Haven, CT: Yale University Press, 2015), 17; Kate O'Neill, *The Environment and International Relations* (New York: Cambridge University Press, 2009), 180.

3  Porter, Brown, and Chasek, *Global Environmental Politics*, 3rd ed., 206–07.

4  Ibid., 38, 57–59; Tolba and Rummel-Bulska, *Global Environmental Diplomacy*, 130.

5  Hough, *Environmental Security*, 108–09; Porter, Brown, and Chasek, *Global Environmental Politics*, 3rd ed., 132–33.

6  Porter, Brown, and Chasek, *Global Environmental Politics*, 3rd ed., 133–34.

7  Ibid., 130, 134–35; Narendra P. Sharma, "The Political Economy of Water Resource Management in Africa: Choices and Tradeoffs," in *The Environment*

  *and Development in Latin America,* ed. Moses K. Tesi (Lanham, MD: Lexington Books, 2000), 130.

8 Porter, Brown, and Chasek, *Global Environmental Politics,* 3rd ed., 128; Peter Andrée, *Genetically Modified Diplomacy: The Global Politics of Agricultural Biotechnology and the Environment* (Vancouver: University of British Columbia Press, 2007), 113.

9 Robert Falkner, "Negotiating the Biosafety Protocol: The International Process," in *The Cartagena Protocol on Biosafety: Reconciling Trade in Biotechnology with Environment and Development?,* eds. Christoph Ball, Robert Falkner, and Helen Marquard (London: Earthscan, 2002), 4, 6–7, 9; Porter, Brown, and Chasek, *Global Environmental Politics,* 3rd ed., 129; Andrée, *Genetically Modified Diplomacy,* 114; David Vogel, "Trade and the Environment in the Global Economy: Contrasting European and American Perspectives," in *Green Giants?: Environmental Policies of the United States and the European Union,* eds. Norman J. Vig and Michael G. Faure (Cambridge, MA: MIT Press, 2004), 240–41; Cartagena Protocol on Biosafety to the Convention on Biological Diversity, 2000, accessed October 30, 2017. https://www.cbd.int/doc/legal/cartagena-protocol-en.pdf.

10 Thomas W. Zeiler and Robert E. Wright, eds., *Guide to U.S. Economic Policy* (Los Angeles: SAGE, 2014), 69.

11 Mary Beth Norton, et al., *A People and a Nation: A History of the United States,* vol. 2, *Since 1865,* 7th ed. (Boston: Houghton Mifflin, 2005), 924.

12 Robert Haryse, *Negotiating NAFTA: Explaining the Outcome in Culture, Textiles, Autos, and Pharmaceuticals* (Toronto: University of Toronto Press, 2000), 26–29; Pamela M. Doughman, "Water Cooperation in the U.S.-Mexico Border Region," in *Environmental Peacemaking,* eds. Ken Conca and Geoffrey D. Dabelko (Washington, DC: Woodrow Wilson Center Press/Baltimore: Johns Hopkins University Press, 2002), 200; Schuler, "The NAFTA and the Environment," 354–55; Blanca Torres, "Transnational Environmental NGOs: Linkages and Impact on Policy," in *Latin American Environmental Policy in International Perspective,* eds. Gordon J. MacDonald, Daniel L. Nielson, and Marc A. Stern (Boulder, CO: Westview, 1997), 169; United Nations, "Cartagena Protocol on Biosafety Takes Effect in September," accessed October 1, 2017. https://www.un.org/press/en/2003/envdev735.doc.htm

13 Bonanno and Constance, *Caught in the Net,* 11–13.

14 Porter, Brown, and Chasek, *Global Environmental Politics,* 3rd ed., 189; Bonanno and Constance, *Caught in the Net,* 200.

15 Ibid.; Ibid., 13–14.

16 Doughman, "Water Cooperation," 200; Schuler, "NAFTA and the Environment," 354–55; James M. Sheehan, "Sustainable Development: The Green Road to Serfdom?," in *The Greening of U.S. Foreign Policy,* eds. Terry L. Anderson and Henry I. Miller (Stanford, CA: Hoover Institution Press; Bozeman, MT: Political Economy Research Center, 2000), 154–55.

17 Schuler, "NAFTA and the Environment," 355.

18 Porter, Brown, and Chasek, *Global Environmental Politics,* 3rd ed., 97–98.

19 Dorsey, *Whales and Nations,* 282; Sand, "Japan's 'Research Whaling,'" 56–57.

20   Michael Johnson, "Whaling in the Antarctic—The ICJ Decision and Its
     Consequences for Future Special Permit Whaling," *Australian Year Book of
     International Law* 32 (2013): 87, 91; "Japan to Resume Whaling in Antarctic
     Despite Court Ruling," *BBC News*, November 28, 2015, accessed October 14,
     2017. http://www.bbc.com/news/world-asia-34952538.

21   Tolba and Rummel-Bulska, *Global Environmental Diplomacy*, 123;
     Sheehan, "Sustainable Development," 153–54; Julian Morris, "International
     Environmental Agreements: Developing Another Path," in *The Greening of
     U.S. Foreign Policy*, eds. Terry L. Anderson and Henry I. Miller (Stanford,
     CA: Hoover Institution Press; Bozeman, MT: Political Economy Research
     Center, 2000), 282–83. For details on shipments of hazardous waste from the
     United States and other nations in the North to LDCs, see Francis O. Adeola,
     *Hazardous Waste, Industrial Disasters, and Environmental Health Risks:
     Local and Global Environmental Struggles* (New York: Palgrave Macmillan,
     2011), 70, and "Where Does America's E-Waste End Up?: GPS Tracker Tells
     All," *PBS News Hour*, accessed September 24, 2016. http://www.pbs.org/
     newshour/updates/america-e-waste-gps-tracker-tells-all-earthfix/.

22   Katharina Kummer, *International Management of Hazardous Wastes: The
     Basel Convention and Related Legal Rules* (New York: Oxford, 1995), 101;
     Porter, Brown, and Chasek, *Global Environmental Politics*, 3rd ed., 107.

23   "Why China is Sick of Foreign Garbage," *Economist*, August 21, 2017,
     accessed September 4, 2017. https://www.economist.com/blogs/economist-
     explains/2017/08/economist-explains-8; Clapp, *Toxic Exports*, 61–64, 153;
     Tony Carnie, "Thor to Pay R24m for Mercury Clean-up in KZN," accessed
     September 24, 2016. http://www.iol.co.za/news/south-africa/thor-to-pay-r24m-
     for-mercury-clean-up-in-kzn-110071.

24   Andrew K. Jorgenson and Kennon A. Kuykendall, "Globalization, Foreign
     Investment Dependence and Agriculture Production: Pesticide and Fertilizer
     Use in Less-developed Countries, 1990-2000," *Social Forces* 87 (2008):
     532; Robert Boardman, *Pesticides in World Agriculture: The Politics of
     International Regulation* (New York: St. Martin's, 1986), 48; Katharina
     Kummer, "Prior Informed Consent for Chemicals in International Trade: The
     1998 Rotterdam Convention," *RECIEL* 8 (1999): 323–25.

25   Kummer, "Prior Informed Consent," 325–29.

26   Peter J. Lallas, "The Stockholm Convention on Persistent Organic Pollutants,"
     *American Journal of International Law* 95 (2001): 692n4, 695–97.

27   Hough, *Environmental Security*, 15; Lallas, "Stockholm Convention," 697–707;
     Elizabeth R. DeSombre, "United States International Environmental Policy," in
     *The Oxford Handbook of U.S. Environmental Policy*, eds. Sheldon Kamieniecki
     and Michael E. Kraft (New York: Oxford University Press, 2013), 214.

28   Jorgenson and Kuykendall, "Globalization, Foreign Investment Dependence
     and Agriculture Production," 533; Hough, *Environmental Security*, 69.

29   Herrick, with McRae, *Issues in American Foreign Policy*, 289; Porter, Brown,
     and Chasek, *Global Environmental Diplomacy*, 3rd ed., 90–91.

30   Porter, Brown, and Chasek, *Global Environmental Politics*, 3rd ed., 120,
     122; James Ciment, *Postwar America: An Encyclopedia of Social, Political,*

*Cultural, and Economic History* (New York: Routledge, 2006), 606; Miranda A. Schreurs, "The Climate Change Divide: The European Union, the United States, and the Future of the Kyoto Protocol," in *Green Giants?: Environmental Policies of the United States and the European Union*, eds. Norman J. Vig and Michael G. Faure (Cambridge, MA: MIT Press, 2004), 216; Miranda Schreurs and Yves Tiberghien, "European Union Leadership in Climate Change: Mitigation through Multilevel Reinforcement," in *Global Commons, Domestic Decisions: The Comparative Politics of Climate Change*, eds. Kathryn Harrison and Lisa McIntosh Sundstrom (Cambridge, MA: MIT Press, 2010), 23; Matt McDonald, "Fair Weather Friend?: Ethics and Australia's Approach to Global Climate Change," *Australian Journal of Politics and History* 51 (2005): 226, 227.

31  Schreurs, "Climate Change Divide," 207; Porter, Brown, and Chasek, *Global Environmental Politics*, 3rd ed., 121–22; Kate Crowley, "Climate Clever?: Kyoto and Australia's Decade of Recalcitrance," in *Global Commons, Domestic Decisions: The Comparative Politics of Climate Change*, eds. Kathryn Harrison and Lisa McIntosh Sundstrom (Cambridge, MA: MIT Press, 2010), 203; Porter, Brown, and Chasek, *Global Environmental Politics*, 3rd ed., 122; Weart, *Discovery of Global Warming*, rev. and expanded ed., 167.

32  Schreurs, "Climate Change Divide," 218; Daynes and Sussman, *White House Politics and the Environment*, 203.

33  Hough, *Environmental Security*, 16; James Dao, "Protestors Interrupt Powell Speech as U.N. Talks End," *New York Times*, September 5, 2002.

34  "World Summit Adopts Voluntary Action Plan," *Science*, September 13, 2002, 1785; Rachel L. Swarns, "U.S. Is Not the Only Nation Resisting a Strong Pact at the Summit Meeting on Global Warming," *New York Times*, August 31, 2002; John S. Seitz and Kristen A. Hite, *Global Issues: An Introduction*, 4th ed. (Malden, MA: Wiley-Blackwell, 2012), 165.

35  Hough, *Environmental Security*, 43; United Nations Population Fund, International Conference on Population and Development, accessed February 17, 2017. https://www.unfpa.org/icpd.

36  "About Roundup Ready Crops," accessed September 30, 2017. http://web.mit. edu/demoscience/Monsanto/about.html; "Argentines Link Health Problems to Farming Chemicals," *USA Today*, October 20, 2013, accessed October 20, 2013. https://www.usatoday.com/story/news/world/2013/10/20/argentines-link-health-problems-to-agrochemicals/3094113/.

37  "About Roundup Ready Crops"; "Argentine Link Health Problems to Farming Chemicals," *USA Today*, October 20, 2013, accessed October 20, 2013. https://www.usatoday.com/story/news/world/2013/10/20/argentines-link-health-problems-to-agrochemicals/3094113/.

38  Olof Linden, "Human Impact on Tropical Coastal Zones," *Nature and Resources* 26 (1990): 5–6; Malcolm J. Foster and Denis D. Gray, "Cambodia's Zeal for Rubber Drives Ethnic Group from Land," *Daily Mail* (London), March 26, 2016, accessed March 26, 2016. http://www.dailymail.co.uk/wires/ap/article-3505777/Cambodias-zeal-rubber-drives-ethnic-group-land.html.

39  Joe McDonald, "China Recycling Cleanup Jolts Global Industry," *Philippine Star*, October 4, 2013, accessed October 20, 2013. http://www.philstar.com/

world/2013/10/04/1241425/china-recycling-cleanup-jolts-global-industry; Eric V. Hull, "Possessing the Poor for Profit," *Duke Environmental Law and Policy Forum* 21 (2010): 2; "UN Environment Chief Warns of 'Tsunami' of E-Waste at Conference on Chemical Treaties," May 4, 2015, accessed September 24, 2016. http://www.un.org/apps/news/story.asp?NewsID=50763#.V-ayVfArLIU.

40  Hough, *Environmental Security*, 98.

41  Weinthal, "The Promises and Pitfalls of Environmental Peacemaking in the Aral Sea Basin," 96; Ankit Panda, "How the Soviet Union Created Central Asia's Worst Environmental Disaster," *The Diplomat*, October 3, 2014, accessed September 30, 2017. http://thediplomat.com/2014/10/how-the-soviet-union-created-central-asias-worst-environmental-disaster/.

42  Maude Barlow, *Blue Future: Protecting Water for People and the Planet Forever* (New York: Free Press, 2013), 16, 105; Suleiman Iguda Ladan, "Global Environmental Change as a Human Security Threat: Situation in Nigeria," in *Environmental Change and Human Security in Africa and the Middle East*, eds., Mohamed Behnassi and Katriona McGlade (Cham, Switzerland: Springer, 2017), 112.

43  Dounia Ben Mohamed, "New Urgency in Battle to Halt Spread of Desertification," *New African*, 556 (2015): 20–21. See also http://www.esa.int/var/esa/storage/images/esa_multimedia/images/2013/10/lake_chad_water_extent_increase/13371177-1-eng-GB/Lake_Chad_water_extent_increase.gif, accessed August 30, 2017.

44  Barlow, *Blue Future*, 16–17.

45  Ibid., 148.

46  Suraje Dessai, Nuno S. Lacasta, and Katharine Vincent, "International Political History of the Kyoto Protocol: From The Hague to Marrakech and Beyond," *International Review for Environmental Strategies* 4 (2003): 184–85; Weart, *Discovery of Global Warming*, rev. and expanded ed., 181–83, 95.

47  Hough, *Environmental Security*, 27, 29.

48  Ibid., 52; Dalby, *Security and Environmental Change*, 87; Duyck, "Polar Environmental Governance and Nonstate Actors," 27; Rebecca Pincus, "Security in the Arctic: A Receding Wall," in *Diplomacy on Ice: Energy and the Environment in the Arctic and Antarctic*, eds. Pincus and Salem H. Ali (New Haven, CT: Yale University Press, 2015), 164, 167.

49  United States Environmental Protection Agency, "Methyl Bromide," accessed September 4, 2017. https://www.epa.gov/ods-phaseout/methyl-bromide; Weart, *Discovery of Global Warming*, rev. and expanded ed., 189; O'Neill, *Environment and International Relations*, 198.

50  Daynes and Sussman, *White House Politics and the Environment*, 239.

51  Hough, *Environmental Security*, 17; Klein, *This Changes Everything*, 12–13.

52  Doyle Rice, "Record! 2014 was Earth's Warmest Year," *USA Today*, January 16, 2015, accessed January 16, 2015. https://www.usatoday.com/story/weather/2015/01/16/record-warm-year-climate-change/21857061/; Henry Fountain, "Researchers Links Syria Conflict to a Drought Made Worse by Climate Change," *New York Times*, March 3, 2015; Jim Yardley and Laurie

Goodstein, "Pope Offers Radical Vision to Address Climate Change," *New York Times*, June 19, 2015.

53   Avinash Godbole, "Paris Accord and China's Climate Change Strategy: Drivers and Outcomes," *India Quarterly* 72 (2016): 362–63, 364–65; Klein, *This Changes Everything*, 350, 351–52; "China's Air Pollution Again at Danger Levels," *Guardian*, January 29, 2013, accessed October 1, 2017. https://www.theguardian.com/world/2013/jan/29/china-air-pollution-danger; Matt McGrath, "China's Per Capita Carbon Emissions Overtake EU's," *BBC News*, accessed October 1, 2017, http://www.bbc.com/news/science-environment-29239194; Li, "Hopes of Limiting Global Warming," 51.

54   "The Road to a Paris Climate Deal," *New York Times*, December 12, 2015, accessed October 1, 2017. https://www.nytimes.com/interactive/projects/cp/climate/2015-paris-climate-talks/key-points-of-the-final-paris-climate-draft.

55   "Road to a Paris Climate Deal"; Simon Chin-Yee, "Briefing: Africa and the Paris climate Change Agreement," *African Affairs* 115 (2016): 365; Godbole, "Paris Accord," 369.

56   Chin-Yee, "Briefing," 362, 364, 367.

57   Columbia University, "France: A Study of French Nuclear Policy after Fukushima," July 17, 2012, accessed October 14, 2017. https://k1project.columbia.edu/news/french-nuclear-policy-after-fukushima; "Top Climate Change Scientists' Letter to Policy Influencers," *CNN*, November 3, 2013, accessed October 14, 2017. http://www.cnn.com/2013/11/03/world/nuclear-energy-climate-change-scientists-letter/; International Atomic Energy Agency, *Nuclear Power and the Paris Agreement*, undated, accessed October 14, 2017. https://www.iaea.org/sites/default/files/16/11/np-parisagreement.pdf.

58   See Brad Plumer, "Sweden Decides It's Not So Easy to Give Up Nuclear Power," *Vox.com*, June 17, 2016, accessed February 2, 2018. https://www.vox.com/2016/6/17/11950440/sweden-nuclear-power; Ken Silverstein, "Japan Circling Back to Nuclear Power after Fukushima Disaster," *Forbes*, September 8, 2017, accessed February 2, 2018. https://www.forbes.com/sites/kensilverstein/2017/09/08/japan-may-be-coming-full-circle-after-its-fukushima-nuclear-energy-disaster/#7c7d22c830e8; Attila Somfalvi, "Netanyahu: We'll Reconsider Nuclear Power Plans," *Ynetnews*, March 17, 2011, accessed October 14, 2017. https://www.ynetnews.com/articles/0,7340,L-4043982,00.html.

59   Robin Kundis Craig, *Comparative Ocean Governance: Place-Based Protections in an Era of Climate Change* (Cheltenham, UK: Edward Elgar, 2012), 39; "Great Pacific Garbage Patch," *National Geographic*, accessed October 14, 2017. https://www.nationalgeographic.org/encyclopedia/great-pacific-garbage-patch/; Tolba and Rummel-Bulska, *Global Environmental Diplomacy*, 36; Eric Lombardi, "What Does the Paris Climate Agreement Say about Waste?," accessed October 14, 2017. http://www.waste360.com/waste-reduction/what-does-paris-climate-agreement-say-about-waste.

60   Paul J. Crutzen and Eugene F. Stoermer, "The Anthropocene," *Global Change Newsletter* no. 41 (2000): 17–18; Doyle Rice, "Study: Earth in the Midst of Sixth Mass Extinction," *USA Today*, July 24, 2014, accessed October 14,

2017. https://www.usatoday.com/story/tech/2014/07/24/mass-extinction-study/13096445/.

61  Joseph Stromberg, "What Is the Anthropocene and Are We in It?," *Smithsonian*, January 2013, accessed February 17, 2018. https://www.smithsonianmag.com/science-nature/what-is-the-anthropocene-and-are-we-in-it-164801414/; Earth Systems, "The Anthropocene—A New Geologic Epoch?," accessed February 17, 2018. http://www.earthsystems.com/the-anthropocene/.

# Conclusion

1  "Rio 2016: Opening Ceremony Features Environmental Rallying Cry," *ABC News* (Australia), August 6, 2016, accessed October 25, 2017. http://www.abc.net.au/news/2016-08-06/green-theme-runs-strong-through-opening-ceremony/7697316; Andrew McKindy, "Rio Olympics Open with Ceremony Focused on Environment," *Japan Times*, accessed October 25, 2017. https://www.japantimes.co.jp/sports/2016/08/06/olympics/summer-olympics/rio-olympics-open-ceremony-focused-environment/#.WoBi9ujwbIU.

2  Edward Wong, "China Blocks Web Access to Video About Country's Rampant Air Pollution," *New York Times*, March 7, 2015; "Brazil Court Blocks Amazon Mining Decree," *BBC News*, August 30, 2017, accessed August 30, 2017. http://www.bbc.com/news/world-latin-america-41100541.

3  Mary L. Dudziak, *Wartime: An Idea, Its History, Its Consequences* (New York: Oxford University Press, 2012); Karl Mathieson, "What's the Environmental Impact of Modern War?," *The Guardian*, November 6, 2014, accessed November 7, 2017. https://www.theguardian.com/environment/2014/nov/06/whats-the-environmental-impact-of-modern-war; Harry J. Kazianis, "8 Million Dead—What Nuclear War with North Korea Could Look Like," *Fox News*, August 14, 2017, accessed November 7, 2017. http://www.foxnews.com/opinion/2017/08/14/8-million-dead-what-nuclear-war-with-north-korea-could-look-like.html; James Macdonald, "The Environmental Impact of Nuclear War," *JSTOR Daily*, August 26, 2017, accessed November 7, 2017. https://daily.jstor.org/the-environmental-impact-of-nuclear-war/.

4  O'Neill, *Environment and International Relations*, 5.

5  Jareen Imam, "Microbead Ban Signed by President Obama," *CNN.com*, December 31, 2015, accessed September 12, 2017. http://www.cnn.com/2015/12/30/health/obama-bans-microbeads/index.html; Dan Bloom, "Microbeads to Be Banned in Face and Shower Gel from 2018, Government Confirms," *Mirror* (London), July 21, 2017, accessed September 12, 2017. http://www.mirror.co.uk/news/politics/microbeads-banned-face-scrubs-shower-10844111; Fredric C. Menz and Hans M. Seip, "Acid Rain in Europe and the United States: An Update," *Environmental Science and Policy* 7 (2004): 253–65.

6  "Poachers Have All But Emptied This 'Sanctuary' of Forest Elephants," Huffington Post, February 20, 2017, accessed February 20, 2017. https://www.huffingtonpost.com/entry/poaching-forest-elephants-

mink%C3%A9b%C3%A9-gabon-africa_us_58ab4c3ae4b0a855d1d8bfe5;
Jeffrey Gettleman, "Taking on Poachers, Kenya Burns Ivory," *New York
Times*, May 1, 2016; "Elephant Poaching in Africa Falls But Ivory Seizures
Up: Study," *News 24*, October 24, 2017, accessed October 28, 2017. https://
www.news24.com/Green/News/elephant-poaching-in-africa-falls-but-ivory-
seizures-up-study-20171024; Sara F. Oldfield, "The Evolving Role of CITES in
Regulating the International Timber Trade," *RECIEL* 22 (2013): 298; Forest
Stewardship Council, "Facts and Figures," June 2017, accessed July 2, 2017.
https://ic.fsc.org/en/facts-and-figures.

7   Doyle Rice, "Study: Ozone Hole over Antarctica Beginning to Heal," *USA
    Today*, July 30, 2016, accessed July 1, 2016. https://www.usatoday.com/
    story/weather/2016/06/30/ozone-hole-healing-antarctic/86552814/; Michael
    Forsythe, "China Halts Plan to Build Power Plants Fired by Coal," *New York
    Times*, January 19, 2017; "China to Plow $361 Billion into Renewable Fuel
    by 2020," Reuters, January 4, 2017, accessed October 21, 2017. https://www.
    reuters.com/article/us-china-energy-renewables/china-to-plow-361-billion-into-
    renewable-fuel-by-2020-idUSKBN14P06P; Alanna Petroff, "These Countries
    Want to Ditch Gas and Diesel Cars," *CNN*, July 26, 2017, accessed July 28,
    2017. http://money.cnn.com/2017/07/26/autos/countries-that-are-banning-gas-
    cars-for-electric/index.html; John D. Stoll and Tim Higgins, "Volvo Gives Tesla
    a Shock, As Others Plan Electric Push," *Wall Street Journal*, July 6, 2017.

8   Barlow, *Blue Future*, 150; Rachael Bale, "Japan Kills 200 Pregnant Minke
    Whales," *National Geographic*, March 25, 2016, accessed November 8, 2016.
    http://news.nationalgeographic.com/2016/03/160325-Japan-whaling-minke-
    whales-Antarctica/; Carla Herreria, "NOAA Removes Most Humpback
    Whales from Endangered Species List," *Huffington Post*, September 7, 2016,
    accessed September 7, 2016. http://www.huffingtonpost.com/entry/humpback-
    whales-removed-endangered-species-list_us_57cdbac1e4b0a22de096a4c9.

9   Simon Denyer and Emily Rauhala, "Beijing's Claim to South China Sea
    Rejected by International Tribunal," *Washington Post*, July 12, 2016,
    accessed July 12, 2016. https://www.washingtonpost.com/world/beijing-
    remains-angry-defiant-and-defensive-as-key-south-china-sea-tribunal-ruling-
    looms/2016/07/12/11100f48-4771-11e6-8dac-0c6e4accc5b1_story.html?utm_
    term=.5b1fae9e2f61.

10  Kevin Krajick, "Human Population Footprint May Be Growing More Slowly,"
    phys.org, August 24, 2016, accessed August 24, 2016. https://phys.org/
    news/2016-08-human-population-footprint-slowly.html.

11  "Poachers Have All but Emptied This 'Sanctuary' of Forest Elephants";
    "Elephant Poaching Drops in Africa but Populations Continue to Fall,"
    *The Guardian*, October 24, 2017, accessed October 27, 2017. https://www.
    theguardian.com/environment/2017/oct/24/elephant-poaching-drops-africa-
    but-populations-continue-to-fall; Christopher Torchia, "Poachers Target
    Africa's Lions, Vultures with Poison," *Fox News*, September 27, 2017,
    accessed September 27, 2017. http://www.foxnews.com/world/2017/09/27/
    poachers-target-africas-lions-vultures-with-poison.html; "Rhino Horn Auction
    to Go Ahead in South Africa after Court Lifts Ban on Sales," *The Guardian*,
    June 26, 2017, accessed June 26, 2017. https://www.theguardian.com/
    environment/2017/jun/26/rhino-breeder-auction-horns-south-africa-rhinoceros.

12 Steve Ellis and Erich Pica, "A Real Buzzkill," *US News and World Report*, November 13, 2015, accessed October 1, 2017. https://www.usnews.com/opinion/articles/2015/11/13/honeybees-are-dying-and-our-food-supply-will-go-with-them; Chelsea Harvey, "Nearly Two Decades of Data Reinforce Concerns that Pesticides are Really Bad for Bees," *Washington Post*, August 16, 2016, accessed August 16, 2016. https://www.washingtonpost.com/news/energy-environment/wp/2016/08/16/nearly-two-decades-of-data-reinforce-concerns-that-pesticides-are-really-bad-for-bees/ and Erik Stokstad, "Pesticides Found in Honey Around the World," *Science*, October 5, 2017, accessed October 5, 2017. http://www.sciencemag.org/news/2017/10/pesticides-found-honey-around-world.

13 Josephson, "War on Nature as Part of the Cold War," 47–48; "Tunnel Collapse Renews Safety Concerns about Nuclear Sites," *US News and World Report*, May 10, 2017, accessed May 15, 2017. https://www.usnews.com/news/best-states/washington/articles/2017-05-10/tunnel-collapse-latest-safety-issue-at-nuclear-site.

14 Hough, *Environmental Security*, 38–39.

15 Rob Vos, "Green or Mean: Is Biofuel Production Undermining Food Security," in *Climate Change and Sustainable Development: New Challenges for Poverty Reduction*, ed. M. A. Mohamed Salih (Cheltenham, UK: Edward Elgar, 2009), 245; Lynton Keith Caldwell, *International Environmental Policy: Emergence and Dimensions*, 2nd ed. (Durham, NC: Duke University Press, 1984), 254.

16 "Why China Is Sick of Foreign Garbage," *Economist*, August 21, 2017, accessed September 4, 2017. https://www.economist.com/blogs/economist-explains/2017/08/economist-explains-8.

17 Clint Peinhardt and Todd Sandler, *Transnational Cooperation: An Issue-Based Approach* (New York: Oxford University Press, 2015), 275; Harold Borchgrevink, "Acid Rain Still Affects Water Quality," *ScienceNordic*, May 15, 2014, accessed October 28, 2017. http://sciencenordic.com/acid-rain-still-affects-water-quality; Klein, *This Changes Everything*, 136; Michael Forsythe, "China Cancels 103 Coal Plants, Mindful of Smog and Wasted Capacity," *New York Times*, January 18, 2017, accessed May 18, 2017. https://www.nytimes.com/2017/01/18/world/asia/china-coal-power-plants-pollution.html; Alexandra Sifferlin "Here's How Many People Die from Pollution around the World," *Time*, October 19, 2017, accessed May 18, 2017. http://time.com/4989641/water-air-pollution-deaths/; Vikram Barhat, "The Entrepreneurs Making Money Out of Thin Air," *BBC News*, May 16, 2017, accessed May 18, 2017. http://www.bbc.com/capital/story/20170515-the-entrepreneurs-making-money-out-of-thin-air; "Air Pollution: 'Heart Disease Link Found,'" *BBC News*, April 26, 2017, accessed April 26, 2017. http://www.bbc.com/news/health-39710321.

18 Vos, "Green or Mean," 235, 239–40; Barlow, *Blue Future*, 175.

19 David Biello, "Electric Cars Are Not Necessarily Clean," *Scientific American*, May 11, 2016, accessed September 2, 2017. https://www.scientificamerican.com/article/electric-cars-are-not-necessarily-clean/.

20 Michael Greshko, "It's Official: 2016 Hottest Year on Record," *National Geographic*, August 11, 2017, accessed October 28, 2017. https://news.nationalgeographic.com/2017/08/2016-hottest-year-on-record-climate-environment-spd/; Brian Kahn, "Earth's $CO_2$ Passes the 400 PPM Threshold—

Maybe Permanently," *Scientific American*, October 27, 2016, accessed October 21, 2017. https://www.scientificamerican.com/article/earth-s-co2-passes-the-400-ppm-threshold-maybe-permanently/; "Methane from Livestock Underestimated," *The Nation*, September 30, 2017, accessed September 30, 2017. http://nation.com.pk/30-Sep-2017/methane-from-livestock-underestimated.

21  Simon Dalby, "The Politics of Environmental Security," in *Green Security or Militarized Environment*, ed. Jyrki Käkönen (Aldershot, UK: Dartmouth, 1994), 27–31; Hough, *Environmental Security*, 48–51; Conca, "The Case for Environmental Peacemaking," 1, 5–7.

22  "Global Sea Levels Could Soon Rise 20' as Climate Warms," *Environment News Service*, July 12, 2015, accessed July 12, 2015. http://ens-newswire.com/2015/07/12/global-sea-levels-could-soon-rise-20-as-climate-warms/; Mike Ives, "Remote Pacific Nation, Threatened by Rising Seas," *New York Times*, July 3, 2016; Marcus Stephen, "On Nauru, a Sinking Feeling," *New York Times*, July 19, 2011; Olivia Yasukawa and Thomas Page, "When Corals Die Off, We Die Off," *CNN*, July 10, 2017, accessed October 22, 2017. http://www.cnn.com/2017/07/10/africa/seychelles-climate-change-coral/index.html; Joanna Zelman, "50 Million Environmental Refugees by 2020, Experts Predict," February 22, 2011, accessed October 22, 2017. https://www.huffingtonpost.com/2011/02/22/environmental-refugees-50_n_826488.html; Betsy Hartmann, "From Climate Refugees to Climate Conflict: Who Is Taking the Heat for Global Warming?," in *Climate Change and Sustainable Development: New Challenges for Poverty Reduction*, ed. M. A. Mohamed Salih (Cheltenham, UK: Edward Elgar, 2009), 142–43, 145–49; Rebecca Boyle, "Maldivian Leaders Might Move the Entire Nation to Australia If Sea Keeps Rising," *Popular Science*, January 10, 2012, accessed October 22, 2017. https://www.popsci.com/science/article/2012-01/maldivian-leaders-are-buying-foreign-land-future-climate-refugees.

23  Barlow, *Blue Future*, 228; Paul G. Harris, "International Development Assistance and Burden Sharing," in *Green Giants?: Environmental Policies of the United States and the European Union*, eds. Norman J. Vig and Michael G. Faure (Cambridge, MA: MIT Press, 2004), 257.

24  Ludwig Krämer, "The Roots of Divergence: A European Perspective," in *Green Giants?: Environmental Policies of the United States and the European Union*, eds. Norman J. Vig and Michael G. Faure (Cambridge, MA: MIT Press, 2004), 66–70; Brian Palmer, "What Does Vladimir Putin Really Think about Climate Change," *Pacific Standard*, December 9, 2015, accessed October 28, 2017. https://psmag.com/environment/what-does-vladimir-putin-really-think-about-climate-change.

25  Seth Borenstein, "Divided America: Temperatures Rise, US Splits," Associated Press, August 15, 2016, accessed August 15, 2016. https://apnews.com/d4c668bce0f54091b31e2f70fdd3bd16/divided-america-global-warming-polarizes-more-abortion.

26  Johannes Friedrich, Mengpin Ge, and Andrew Pickens, "This Interactive Chart Explains World's Top 10 Emitters, and How They've Changed," *World Resources Institute*, April 2017, accessed November 7, 2017. http://www.wri.org/blog/2017/04/interactive-chart-explains-worlds-top-10-emitters-and-how-theyve-changed.